Diary of a Cycle Path

John Strater Brown

John Strater Brown

How SeaBos Pushed My Pause Button

ISBN: 978-1-7374129-0-8

For Mom and Dad, who inspired and taught me how to:
**

ski;
sew;
fish;
camp;
cook;
canoe;
garden;
tie knots;
be frugal;
love dogs;
play music
use a knife;
shoot a gun;
meet strangers;
be a leader;
say the Lord's Prayer; and
ride a bike,
Among many other things

And

for Strater, Shannon, and, Andrew
Who inspired and taught me how to be a Father

For all the Bikepackers Everywhere

Figures

ACKNOWLEDGMENTS

Thanks to:

My Family – God bless you for your support
Steve Johnson - My incredible Editor in Chief
Liliana Guia – Master Graphics Coordinator
Andy – For facilitating what was already inside me
Griffin – For getting SeaBos ready to roll
David and Amanda – For getting me out of Seattle
Danny and Jules – Forever friends
Bill, Jeff, and Tom – For having my back
Jolene – For everything

Foreword

This book is not about how to plan a bike ride across the country. There are plenty of internet logs, journals, and books available on the subject. This is a story of the collision of childhood fantasy and an overwhelming desire as an adult to break away; a tale that borders more on the edge of monomaniacal madness.

This is not a tutorial about bikes, bike repairs, or to profess I am a bike expert or even a knowledgeable bike rider. I am not an experienced biker. I can't hold a candle to riders with chiseled bodies and sobering credentials who have logged serious mileage across America, across multiple continents, and around the world in record times. I have no mad biking-skills credibility. My qualification as a biker is more of a matter of the heart, and that love for riding a bicycle has stuck with me since childhood.

My curiosity for exploring and pushing geographic boundaries began early. When I was not quite two years old, a neighbor found me wandering down the street, lost and bewildered, and carried me safely home. Years later, I learned to read maps and keep my wanderings to the self-professed variety. Maps showed me endless roads connecting to others in an irresistible "dot to dot" pattern between towns across the country. Looking through an atlas of the US, I daydreamed of long-distance bike riding through thick forests, past lakes, fish-filled rivers, and faraway mountains—I would pedal towards unknown horizons and beyond, never turning back. These fantasies packed my mind as a young boy. Lying awake in bed, I knew that Pleasant Street, just outside my front door, led somewhere.

Boy Fishing the Charles River – Irene Strater Brown, 1963

CHAPTER 1 - I FLY AWAY

Our car pulled up to the unloading zone. I held back tears, reservations, and stifled an avalanche of emotions. I stoically hugged my son Andrew. My daughter Shannon locked eyes with me and reiterated her faith in me. Her hands gripped my shoulders with a gentle shake.

"Dad, I know you can do this!" she whispered, teary-eyed, somehow she had a sense of what I was going through.

A lump formed in my throat as I prayed that she knew more than I did. She was my rock. I stared into her eyes for assurance and realized that my 19-year-old daughter admired my passion for confronting unreasonable, self-imposed challenges. I saw there was no doubt in her mind but in my mind, in my reality, was this something I could do? Ride my bike across the country? I was clueless and had little idea of what might lie ahead.

My wife of nearly 22 years stood on the opposite side of the car, looking away, seemingly studying the concrete parking garage structure with great interest. I walked into the terminal, not looking back, towing an overstuffed suitcase and pushing a tall, skinny cardboard box filled with a dismembered bicycle. I felt a chill.

"These are not the right clothes for flying. Who dressed me this morning?" I thought.

The sliding glass doors closed behind me and I was on my own. Mild confusion set in. Standing in the airport with a box and a suitcase was my newfound self-inflicted reality—this was not the time for panic. One week had passed since I bought the plane ticket, but I never doubted the decision. Why start now? I turned around and looked back at the door. My family was gone. It was time for check-in, leaving Salt Lake City and the life I had known for the Pacific Northwest. But why Seattle? My brother-in-law lived there, so that made some sense. More importantly, wind patterns across the U.S generally blow from west to east, and I'm not too fond of a headwind on a bike.

It all happened in such an abrupt instant when those doors closed that I can hardly remember it but I distinctly recollect dragging that big box into the terminal, sliding it across the smooth floor to the check-in desk, and being immensely proud of my excellent packaging job. Thanks to TSA and their general suspicion of passengers with one-way plane tickets, my belongings immediately came under scrutiny and extra screening. Despite my meticulous work with packing tape, a pair of TSA agents chopped the box open in less than ten seconds with the inelegance of a hatchet and my bike and its parts spilled from the box like roadkill. They removed the contents and wiped everything down with a sampling pad, then checked the wipe for chemicals while I stood there gaping at the grisly scene because the box was no longer sound.

"Hey, I don't have any tape with me! How will you secure the box again so the contents don't get lost on the plane and in baggage?"

"Oh, we'll take care of it. I worked for UPS," said one of the TSA agents with a sarcastic chuckle that got both of them laughing in my face.

The bike was my essential piece of equipment; what jackasses. I watched as an agent patched up the gaping wound with flimsy masking tape in a couple of spots, but not with the care I exercised the night before or near enough sturdiness to keep everything inside the box. I grabbed my pedals and a bag of screws, nuts, and bolts—at least I could keep something safe. Walking to the gate, I downed a quick beer, prayed to God that my bike and parts would make it, and boarded the plane. It was 10 a.m.

The day's dismal start continued when my suitcase's weight exceeded the limit, so I had to remove the tent, sleeping bag, Camelbak, pump, and helmet and hold them on my lap before takeoff. I wore summer bike riding clothes, so the air conditioning chilled my skin and I felt out of place alongside the other passengers. A text came through from my wife:

4

"I'm sure you are on the plane now. I'm in a daze thinking how strange it's going to be without you here. We have never been apart for more than a few weeks continuously. Happy trails, JB."

I sat by the window next to a couple of millennials. They gave me, a slightly unfit Boomer, a quick once-over and probably concluded that they didn't want to converse with a guy in Lycra shorts on a plane with camping gear and bike parts piled on his lap. But after a beer, I had no reservations about making friendly conversation. I discussed some of my hobbies and interests as the plane took off sharply over the Great Salt Lake, climbing northwest into the clouds. I acknowledged that I was wearing bike clothes because I intended to pedal my bicycle across the country. The young man looked a little surprised, while the young woman made some snotty comments behind the back of her hand.

"Well, I guess you do just about everything, don't you," she whispered sarcastically to the man seated beside her and snickered.

That really meant, *"You can shut up your pie-hole now. You will never get your fat ass out of Seattle on that bike of yours."*

I craned my neck to gaze out both sides of the plane at the thick cloud cover below. Our plane passed over Mount Rainier, while Mounts Adams and St. Helens prominently stood above brilliant silvery clouds to the south. Interestingly, my long-term admiration of Washington's volcanic peaks began in 1980, evading the police on a high-speed motorcycle chase near Spirit Lake after the first Mount St. Helens' eruption, ditching my R/75 BMW in the woods near the North Fork of the Toutle River and dodging a 10-day jail sentence.

I saw Mount Baker and Glacier Peak protruding through the clouds to the north. I'd been up Mount Baker three times, once solo, and love the challenge of the high peaks. Before long, the plane circled and headed south, dropping below the clouds, and suddenly I could make out green treetops. Seattle was just below us, and Amanda would be waiting to pick me up.

CHAPTER 2 - LIGHTNING STRIKES

I love riding my bike in the Wasatch Canyons and I could get there from my driveway, following a short hop downhill to the Lake Bonneville Shoreline Trail. This trail roughly follows near the topographic contour along the lake bench of glacial Lake Bonneville[i], the ancient lake that once filled the Salt Lake Valley during the Ice Age[ii]. This paved bike trail connects with a half-dozen river or glacial-cut canyons that meander deep into the Wasatch Range.

The canyons are a great place to train on a bike. Each canyon has its character and unique range of riding challenges showcasing spectacular geology and mountain scenery. Best of all, the wind is predictable, blowing down the canyons in the morning and up the canyons in the afternoon. Riding into the canyons in early mornings, I feel like a salmon swimming upriver.

One especially magnificent bluebird summer morning, I headed up Emigration Canyon on Little Mountain towards Big Mountain. This enjoyable ride follows the historic route blazed into the Salt Lake Valley by Brigham Young and the ill-fated Donner Party. Today the road is agreeably graded and paved and in places, you can still see some of the original pioneer trails in the woods. It is a ride for bikers who enjoy a few steep grades and the total round-trip effort from my house entails more than 3,500 feet of climbing.

The moment I rounded the first switchback on Little Mountain, a most unusual desire took hold of my thoughts. It was triggered by a conversation with my friend Andy, an avid rare guitar collector in Hollywood, just weeks before as we picked tunes late into the night. "John Brown," said Andy, "Is there something you especially want to do in life that you haven't done yet? Is there something that you want to do before you croak?"

I laughed off the question. It was a complete non-sequitur from our discussions of artists and music styles. "I don't know Andy, where is this coming from?" I replied, somewhat uncertain of his line of questioning.

"Maybe something that's been on your list of things to accomplish before you get too old?" he continued.

"I don't know, maybe ride a bicycle across the country or something. As a kid, I thought it would be the coolest thing to do, but I haven't thought about it in years."

At that moment riding up Little Mountain, remembering that conversation back in LA prompted a rising tide of emotion that felt like a tsunami wave bearing down upon slack-jawed tourists staring at the ocean in disbelief. I became moonstruck, so overcome with a certainty of purpose that I was convinced I had to ride my bike from coast to coast. An undeniable adrenaline-infused ecstasy, more euphoric than a hospital dose of morphine, filled my veins. The notion of riding cross-country burst from my obscured childhood subconscious to my adult reality with the urgency of lightning to the ground. This was it! For some reason, the idea became so convincing, so overcoming, I couldn't *not* think about it. I had to do this. I didn't know how or where it would happen, but I wanted to ride across the country more than I ever wanted anything. And I wanted it now.

The phrase *"I would rather be dead than not do this"* repeated in my mind. An instant feeling of satisfaction swept over me as if I had just received the highest grade on a test. I didn't have a clue why, but it was an epiphany. I became convinced that I had to do it. I was infected. I stopped riding and sent a text to my wife, asking what she thought of the idea.

"Ride a motorcycle across the country?" she texted back quizzically.

"No, ride a bicycle," I replied.

More than ten minutes passed. "Are you kidding, ride across the country? You are going to need a new bike," came her final reply.

7

I sensed that she wasn't overjoyed with the idea.

Returning home, my legs cramped, so I slugged down Gatorade in the kitchen. The best way that I can describe my wife's reaction was she was not exactly thrilled. She knew this ridiculous undertaking would require missing a lot of upcoming family events. Shannon's summer break from college, her boyfriend Dani's first visit, and my granddaughter's first visit with my son Strater and his wife Christina would all be unattended by me. Then there were two more landmines: my wife's birthday and our twenty-second wedding anniversary. Missing these events would be an enormous sacrifice.

But I rationalized to push ahead as she begrudgingly gave me the proverbial green light. I was excited but couldn't know what she was thinking. She probably felt that I had lost my mind. Riding Big Mountain in a day is nothing compared to a long-distance solo bike adventure. I knew not what I was asking of myself. But I had to go. Somehow, I knew this ride, this journey into the unknown on an unproven marginally-conditioned body might help me in some intangible way.

I didn't dare to announce my scheme to anyone else for about five days. I thought it would be a monumental achievement if I made it and told everyone afterward. If this ride would be an epic disaster with no backup plan, I would genuinely look and feel foolish.

[i] Lake Bonneville - A Pliocene Lake that occupied almost 20,000 square miles of the Great Basin in Nevada and Utah and southern Idaho that reached nearly 1,000 feet in depth.

[ii] Ice Age - A glacial period or part of a glacial period most frequently refers to the last glacial period of the Pleistocene Age.

CHAPTER 3 - THE NO-PLAN PLAN

I purchased a one-way airline ticket to Seattle for the following Wednesday without considering which route I would take. I didn't want to think about this too much. The plan made little sense for someone like myself with novice skills but I was too foolish to know any better. I never rode a bike on tour with panniers, so my next stop was the bike shop to figure out precisely what would be necessary to get the bike prepared for long-distance riding. I also needed to determine which accessories would be required to make the journey.

Although I had ridden various bicycles since the age of five, I didn't know a lot about bikes or biking equipment. I could do minimal damage with a screwdriver, fix a flat, and change a tire; however, I never rode a bicycle for more than 41 miles in one day and that ride didn't end well.

I threw the bike in the pickup truck and headed to a bike shop down in the city. A twenty-something employee named Griffin greeted me.

"What's up?" he said as I wheeled the bike into the shop.

"I want to ride this bike across the country from Seattle to Boston."

He sized me up and appeared puzzled because I was in my late fifties, possibly a little on the overweight side by body mass index standards. But didn't I look like I could at least make it across Washington? Entertaining the notion of a solo cross-country bike ride was a young man's ambition, not a middle-aged man's delusion of grandeur and vision of glory. Seriously, it was time for a reality check. He continued with his questioning to examine the sincerity of my intentions.

"Have you ever done a big bike tour before?" he asked.

"I rode 41 miles one day." I didn't mention to Griffin that I carried no gear, and there was a subsequent trip to the emergency room on the following day when my back seized.

"How many riders are going with you?" he asked.

"I am going to ride solo."

"What about a support vehicle? Do you have anyone in a car or van following you?"

"No, what fun would that be?" I responded with a smile, half-kidding, half smart-ass.

"No, it's a good idea from a basic safety standpoint. If you have never done this before, you should have some means of support. Somebody should carry your supplies and watch your stuff when you go into stores. Someone should be there to go for help in case you have a breakdown or to take you to a hospital if you get hurt."

"Hurt? Well, I don't know anybody who would want to do this with me, or at all for that matter, and it's too late now because I already bought a plane ticket for next Wednesday."

"How long have you planned out this trip?"

"I just thought about doing it yesterday."

Griffin recoiled, rolled his eyes, and his head bounced back slightly. Undoubtedly, he was thinking about a big mistake this fifty-something Boomer was making with his lack of preparation. It was not smart or rational. Griffin laughed and looked at the shop floor, shaking his head.

"People usually plan out these large tours for months, sometimes years in advance. You can't just hit the road on a whim. It takes planning, strategy, mapping out routes, and considerable forethought. It's not as simple as just following a map."

"Well, I don't want to give it too much thought. I might change my mind. I am going. So, if this was your bike, what would you do to it to make it more comfortable and road-worthy, so you wouldn't have to worry about it breaking down?"

Seeing what a fool I was about to become, Griffin changed his attitude from a doubting Thomas into a proactive mode. We went to the counter and he pulled out a massive bike catalog. Flipping through the pages, Griffin pointed out the most critical types of bike equipment, bivouac, and survival gear that I should have on a long tour, at a bare minimum. He recommended two extra cages for carrying as much water as possible. There would be long stretches in the West without water. He insisted that a small sewing kit would be necessary, although I wasn't sure why he recommended it at the time. I wrote everything down because I had much to learn in a short period.

I left the bike at the shop for two days. On Friday, Griffin called me and told me it was ready to be picked up. He said the chain and cassette cluster, worn beyond the duty point, might make it across the country but possibly not. I knew the bike always shifted well and never skipped teeth but I told them to replace the components, as chains and cassettes get swapped out at the same time.

I broke away from work and drove to the Sugar House area of Salt Lake to pick up the bike. I was indeed pleased to see all the changes and upgrades. They raised the headset slightly, added a new touring seat, a new rack, new lights, a new chain, a mirror, a new cluster, and new tires. I picked up spare tubes, a lock, a repair kit, and a new helmet that somewhat resembled a cop motorcycle helmet. The total cost was about $600 to get all the changes made to the bike. Griffin told me the new Gatorskin tires would make it across the country. Little did I know how wrong he would be about that.

At REI, I purchased a North Face sleeping bag that weighed 1.8 pounds and an MSR one-person tent that weighed under 3 pounds. I bought an inflatable pad, stainless water bottles, a 3-liter CamelBak, and two extra bottle cages. I picked up one large can of Recoverite (a must), which had electrolytes, protein, and glycogen to replenish muscles after each daily pounding. Twenty-five packs of GU energy gel. Twenty tubes of Zip Fizz, which would help to keep me from bonking. Emergen C's for the ride for a vitamin boost. A canister of dried Gatorade. New riding shorts, a new shirt, and some clothes that I probably thought I would wear. Later, I bought a water filter, a small solar panel to charge the phone and lights, a new tire pump, a bottle of sunscreen, a tarp, and some butt-lube for my chamois, but not nearly enough. How would all this stuff even fit on the bike?

I bought Axiom Randonnee panniers, 20 liters in capacity and, hopefully, big enough to carry whatever I needed. The total cost of all those necessities was about $1,100. The remaining gear went into a well-used river dry bag strapped on the top of a rack behind the seat. I jam-packed anything and everything I thought I could fit or needed into a large suitcase that weighed about 65 pounds. I decided against taking a stove or cooking gear because that would add too much weight. I would eat from gas stations.

Five busy days passed while I worked, packed, and assembled gear before informing a handful of closest friends that I was attempting this ride. Work was hectic, mostly completing reports for clients in advance to transmit them from my phone while on the road without anyone knowing I wasn't working in the office. On several occasions, I asked my wife to help me get ready for the trip, but I sensed an avoidance to even talk about it. The final night, she helped me take the bike apart and work out how to get the bike and components into a big cardboard bicycle box. These unique boxes are required by the airlines for cargo transport and obtained from a bike shop. My wife directed me to run the tape in about ten different directions, using up nearly four packing tape rolls. It looked ridiculous.

It was hard to sleep that last night. Thoughts of what I was about to do sunk in more than before. I had no idea what I was physically capable of doing. I'd never ridden with panniers or for long distances. Doubt tiptoed into the bedroom to tease and unnerve me with a string of questions, one after another.

What distance could I travel before I decided to give up? Give up? What am I thinking? What if I couldn't even get over Snoqualmie Pass (the lowest highway pass) in the Cascade Mountains? What if I had an accident? Why did Griffin mention getting hurt? I had no backup plan. No backup plan whatsoever. Did I need one?

But what if I made it? Just the thought of making it to Boston gave me a rush of adrenaline. I looked at the clock and it was almost 3 a.m. Getting closer to start time.

CHAPTER 4 - SEATTLE TO THE ROCKIES

When I landed in Seattle, it was a cloudy day, about 75 degrees, ideal for July. Amanda, my brother-in-law's girlfriend arrived with a small red Volkswagen and we opened the hatchback and pushed in the bike and huge suitcase. My gear barely fit but we made it work and drove across bustling Seattle to a small eclectic cafe in the Fremont neighborhood for lunch. Afterward, Amanda took me to the beach to stand in the icy ocean water. Offshore, I watched ocean kayakers and sailboats playing in waves that glinted like diamonds in the late afternoon sun. It was exhilarating to feel the cold Pacific waters before starting the journey but ten seconds was long enough.

We went back to Amanda's house, picked up a growler of Red Hook ESB, Pliny the Elder Double IPA, and fresh food for Amanda's grand dinner plans. I love Seattle; there are so many good beers to choose from. Amanda was a professional chef before becoming a registered nurse, so I looked forward to one more great meal before hitting the road. We drove to her friend's apartment, where we met up with my brother-in-law, David. The three of them were planning a weekend hike in the North Cascade Mountains while I would be making my way south and east out of Seattle. It was a great evening of looking at maps, drinking, and planning an adventure. While they were preparing every logistical detail of their trip, I hadn't yet looked at a map to this point and wasn't even sure how to get from their house in Ballard to Seattle. Bad luck before the ride? A portent of doom? Perhaps, I thought the route would magically become obvious while riding.

Late that night, we drove to their house and I checked the gear, loaded up the panniers, and had David look them over to make sure they were balanced correctly before drifting off to sleep.

July 23rd - Seattle to North Bend, Washington

On the morning of July 23rd, I was up at 5:30 a.m. with David. I hardly slept, waking every few hours to check the time. The bed was hard, the covers were thin and short, and I shivered from the foggy cold Seattle night air wafting through an open bedroom window. In the kitchen, I was nervous and excited, brimming, chattering in whispers so as not to wake Amanda. The smell of coffee brightened the room. Dave and I downed a quick oatmeal breakfast punctuated with strong, hot, steamy cups of black coffee. That resuscitated me from a foggy night of little sleep, growlers of beer, and tequila shots. Before leaving the house, we clicked off some last-minute selfies in the living room.

David was off to work, Amanda was asleep, and I was at last on my own. This was it. I compulsively checked the bike for issues, brake clearances, and weight distribution. Gear weighed in at about 62 pounds, including liquids, and the bike felt strangely heavy and awkward. How on earth would I propel this portly, ungainly beast across the country? Ironically, I started the ride by not riding. I pushed the bike straight up a steep hill from the house, maybe two blocks to a coffee shop at the top. In less than five minutes, I was taking my first break. Inside the coffee shop, the smell of roasting coffee beans permeated the air. I dropped five bucks on a tasty latte with an exquisite cream design adorning the top.

Suddenly, I sensed that I was stalling. "*How long am I delaying the inevitable?*" I drank my coffee outside on a wooden bench by the bike and called my mom to reassure her I was okay. I told her about my plans three days before and my parents provided a strong warning not to attempt this ride.

"Hi Mom, I'm fine. I've come more than a whole block already," I told her.

"We have some friends whose grandkids in their 20s tried to do this kind of thing a few years ago, and only one out the four bikers made it. Maybe you can ride across Washington this year, then next year, you can ride across the next state," she implored.

"There isn't going to be *a next year*," I replied. "I'm doing this.

I'd rather be dead than not do this." I failed to mention I pushed the bike uphill the whole way. I also noticed that it was extremely challenging with all that weight. I savored my coffee, and then it was time to clip in and roll south to downtown Seattle.

I had only been riding in the clipless pedal system for less than two months. Clipless bike shoes have cleats that connect the shoe to the pedal, much like a ski binding connecting boot to ski. A quick ankle rotation shakes the foot loose from the bike pedal and while this system is an efficient way to pedal a bike, you must make a determined effort to unclip just before stopping or you and your steed hit the deck.

My bike felt extremely shaky and unstable. It seemed like the frame was flexing under the load, a feeling that was entirely unfamiliar to me. I had never ridden a bike with heavily loaded panniers. I was in for a treat. Crossing over the Lake Washington Ship Canal on Fremont Bridge, I was overtaken by a squadron of urban bikers. Most of them looked like young professionals, well dressed with laptops shouldered, each sporting a single pannier. These guys blew past buses and heavy traffic into town.

"Wow, this is great. I'm doing this!" I yelled aloud to them with a broad smile. Amanda's directions from Westlake to 5th Avenue were excellent and accurate enough to get me into busy downtown Seattle. To the west, the iconic Space Needle pushed up into the gray ceiling. Tall buildings with multicolored glass, busy streets, and buzzing intersections engulfed me. The traffic was outrageous. The smell of weed and coffee permeated downtown near alleyways. Diesel exhaust from commercial trucks left noxious clouds hovering just above the pavement.

I had never ridden a bike in a big city in traffic and felt a bit intimidated. I knew I had to keep a distance from parked cars to avoid getting doored; an unexpected opening of a car door can seriously injure or kill a biker in traffic. Best to take up a lane and piss off a driver. I soon passed south of downtown and a young African-American woman stopped me and gave me a big hug. I wondered why that happened but appreciated it and carried on.

Shortly afterward, I found my location on a seedier side of town looking for Rainier Avenue South to the I-90 Trail. Amanda told me this trail led towards Snoqualmie Pass in the Cascades. I missed the turn and was temporarily lost in the city, then backtracked and found the I-90 Trail. My phone navigation was terrible in the city, and my Google Map version didn't show bike trails. Maybe it was harder to get around back in the pioneer days but they didn't have neighborhoods, streets, and freeways in the way. Fortunately, the I-90 Trail made modern-day travel through these areas easier as I enjoyed a fun ride on pavement through green space. I-90 traveled through a tunnel 50 feet below the park. On the trail, I came upon and stopped at a Korean pavilion to investigate. The unusual structure was dark red, emerald green, and turquoise with intricate and ornate detail.

It's going to take a long time to cross the country at this rate, I thought.

Soon I was coasting through the 1300-foot-long Mount Baker Tunnel, emerging from the east side to be greeted by a spectacular unfolding panorama view of Lake Washington, the second-largest freshwater lake in the state. Known to limnologists[i] as a "ribbon lake," Lake Washington's shape is long and lenticular, carved into bedrock about 14,000 years ago by continental glaciation. As the glacial ice melted and retreated north, meltwater filled the lake.

Giggling with excitement, I thought this was hands-down the most rad bike trail I had ever ridden. I only wanted to go back through the tunnel and do it all over again but there was time for do-overs because a long ride awaited me.

The I-90 Trail bike trail parallels the westbound lanes of Interstate 90 on the north side of the bridge. I merrily pedaled across the floating bridge towards Mercer Island, accompanied by the roar of eight lanes of heavy, high-speed interstate traffic. This particular bridge designed by Homer Hadley is one of the longest floating bridges on Earth, over 6,600 feet in length, floats on hollow concrete pontoons, and cost nearly nine million dollars to complete in 1940. To the design engineer, the bridge was the best transportation crossing option for Lake Washington due to the excessive span across the Lake. Apparently, it was unfeasible to use conventional bridge foundation support such as caissons or pilings. The lake is deep, and the lake bottom is covered in gooey, thick, soft sediment left behind from the ancient glacier.

The ride east to Mercer Island was unbelievably sublime. Sky and water reflected similar hues of blue-gray and the strong wind pushing me from the north felt like an ocean gust whipping up ripples and whitecaps. Trees cloaked in dark shades of green contrasted against sky and water, clouds hung low in the air, and distant hills to the east stair-stepped higher into a blue haze masking the Cascades from view.

I-90 Trail Lake Washington

Once off the bridge and onto Mercer Island, I realized that lack of route planning would be a problem. I had no directions off of the bridge. Amanda's instructions had pretty much run out at this point, and I was lost in a verdant park. Fortunately, I spotted a group of county workers who gave me directions eastbound back to the I-90 Trail. I stopped in a park and mixed up some Zip Fizz because I'd already expended far more energy than I anticipated just getting across part of Lake Washington.

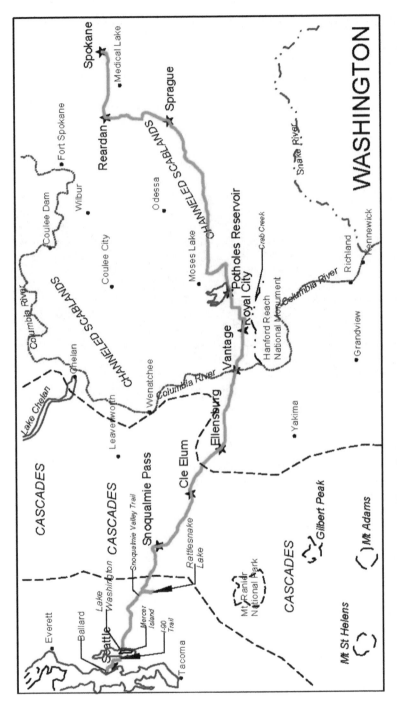

Figure 1 Seattle to Spokane

While resting in the park, I met an older Japanese man walking his dog. He described how he lived on Mercer Island for about 40 years. He never left the island because it was such a quiet and peaceful place to live, but I could barely hear what he said above the I-90 traffic rush. By afternoon, I traveled the I-90 Trail off the east side of the island, past the south end of Sammamish Lake, and through Sammamish and Issaquah. Issaquah is a growing, bustling town occupied by many apartment complexes, strip malls, and big-box stores carved out of the forest. I stopped at Best Buy to possibly purchase a GPS unit. Nothing they offered for sale was as helpful as my iPhone, so I returned to the trail. I followed the Issaquah-Preston Trail and the Highpoint Trail along the north side of I-90 through Preston. A turn back on the Preston-Snoqualmie Trail had me even more bewildered. One trail left me on a dead-end into deep woods.

I backtracked and connected with Preston-Fall City Road, turned left off the road back onto the trail, and pushed the bike on dirt up the steep Preston-Snoqualmie Trail switchbacks. I stopped at the eighth switchback for photos. The path was utterly wild and continued through a magnificent forest. By late afternoon, I followed a combination of wooded trails and confusing road connections to Lake Alice Road. A detour sent me one mile uphill on a 15-percent grade. I dismounted the bike, pushed it up what seemed like an endless hill while groaning under the heavy strain, and laughing at myself for my self-inflicted predicament. I don't get lost often, but I was way off course in the Cascade foothills' dense forests, and strangely, it didn't feel all that bad.

I knew from checking navigation that this was not the shortcut to Snoqualmie Pass. My legs began to cramp so I stopped to suck some GU gel packs. I picked up the Snoqualmie Parkway, took a right turn, and rode into Snoqualmie on Railroad Avenue, following the town's route along old rail tracks and brick sidewalks. To the right side of the road were old, historic railroad cars abandoned on the tracks, with signs describing the utility of the various railcars, part of the Northwest Railway Museum. I was particularly impressed by one of the old rusty locomotives painted by many colorful oxidization shades.

I was famished and stopped at a local burger joint for food and rest. My lights and phone batteries were on fumes and my butt was beyond sore. I had no prior experience with the daily battery recharging maintenance cycle; I had not taken the time to set up the solar panel behind the seat. Still, it didn't matter anyway because of the extensive cloud cover. I wolfed down a delicious hamburger, ordered another, and charged the lights and phone for about an hour. Food tasted better than ever before.

Locals in the restaurant told me the best way over Snoqualmie Pass was on the Iron Horse Trail from Rattlesnake Lake, which led through the long Snoqualmie Tunnel in Iron Horse State Park. I wanted to avoid the interstate and this was said to be the only alternative. They told me the ride was challenging beyond Rattlesnake Lake. They failed to mention that the Iron Horse Trail is loose gravel. I went into the bathroom, smeared some butt lube inside my shorts, loaded up the gear, and pedaled off to the southeast along the Snoqualmie Valley Trail towards North Bend.

The smooth asphalt pavement on the Snoqualmie Valley Trail is one of the most pleasurable rides I have ever pedaled, on a marvelously scenic trail. The Middle Fork of the Snoqualmie River danced to the left, beautifully framed against Mt. Si in the background. The mountains grew more prominent and closer as the valley width diminished. I approached the Cascades with a shiver of delight. I was beyond stoked. Somewhere before North Bend, the trail passed through multiple open fields with immense mountain views and I saw a small elk herd grazing at the edge of the woods.

Two large bulls, each with a few cows and a sprinkling of yearlings, brought me to an immediate halt for pictures. The bulls were the size of a small horse and large enough to make any hunter's bow shake on the draw. Each bull had six points and both were dressed in full light brownish-tan velvet, soaked with sunrays and gleaming against a forest green backdrop. They seemed aware but unfazed by my presence on the noiseless bike. The moment was memorable and magically euphoric.

This time is and always has been my favorite time of day to be outdoors. The picture-perfect near-sunset red lighting colors and dramatically steep Cascade Mountain slopes took on higher contrast in every direction, capped by the darkening clouds. The air temperature couldn't have been more ideal. Late afternoon sunbeams broke through the clouds for the first time. Despite body pains, cramping legs, and a butt that felt like it was sitting on a sandpapered pole, I was ecstatic and besieged by visual overstimulation. All of my senses became aroused and I fell into a blissful, joyful state of mind.

The Snoqualmie Valley Trail

When the sun's elevation fell within four fingers above the horizon at arm's length, I hunted for a campsite in earnest. Before dark, I spied a thick forest of straight pines near a power line corridor and followed a faint trail under the lines that branched off into the trees. I carried the bike to the woods, past deer and elk droppings scattered about the trail, and camped in dense woods. I wasn't quite sure of the location due to my crazy wanderings throughout the valley, it was the first night on the road, and I had not yet set up the new tent.

I camped right on the trail because the woods were astoundingly dense and brushy. Setting up camp should have been simple, but after a long day of riding a bike laden with gear, every task took more effort.

I stretched out and downed 800 mg of ibuprofen with a liter of Recoverite. The combination would replenish my muscles and proactively assuage back issues. I assigned locations for all the cargo contents, which would facilitate locating needed items during the day. I accidentally zeroed out the odometer, but I estimated the day encompassed 68 miles of circuitous meanderings from Ballard. I was alone, yet I did not feel alone and contemplated my situation—I was on track for slightly over two months of riding at this rate. *Could I make it? What am I doing?* I laid on my back and raised my knees. The deafening roar of the interstate traffic while crossing Lake Washington played in my mind. It was terrifying to be so close to traffic. Instantly my calf muscles contracted involuntarily into severe, agonizing cramps. I pushed out my heels and laid on my side until the pain subsided. Note to self, "*Don't do that again.*"

Sometime in the middle of the night, I was awakened by the loud breaking of branches. Several large animals were moving within close range and then large brushwood snapped closer to the tent. I panicked at the thought of an animal stepping on (or eating) me in the dark. The only "weapon" I had was a 14-inch piece of 3/4-inch PVC, which I used as a cheater bar for the bike pedals. One of the beasts whistled and I recognized it to be an elk call. I smacked the pipe on the floor of the tent and yelled, then heard the creatures scatter, providentially not in my direction.

July 24th - Snoqualmie Pass

I woke at 5:30, just ahead of sunrise, feeling surprisingly sporty and not too sore. A few sprinkles fell during the night and everything was wet. I kept thinking about the elk in camp. *Did that happen?* I got up, caffeinated up, packed up, said a morning prayer for safe travels, and hit the Snoqualmie Valley Trail. About 2.5 miles south of the interstate, the trail turned to the south and southwest and I realized I was traveling in the wrong direction on a dirt trail. Once again, I became more or less lost in an unfamiliar forest. The trail was compacted gravel but not hard to ride despite my road tires and I soon intersected Iron Horse State Park at Rattlesnake Lake.

The lake had an unusual blue-green hue and gravel beaches littered with dozens of 3- to 4-foot-high tree stumps, bleached gray and ringed with watermarks. The mystery behind the petrified stumps started as a slow-motion catastrophic flood in 1915 in a railroad village named Moncton. The town surrounded a much smaller lake at that time. In 1914, the river above Rattlesnake Lake was dammed by the City of Seattle, creating the Chester-Morse Lake. When filled, the dam leaked into the porous underlying glacial moraine[ii]. Water flowed downhill underground to Moncton and into Rattlesnake Lake, raising the level by about one foot per day. By mid to late 1915, hillsides around Moncton popped open with geysers, and homes floated away. They eventually condemned the town and burned the remaining structures.

The Snoqualmie Valley Trail intersects with the Iron Horse Trail at the northeast corner of the lake. I pushed the bike up onto the trail and realized I couldn't ride in the loose, uncompacted gravel. I wanted to cycle through the Snoqualmie Tunnel but it would not be possible on this bike. My only alternative was the interstate. I quickly backtracked on paved roads and descended 500 feet towards the town of Riverbend, hitting the on-ramp and launching out onto the noisy and frenzied Interstate 90. Snoqualmie Pass was my most direct way through the Cascades and a 2,500-foot climb in a 20-mile stretch.

What is the first thing you think of when you are in a vehicle and see someone biking on the interstate? Idiot comes to mind. I had never ridden a bike on an interstate highway, but one thing with certainty is that it sucks. It takes the ability to filter everything out, including noise and high-speed vehicles at close range. All of the worst debris on the highway is right where you have to ride. There are narrow bridges, and obstacles such as large storm drains and broken down cars that force you close to passing vehicles. Then there is the most chaotic and deadly part, crossing on-ramps and off-ramps at exits, where fatal contact with a car can occur. My right arm always went straight into the air, waving to alert vehicles. Sometimes I took the off-ramps to get off the highway.

"*Good God!*" I thought on the first few miles on the interstate. I was picking up speed, and the breakdown lane was rough. Then my first near-fatal mistake happened. I didn't make sure that everything on the bike was secured enough to endure the road vibration. The 64-ounce Mt. Dew bottle flew out of its cage and nearly went under my rear tire. If it did, it could have thrown me out in front of a vehicle. I stopped and secured it back in the cage with duct tape.

I prayed for safety in a near-constant refrain as I walked around trucks and cars blocking the breakdown lane. One of the bridges narrowed so much that I had no room to cross. It was all traffic lanes and just a white stripe along a Jersey barrier and a low railing. The apprehension was akin to crossing steep snowfields in the backcountry with considerable avalanche danger: Go real fast, be deliberate, and don't stop.

The ride to the pass on I-90 is a long grade with four steep sections averaging three to nine percent. Up....up...up, I groaned on the bike, standing on the pedals, willing the bike forward. The staccato thrum of downshifting semi-trucks was deafening, the exhaust nauseating. In many places, the breakdown lane was as wide as a traffic lane, and tens of thousands of metal wires littered my path. Several dozen motorcycles passed by in formation. A few of the bikers pretended to pedal as if they were on bicycles.

"Pretty amusing, thanks, guys!" I chuckled.

The ride was a long and arduous grunt. It wasn't the steepest climb I'd ever encountered on a bike, but positively the most terrifying. Deafening noise and diesel fumes invaded my senses. I could taste it; so many trucks, all groaning under the strain of summiting Snoqualmie Pass at 30 mph. I continually checked the GPS on the phone to see how close I was to the summit. When I got tired, I sat down and pedaled in second gear. Then the muscle pain reached its limits and I stood back up, repeating the process dozens of times. I couldn't stop because I didn't know if I could get going again.

I felt every ounce in the panniers. Did I need all this stuff? I was pushing my physical limits, my muscles fatigued, my hips burned. I took some solace in a light rain dotting my Ray-Bans and cooling my face but I had to think of something else. My thoughts drifted to my boyhood bike adventures. I keenly remembered my first two-wheeled ride sensation on a black, rusty 20-inch bike, discovered in a barn down the street. I recalled the joy and excitement of riding along the sidewalk for the first time on only two wheels, how quickly it traveled, freeing and graceful, compared to the tricycle I was used to. On the new bike, I could stay up and balanced as if I were flying on a fast-moving gyroscope. Then, the rusty handlebars broke off one day while riding around the block. After shedding a few tears, my parents bought me a 24-inch bike with wire basket panniers. That get-a-way Schwinn bike explored deep into neighboring towns and I was hooked. Chased by mad dogs and lawlessly trespassing on private properties, I would disappear to the woods with fishing rod and tackle box, seeking out bass and pickerel ponds with the fewest lily pads. I frequently returned home after dark with dirty or torn school clothing, and frantic parents who had no idea of my whereabouts grounded me. It was all worth it; rinse and repeat.

At last, the summit was in sight! I felt overwhelming relief as the grade lessened and the climb rounded off. Near the exit, the Iron

Horse Trail emerged from the 2.3 mile-long Snoqualmie Tunnel just south of the interstate. While it seemed like a good idea to go through the tunnel, I knew it would have been torture to attempt the ride from Rattlesnake Lake, and I would have walked most of it in darkness. I stopped to rest, take in spectacular views near the Pacific Crest Trail and suck down some GU and Shot Blocks. It was hard to believe I was only 3,015 feet above sea level. The impressive peaks all around gave me a sense of higher alpine elevation, revelation, salvation.

"That wasn't so bad of a climb," I said aloud to no one.

On the phone in Seattle, I told my mom that I would recalibrate the riding plan once I made Snoqualmie Pass. Well, I made the pass on Day 2 and I felt good. I guess I concocted some cross-country schedule at that point, although I didn't know what the program would be or even why I invented a plan. Eventually, I knew that my disappearance would be noticed by my clients, various friends, and family. If I made it back before discovering my boondoggle, I could complete a seamless re-entry back into my life. Yeah, that could happen.

The next logical geographic point for plan decision-making would be Helena, Montana, more than 650 miles away. I rolled eastbound with a newfound surge of energy. I was weirdly optimistic in totally unfamiliar territory. I pedaled over to the East Summit and stopped in at the US Forest Service building. The ranger told me I couldn't continue on I-90 eastbound because of road construction. The Highway Patrol prohibited bicycles from this point east past Keechelus Lake. Instead, I had to ride on the John Wayne Trail, an extension of the Iron Horse Trail, which detoured along the west side of Keechelus Lake.

Keechelus Lake (in Native American, meaning "few fish") is the headwaters of the Yakima River and one of three large natural lakes (Keechelus, Little Kachess (more fish), and Cle Elum (swift water). Naturally, the trail was not built for road biking; it is more suitable for mountain biking. I noted a few fat tracks, but the path did not seem as if it had seen much traffic.

"I am over the Cascades!" I giggled. I stopped to text pictures to my wife and kids. The John Wayne Trail started with reasonably decent riding conditions. Over the next six miles, the gravel became deeper, then deeper, then nearly unrideable in three inches of loose gravel. I tried riding different sides of the road. I tried looking for a sweet spot of firmer riding. I tried riding off on the edge of the road on bright green moss, rocks, and logs at 1/2 mph. Nothing worked and pleasurable riding became complete torture.

The lake views and a dramatic Cascade backdrop coalesced into a beautiful landscape. The steep, rugged terrain cut by avalanche paths, and green-carpeted slopes was breathtaking. Then suddenly, after gaining some speed with my attention on scenery, I crashed down hard to my left, auguring into the gravel. My mirror snapped off the handlebars. I cut my face, my left arm, and my left leg. Blood poured out, and I grabbed a bandana to slow the blood flow.

Keechelus Lake - First Crash

"Dammit, that really hurt!" I screamed out at the lake. The trail seemed frustratingly endless. I wanted desperately to get back on pavement, even if it meant illegally pedaling back onto the interstate. I stopped many times to glance back to the west at the Cascade Mountains. After 6.5 miles of miserably slow riding, I crossed the dam and returned to I-90. A text came through from my wife, *"Happy Pie and Beer Day! I love you, looking good. How many miles have you gone?"*

I rode I-90 for about 10 miles through the Wenatchee National Forest to Easton just south of Little Kachess Lake, then rode another 12.5 miles into Cle Elum for groceries. Cle Elum is a delightful town with tall pines, surrounded by the Wenatchee National Forest. I shopped for camping supplies, rolling my bike through the store, then headed out of town, first stopping at McDonald's. I needed protein and fat nourishment to replenish an empty well. I decided then to make one hot meal a day part of my routine. I rode through the drive-thru lane between cars and ordered. They didn't like the fact that I was on a bike. They said they couldn't give me the meal and needed special permission from the manager after paying for it. The manager came outside and handed me the food with a stern scolding.

"We only serve motor vehicles in the drive-thru!"

"Whatever," I thought, as I wolfed down 1400 calories, not what I would typically eat but twice as fast. I felt a twinge of nausea and threw water in my face.

"Try not to vomit," I thought.

After settling my stomach for 20 minutes, I pedaled down Highway 903 to Highway 10 through Teanaway and Ellensburg. It was late in the day and I caught glimpses of the Yakima River's picturesque rapids dancing in the sunlight. I entered a desert of 15 million-year-old lava flows that stretched from the eastern half of Washington to Idaho's Rocky Mountains with the Cascades behind me. With my hand stretched out against the sky, the sun at a four-finger gap, it was time to look for a campsite. I crossed the railroad tracks near a horse ranch in Bristol and located a concealed spot on the riverbank in the willows. Then, I took a slow-speed dump from the bike and landed hard. I was more embarrassed than suffering from pain and hoped my crash went unnoticed. I was in the wrong gear and still getting used to the new clipless shoes, and not paying attention to unclipping first.

I pushed the bike over a massive pile of old, bleached horse bones to the river bank. There must have been five or more horses' worth of bones here, based on the number of skulls. *"That was weird. Don't they bury horses?"* I thought. I quickly set up the tent as the site was rampant with mosquitoes. I donned my black Gore-Tex pants and a light green down jacket, my *"after-riding"* camouflage attire for the remainder of the trip. I mixed up Recoverite and downed an appetizer of ibuprofen.

I had just settled in when the approaching roar of engines overwhelmed the sounds of the river rapids. Two 4-wheelers pulled up above me and stopped. *Damn it!* My camp had been discovered by the ranch owners, both sporting cowboy hats and western clothing. The older man introduced himself as Shane and his associate as his son Beau. Real cowboy names indeed.

"You are trespassing on our ranch, and we want to know why," said Shane sternly.

"I needed a place to crash for the night, and I didn't see any No Trespassing signs, so I thought it would be okay to camp by the river. I saw that there is a self-pay boat launch sign about 400 feet upriver. I thought it might be public land."

"This is our ranch, our property, and it's private property," said Shane sternly.

I should have asked before camping, I guess. I should have been worried. But, for some reason, I couldn't stop wondering if they saw me turf it onto the gravel road right before they showed up. I don't even know why I fixated on that thought. I couldn't even think of what to say.

"Don't worry, I am an ethical and experienced camper, and my parents raised me right, so I won't be any trouble, and I will leave no trace of my stay, just some flattened grass. If you want, I can pay you."

Shane entered my personal space, looking me straight in the eye.

"Well, you'd better be good, or we will come down here in the middle of the night, kill you and throw your body into the Yakima."

Just as he said this, he lurched towards my face and crushed a mosquito on my cheek.

"Oh, that one almost got you," he said as he flicked the bug from his fingers. He faintly smiled. The two left on the 4-wheelers in a cloud of dust, and I went back over the bone pile to my river spot, somewhat relieved. I hate being busted while poaching a camp. I prefer seclusion to discovery.

It was the first quarter of a waxing July moon. I stripped off my clothes and slipped into the shallow rocky, fast-moving river to wash off the sweat and dried blood. Darkness concealed most of my surroundings, but the moonlight lit the tent and danced on the Yakima's ripples. It was wonderfully pleasing. I was alone but it did not feel that way. The moment was magic, much more so than the previous night in the forest. I called my parents to reassure them that everything was fine, and crawled back into the tent and checked the map to see where I was headed in the morning. I rested well that night with the moon shining brightly through the fabric, listening to the ebb and flow of buzzing mosquitoes.

July 25th - Yakima River to Pothole Lake

I was up at 5:30 and after a refreshing, uninterrupted sleep, in desperate need of caffeine. I mixed up a powdered caffeine drink. It was sticky, and the bottle leaked gummy, sour half-dissolved powder down the side of the container. My fingers stuck to everything and I hoped that wasn't a harbinger of the day ahead. But I was feeling good and called Mom and Dad again to reassure them I was okay and would be hitting the road with a lot of strength. I pushed the bike up from the river and over the massive bone pile and set out onto Highway 10. I felt fantastic and ready for a 100-mile ride. To the north, I spotted Shane out working in his garden. I waved goodbye and yelled, "God bless you for the campsite!" Shane turned and waved goodbye as well, apparently in a more pleasant mood.

I pedaled southeast alongside the meandering Yakima River on Route 10, pushed along by a robust tailwind. Eighteen miles down the road, I reached Ellensburg, home of Central Washington University. I needed a state road map; unsure of where I was going and getting lost was taking too much time. I stopped at a bookstore on the north side of University Avenue and purchased a Washington State map.

I left the bookstore with greater confidence and a sense of direction. I pedaled east through town, stopping at a "hippie" bagel shop for a delicious latte and breakfast bagel. Sufficiently fueled, I swung by the post office and mailed out a card to my parents because, in just a few more days, it would be their 61st anniversary. I left town pedaling east past the University and took the 29-mile Vantage Road from Ellensburg. The road to Vantage was a two-lane highway with a gentle climbing grade through irrigated farmlands, wind farms, and horse pastures. Riding conditions were beautiful with a strong tailwind that inspired a pleasant couple of hours on the bike.

After crossing an irrigation canal, the scenery changed radically from emerald green farmlands into brown, dry, non-irrigated, remote rangeland and volcanic hills. Then, a relentless climb began, grinding up about 1,000 vertical feet over 12 miles on a sinuous road. It was a desolate sage desert surrounded by naked layers of volcanic tuffs[iii], sediments, and basalts[iv]. This rock is classic Washington volcanic geology and my mind became lost scrutinizing stratigraphic sequences[v] of rock, distracting me from the slog of the climb. Swirling wind and gray cloud-covered sky added an eerie feel to a remote and lonely stretch of Washington. There were no cars on the highway, a welcome treat after the melee of riding on the interstate. As I approached the ridge top, I noted scores of large wind turbines sprouting from the ground across the horizon line. The view was surreal, and I rode around traffic barriers to get a closer look. Each tower was over 300 feet tall, with three, 100-foot-long blades slicing through the air with deep, low, throaty "thumps" generating over a megawatt of energy. I could feel the vibration reverberating through my body. A fascinating, close-up view of renewable energy in motion.

There had been no traffic on the road for at least a half-hour and from the wind farm it was 11.5 miles and over 2,000 feet of downhill coasting to Vantage. I whizzed downhill at speeds up to 45 mph, chin on the headset and adrenaline spiked. The bike felt perfectly stable and I took the traffic lane, attacking the downhill with pure speed and giggles, occasionally looking behind me for cars. Tears beaded up and streaked from my eyes as I flew past Ginkgo Petrified Forest State Park. Soon, the Columbia River came into sight, presenting an impressive backdrop of sparsely vegetated brown volcanic canyon walls.

Across the Columbia loomed large sequences of Tertiary[vi] volcanic lava flows, weathering out to giant, imposing benches. These basalts welled up from deep cracks in the crust of Eastern Washington over 17 million years ago. Up to three miles of lava oozed up from great depths to elevations far above the present-day river. I stopped to examine every detail of the stratigraphic flows and then rounded a large bend into the small village of Vantage. After nearly a dozen miles of downhill, my heart was pounding from excitement. I was already halfway across Washington and I felt strong and confident.

I stopped at a gas station and picked up two Gatorade bottles for later and a large iced tea, which I emptied before reaching the cash register. The cashier told me that I-90 was reduced to one lane across the bridge in both directions. I wasn't sure what that meant but it didn't sound bike-friendly. I guzzled a quart of Gatorade sitting on the picnic table outside the station, staring at the bridge and planning my next move. Crossing a bridge on a bike requires more thought and more exceptional care than one would think.

The I-90 Vantage Bridge is impressive, over 2,500 feet in length and 75 feet above the water, constructed in 1962 across the gorge over Wanapum Lake, a reservoir on the Columbia River formed by a dam just below Vantage. The bridge is a "through-type arch design" because the arch of the bridge starts below the highway deck level. My nerves were shaking because there was no other way across for many miles. This was the only way.

"*Screw it,*" I thought, "*You only live once. I'm having Pop-Tarts and Gatorade for lunch, I'm going for it.*" I jumped onto the bike, hardened off my nerves, and stormed the ramp onto I-90, picking up speed with semi-trucks climbing up behind me. Anxiety welled up from the pit of my stomach. One bump from a vehicle would launch me over a three-foot rail into the Columbia. When I approached the choke point at the bridge, I spotted a small gap between Jersey barriers, not quite wide enough for the bike. I jumped the barriers, lifting the bike over into the closed lane.

"This lane is all mine!" I exclaimed aloud with a great big smile and an immense cry of relief. The entire lane across the bridge was shut down, utterly empty of workers and obstruction because it was a Sunday. I stopped to gaze across the vast expanse of water with magnificent layered basalt cliffs jutting out above lengthy talus slopes. Volcanic plateaus of reddish-brown garlanded in pastel yellow vegetation painted the gorge in all directions. It was so grand that it didn't look real. I spent ten minutes savoring the view from the safety of my private lane and later relished this as one of the most sublime experiences of the journey. Despite the turbulent wind and raucous semi-truck traffic only feet behind me, I was in an enchanting moment far away.

Off of the bridge, I turned right and south onto Highway 26, then east up into Sand Hollow, a desert canyon that climbs towards Royal City. The road grade climbed steeply for a challenging 600 vertical feet over about four miles alongside a raging creek. The water volume in the stream seemed odd, considering the time of year and the desert-like surroundings. After about five miles of riding beside this mystery creek, I reached the canyon's top, where the scenery radically shifted from desert to agricultural. Ahead to the horizon were miles of irrigated fields of corn, groves of apple trees, and rows of grapes. A maze of canals and pumps and myriad pivots soaked each side of Highway 26. This massive irrigation system appeared to be the mystery creek source, return water to the Columbia. This water transformed an otherwise desert into an Eden.

I was drained of energy but made time on the flat with less effort with a rhythm of stand-up pedaling and coasting—ten cranks, coast for 10 seconds, and resume once my speed dropped below 20 mph. I was starting to bonk and my unprepared butt hurt, with visible raw sores after three days of grinding through beautifully brutal Washington terrain.

Finally, relief appeared like a desert oasis: *"Judy's Great Food."* Part roadside stand, part diner, part winery. Out front, fresh produce was on display for purchase and inside, they welcomed visitors to free wine tasting. I met the owner who shared his story. Once a water well driller, he changed professions after a divorce and devoted his life to growing grapes and producing wine. It was, by his account, a better lifestyle. He offered me a taste of his product but I graciously declined; it is dangerous enough riding a bicycle under sober conditions. I decided in Seattle that I wasn't going to drink alcohol on this trip. Staying hydrated can avoid all sorts of ills and my history with drinking and bike riding wasn't injury-free. The last time I tried that combination was on the Slickrock Trail outside Moab, Utah. I ended up in the ER with a broken sternum after one beer.

I laid out all of my gear across the table at the booth, charged the phone, and enjoyed a delicious barbecue brisket sandwich and homemade coleslaw. Protein and fat are what every biker needs for a deep reservoir of go juice. I wolfed it down while sussing out places to camp in the area.

"Go to the Potholes Reservoir to camp because there is a formal campground with showers, and I think it's very popular," said the waitress. Lake camping sounded like a good idea. After a pleasant hour-long break, I went outside to reacclimate in the enticing Columbia Plateau breeze. Adrenaline began pumping again so I went back inside, said my goodbyes, and took to the road with a brisk tailwind and fully reenergized momentum. To the south was Crab Creek Basin, which is so large that I mistook it earlier for the Columbia River Gorge. In fact, the ancient Columbia River once flowed through Crab Creek during the Ice Age. Massive scouring from a phantom flood occurred during the Pleistocene[vii], which created small pothole ponds and ghostly riverbank features where there is no river present. The prehistoric features confounded geologists for decades.

I followed Highway 26 east, passing Royal City. At the junction with Route 262, I turned north towards Potholes Reservoir, through an endless maze of canals, pivots, pumps, and drop structures with massive volumes of water gushing and disappearing into drains. The air had a curious, organic smell, something like camphor. Still, I couldn't recognize it, nor had I ever smelled anything like it before. I rode through miles of crops I couldn't identify and at one point, while grinding away on a steeper section, a feisty blue heeler took chase as his owners watched with amusement. I stood on the pedals to power away and just barely stayed ahead of the miserable mutt's snarling maw.

After six tiring uphill miles, I came to a large bend in the road. Ahead of me lay the Potholes Reservoir, spread over an area known (to some) as the Scablands[viii]. The Scablands area is an ancient flood path that scoured the Columbia Plateau, a true testament to world-class geologic Catastrophism[ix]. The Scablands were formed during the Pleistocene Period by a massive flood originating from glacial Lake Missoula[x] in far-away Montana, resulting in a desert land of buttes, labyrinths of channeled canyons, ethereal piles of giant rocks, prehistoric ripple marks, and scoured pothole lakes[xi]. Erratic boulders[xii] were randomly scattered about. These and other dry phantom waterfall features remained a mystery for over 40 years of geologic study. The Scablands were the subject of considerable controversy because the premise of the cataclysm's sheer magnitude was so unimaginable that the geologic mystery took generations to be understood.

Near present-day Missoula, the glacial lake was over 900 feet in depth and possibly half the volume of Lake Michigan. At one time, Lake Missoula exceeded 3,000 square miles, originating from the melting of the North American glaciers within the northern Rocky Mountains. The lake was dammed to the west by massive ice sheets along the Clark Fork River near the Idaho border and drained when the ice dam broke, submerging east-central Washington to the Pacific Ocean in a flood that would have left Noah duly impressed. A mind-boggling flow on the magnitude of ten cubic miles of water per hour rushed across the landscape. The lake drained not once, but dozens of times, based on the study of sedimentary deposits left behind. J. Harlen Bretz, a geologist from Washington, studied the Scabland area for years and was ridiculed for his premise of a massive flood. It wasn't until satellite photos obtained in the 1970s fully confirmed Bretz's theory about the Scablands.

Potholes State Park is located at the southwestern corner of its namesake reservoir. Although spending the night at a campground with showers sounded good back at Judy's, the $25 campsite fee was a rip-off. The campground was packed with RVs, family reunions, generators and blaring rap music, cars, traffic, drunk teenagers, and screaming kids—everything I detested about pay campgrounds. The ranger assigned me to a site at the farthest north location. These choice campsites included tire-piercing goat heads and dirt, weeds, broken picnic tables, and fire pits full of trash. With no trees and lots of bugs, it was undoubtedly one of the most unappealing places to camp. I was met by a 40-something-year-old substitute teacher named Dex, who had already set up his tent in my campsite. He began his rant.

"I spent 20 minutes setting up this tent; I'm not taking it down. There wasn't anyone at the booth when I pulled into the park, so I thought camping was free," he said. It became apparent he wasn't going to back away.

"Well, I just paid for this campsite and here is my receipt," I told him, pulling it out of the pouch on the handlebars and waving it in his face. I wasn't going to let up either. There were no other open camp spots and it was late in the day. I paid for the site, my ass was sore, my legs were cramping, and I was not in the mood for squatters. I rode 93 miles for the day, and now I was locked in a standoff for a camp spot.

Suddenly he jumped in his car, and it was on. I got on the bike, and we raced back to the ranger station, him on the roads while I blasted through family dinner gatherings in occupied campsites. We arrived at the guard station at the same time. Dex complained that he was at the site first so he should get it. I relented as the ranger assigned me the adjacent camp spot. I returned to find a parked car at my site with a reservation clipped to the site post. I tore off the ticket, ripped it up, and threw it in the fire pit. Problem solved. An attractive and ornately-dressed Polynesian woman strolled across the road and asked to borrow my phone.

"Why are you camping at our site? I made a group reservation for this spot months ago," she said. I ignored her while I unloaded the panniers onto the table. Then her girlfriend came over to make small talk. Noting the increase in female company, Dex invited himself over to investigate. His unsophisticated, mindless banter irritated me and I didn't want him around. Later, he invited me over to his site for a salad, which I construed as a peace offering. What an odd series of events.

As the moon peeked above the horizon, Dex took off on a photographic spree. At the same time, I wandered out into the fields and watched the moon rise above Potholes Reservoir. The panoramic sky above the water and the moment were beautiful. The air was still, and the water was glass. It was close to the full moon, and silver beams of light illuminated green fields around the lake. To the west, a large turbulent creek dropped into the reservoir, so bright that I could see the rapids as clear as day. I headed back to the tent, lay in my bag, and started to drift off. Then I heard Dex snoring. Not a regular snore, no, that would have been fortunate. His snore was being monitored by seismograph stations worldwide. I knew that I didn't want to spend any more nights in a campground.

July 26th - Gravel Roads and Dead Ends
I woke up at first light, around 5:10 a.m., and Dex was still at it. I was anxious to get up and go. Showers weren't part of the camping fee, so I decided to forgo a cleaning and put up with my stench for the day. My clothes were dirty and damp, either from moisture in the tent or sweat, and it felt dreadful to put them on. Making matters worse, the butt lube I applied to assuage saddle sores stung like hell. The day wasn't off to a great start but then a text message arrived from my wife, *"Good morning, how are you feeling? Happy trails, no falling off the bike today."*

I started pedaling at 6:30 a.m. and headed across the O'Sullivan Dam, which forms the Potholes Reservoir. Looking south, I noted the extraordinary erosional features and pothole ponds carved out of the basalt bedrock. The dam is about 200 feet in height and 3.6 miles in length. I crossed the dam with the sunrise, stopping to watch walleye and bass break the surface far below. I felt euphoric in the moment but my exceedingly sore behind was hard to ignore, as was the persistent grade. In an automobile, you hardly notice the change in elevation across this area. But on a bicycle, low spots and grade increases announce themselves by inflicting pain in your legs. I distracted myself with the dramatic scenery all around me. I could see why the tremendous flood rushed through this area, and I was impressed with the bedrock laid bare by scouring, numerous lakes and rock piles. Mt Rainier still dominated the horizon, its snowfields soaring above distant mountainsides in the cloudless blue sky behind me to the west. This would be my last glimpse of the Cascades. The Rockies were somewhere out there to the east, still far from sight.

I immediately wished I was on a different route when I reached Route 17. The highway had recently been chip sealed, and the gravel was loosely spread in thick, uneven swaths that proved difficult to ride on. Although construction signs posted a 45 mph speed limit, most cars and trucks blasted by at highway speeds, spraying me with hailstones of gravel. It appeared there was no oil placed on the road to hold down the gravel surface. It was painful. Pebbles bounced off my face and glasses. At times, it seemed like some cars moved closer to shower me on purpose.

I became anxious. *Find a strip to ride, keep control, turn your head every time a vehicle passes.* There were no other routes available. Not only were road conditions terrible, but I was riding northwest in the wrong direction. I kept checking the navigation until I came to Road O SE and followed it north. After a quick stop to lube the chain, I reached the frontage road along I-90.

The day turned miserably hot and road conditions were dreadful. Sometimes the frontage roads consisted of loosely-packed gravel. On some occasions, I arrived at dead ends way out into dry wheat fields. I backtracked two miles to the south side frontage road, which was just as bad. Following endless miles of loose gravel chip seal and deplorable road-riding conditions, I began to cuss out loud many times. Handling the bike and the load was squirrely at best under these conditions. Then I pedaled roads with no road base. Under the stress of mid-day sun, my mind wandered back to my business. Yes, escape, that's what was happening.

Text messages arrived from my wife, including a picture of my one-year-old granddaughter Siena taking her first steps. This trip was starting to feel like a big sacrifice. I was in physical agony, thirsty, hot with raw sores on my butt, and riding in terrible conditions. But what could I do? I had no backup plan, and I was committed. I continued pedaling thirty-seven unpaved frontage road miles to Ritzville.

Finally, I turned northeast and followed East Danekas Road out of town, around the south side of Sprague Lake to Sprague. The scenery was surreal on a winding road bounded by endless harvested golden wheat fields and fields in fallow interspersed with scoured ponds left behind by the Lake Missoula Flood. At the 90-mile mark, I rolled into Sprague, highlighted with large grain bins in the center of town. I stopped to admire a collection of antique cars and met a friendly older man on a four-wheeler with an Australian Cattle Dog that moved in to kiss my face.

"That will be my next dog," I said to the man.

"She's a sweetie!" he said.

I stopped to pick up water in town and headed north, climbing steeply on Route 23, then I turned onto Route 231 towards Edwall. It was getting late with less than four fingers of sun and not a tree in sight. It was time to go undercover for the night, but where? I located a campsite in some undulating fields off to the north, surrounded by barbed wire fences and miles of harvested grains where I couldn't be spotted from the road. I rode 94 miles for the day and I was reasonably tired. I set up camp in the cheatgrass and gulped down copious amounts of liquids.

July 27th Sprague, Washington, and the Centennial Trail

I awoke at 4:50 a.m. It was cold and beginning to get light under low clouds, prompting me to pack up and go. Coyotes yipped all night and I yelled out to shut them up. "Dammit, I am trying to get some sleep in here!" They were still howling a half-hour after sunrise. I peered out of the tent to see an impressive rainbow against a blue-gray sky to the west. It was inspiring but morning rainbows almost always portend rain. Sure enough, I climbed outside of the tent into light sprinkles. Coyotes were close during the night, and judging by the size of the fresh poop all about, they were pretty big. They left quite a mess behind.

Nevertheless, my spirits were high as I gorged on Pop-Tarts and dry granola, downed cold coffee, then pumped the tires and pushed the bike out of the field down to the road. In light rain, I headed northeast on Route 231 towards Edwall. This was a beautiful stretch of good riding with little traffic and many hills pitched against ancient torrential Lake Missoula Flood features. A strong northwest wind buffeted my progress as I rode through miles of yellow to gold to tan hills. They resembled rolling waves on a sea of grain interspersed with plowed earth that didn't look real. I felt like I was riding through a painting or a rendered photograph. Red barns and wide-open panoramas, cut by lines of tilled land hugging section lines, dotted the countryside.

Heavy rain hit the pavement and pelted my body from a dark ceiling and for the first time, I caught a glimpse of the Rocky Mountains. The road climbed, sometimes steeply, finally topped out, and I enjoyed a long downhill coast into Edwall. The town was settled for wheat farming, but most of it was boarded up. Even the post office was closed down. From Edwall, I pedaled north up towards Reardan, working my way out of the Columbia Basin. The scenery changed at this point when I noted the first stand of ponderosa pine trees. I intersected Route 2 and rode into Reardan in heavy traffic on another recently chip-sealed surface.

I needed a break, so I stopped at a crazy-looking coffee shop named the "*Fist a Cup Java.*" The building facade was adorned with license plates and road signs, many with entertaining content. I downed a latte, gained a renewed strength, and pedaled east out of town on Route 2. A text arrived from my wife: "*I'm having the kitchen cabinets painted today, and I need $3,000.*" I wondered why we suddenly needed to paint oak kitchen cabinets. It seemed like a sizeable cost, but I shook it off and refocused on the road.

After twenty miles, I approached Spokane, passing perfect hexagonal-shaped basalt columns. Spokane is situated at the eastern border of Columbia Plateau volcanic geology and the Rocky Mountain Region's western side. The city is bifurcated by the Spokane River, which flows from Idaho. The city is named after the native Spokan Tribe meaning "*Children of the Stars.*" Spokane is also the birthplace of Fathers Day, founded in 1910, and home to Gonzaga University and the home of basketball star John Stockton, retired point guard and star from our Utah Jazz.

I was overwhelmed with hunger, so I stopped at McDonald's for lunch and free ice and water to fill my CamelBak. I also bought lunch for a traveler who was perched outside the door peddling leather pouches to make his way back to Portland. Feeling good about myself for helping the stranger, I rode two blocks and experienced a flat tire, my first in almost 380 miles.

"Well, no good deed goes unpunished," I said aloud, hoping this was not a metaphor for my trip. So much for my humility. I interpreted it as a signal from beyond. I flipped the bike over and pulled out the back tube, then pedaled into Spokane to a bike shop for supplies and biking directions. While using the shop's pump to top off my tires, the mechanic told me to follow the Centennial Bike Trail. This trail starts northwest of Spokane and follows the Spokane River to Lake Coeur d'Alene. I had no clue about this trail or where I was going, never mind anything about Coeur d'Alene. I rode into the center of downtown Spokane in heavy traffic, then turned left to the north on Washington Street to Riverfront Park with impressive views of waterfalls to the west and a large hydro dam to the east.

I located a trail in Centennial Park that followed the north side of the Spokane River under a bridge on the River Walk Loop, a riverside paved trail with occasional boardwalk and brick-lined sections. The unusual blue-green color of the river caught my eye. It was delightful to ride in the ponderosas after days in the desolate, treeless Columbia Plateau terrain and endless prairie. I followed the trail onto the Gonzaga campus, where hordes of summer students passed by with books. After days of solitude, riding the trail through campus was especially fun. What a huge relief to finally pedal on a decent bike path with bathrooms nearby.

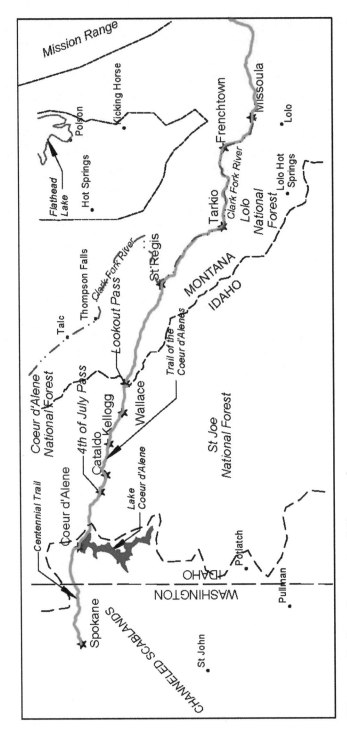

Figure 2 Spokane to Missoula

The Centennial Trail

The Centennial Trail followed the south side of the river in Millwood. Dark gray clouds hung low and the sky took on an ominous character. I donned my Gore-Tex coat and followed the trail through the town of Liberty Lake, where I crossed into Idaho. The Washington-Idaho state line on the Centennial Trail is marked with a bronze plaque mounted on a large granite boulder. I stopped for a selfie and reflected on my achievement as time slowed in an unexplainable way. I had never crossed an entire state on a bike before. I was overwhelmingly emotional, ecstatic, and delighted.

Without warning, a rain shower intensified into a microburst hail storm, pelting me with half-inch ice nuggets, but the euphoria from crossing Washington kept my spirits high. I felt a tremendous sensation of invincibility, driven by giggles of pure foolishness, when I realized how naked bike touring is in bad weather. Even though I've previously been on river and mountain excursions in big storms, I never chose to go bike riding when the weather was terrible. I found sanctuary under a bridge and replenished my burned-up calories. The storm intensified to a pavement-pounding crescendo before diminishing to a drizzle as fog drifted from the woods.

It was late and with no sun to gauge the time, I continued the riding pace on a cold, wet road into Post Falls, Idaho. On 3rd Ave, just off the Centennial Trail, I found a vacant wooded lot and deemed it the perfect urban campsite. I was tired but stoked after a 98-mile day. I quickly went undercover and set up camp close to a small ledge that concealed my location from the road above. Several deer worked their way past me through the wooded park as darkness crept in. I zoomed in on a US map to gauge Post Falls relative to Boston. Many states and miles lay ahead.

July 28th - Centennial Trail to The Trail of the Coeur d'Alenes

Throughout the night, I conversed with one of the deer in the camp. She would let out a short snorting sound, and I'd snort back for a reaction. This comical exchange went on for quite some time. I awoke at 4:30 and attempted to go back to sleep when she snorted again, awaiting a response.

"I need some sleep here!" I shouted. I sensed she was lying next to the tent and I was right. She jumped up and scurried away through the leaves, which completely startled me. I didn't need any more adrenaline. So much for sleep. I rose at 5:15 a.m., packed the gear, and was back on the trail by 6:30 a.m. It was a chilly and foggy July morning, so I bundled up to stay warm.

A text came in from my wife. *"Max is really sick. I think it's time to put him out of his misery. He is constantly hacking."*

"Just take him to the vet and see what is wrong with him," I texted back. I wasn't aware of any health issues with the dog. Messages from home were now becoming more concerning.

The Centennial Trail follows along the Spokane River through open meadows, healthy ponderosa pines, and noisy, short sections along I-90. I arrived at Lake Coeur d'Alene, on River Avenue. This was my first glimpse of Lake Coeur d'Alene, and its magnificence immediately enchanted me. Lake Coeur d'Alene is mostly a natural lake created by flood bars from the catastrophic Lake Missoula flood. Today, the lake is refilled by the Coeur d'Alene and Saint Joe Rivers, which replace the lake's water volume, on average, about twice per year.

A strong wind swept in from the south, whipping up whitecaps. It was a lovely sunny morning, not a cloud in the sky, the wind was warm, and there was that happy feeling evoked by a summer breeze wafting through the pines. I smiled broadly and savored every moment, then found a sandy gravel beach in the trees and rolled the bike onto the sand. I couldn't help but see similarities between Coeur d'Alene and New Hampshire, except for the ponderosa pines.

Lake Coeur d'Alene

I had not been in the water since the Yakima River. No one was around, so I stripped naked and gingerly stepped to the lake's edge and dove out into cool, translucent water. I took a long, refreshing swim and then came back to the beach to wash my dirty clothes with castile soap. I laid clean duds across a picnic table next to the bike and went back into the water. Without any doubt, this beach amenity made the Centennial Trail one of the most delightful bike paths I had ever pedaled. Floating comfortably in the water, I looked back to the beach and saw a man picking up my belongings. I quickly swam in and yelled at him to drop my stuff. Startled by my nakedness, he dropped my clothes and ran back up to the trail above the beach. He probably didn't get chased by crazy naked guys from the water too often.

I was losing time and not making the needed miles for the day, so I tempered my mileage expectations to enjoy the lake.

"Not too much of this type of water across the country, better to enjoy it now." I thought. Several hours passed as my clothes dried. I packed up, put on my road face, and rode beside sandy beaches into town to the elegant Coeur d'Alene Resort. I rode out onto the docks and was stopped by a local who wanted to chat about the bike. When she mentioned biking the Trail of the Coeur d'Alenes, my ears perked up. Her directions were vague, but the trail lay somewhere to the east.

"Where is the Trail of the Coeur d'Alenes?" I wondered. I needed to go east but the only way to connect to the trail appeared to be I-90 and over Fourth of July Pass that divides the two paths. Access onto I-90 was near Leopold (a statue of a photographer with a bellows camera overlooking the lake), over a Jersey barrier and damaged chain-link fence. I stripped the bike of its gear, climbed the barricade, and lifted everything over to the highway. I jumped the fence, packed up the panniers, and rode the freeway. Grunting up noisy I-90 again was not much fun, after riding such a beautiful trail.

"Stay focused," I thought as I struggled to the top of Fourth of July Pass. The hill turned into a real chore under the strain of 60 pounds of gear. It is about a 1,000-foot climb at grades of five percent or more over about six miles, with a summit elevation of just over 3,080 feet. The pass is located at the western end of the Idaho silver mining district. The road was originally a wagon trail cut for the military to travel through the Rocky Mountains to the Pacific Northwest. Captain Mullan named the pass on the 4th of July in 1861 but today, the col was a raucous slog punctuated by roaring Harleys.

I coasted towards the Trail of the Coeur d'Alenes off the Cataldo exit, where I stopped at Old Cataldo Mission State Park. This Jesuit church, built around 1853, claims to be the oldest building structure in Idaho. The guard station woman told me I could proceed into the park for free on a bike. She also gave me free Clif Bars. I rode up across the steep, grassy hill to the mission stairs and set the bike on the front steps. Inside, the ceiling was ornately painted as if it was meant to mimic the Sistine Chapel design. I found the artwork and the construction impressive for this age and the remote Idaho location. I stopped to pray for my safety on the road and quietly left.

I rejoined I-90 for another mile, then crossed the Coeur d'Alene River and picked up the Trail of the Coeur d'Alenes in Cataldo. This is a great bike trail—velvety smooth pavement leads through thick woods, crossing the river several times on old railroad truss bridges, with gradual grades ranging from about one to three percent. For the most part, the trail winds tightly along the lazy Coeur d'Alene River, passing through Enaville, Pinehurst, Smelterville, and then past the Kellogg Superfund Site. A feeling of great happiness passed through me, having escaped from the interstate and gained another beautiful trail.

I passed the historic Snake Pit in Enaville, once a famous brothel for the silver miners, now a popular bar and restaurant for the biking crowd and tourists. After another river crossing, I rode into Smelterville and past several rock dumps and leach piles from mining. From here, the trail wanders through the heart of the Kellogg Superfund cleanup work adjacent to the creek drainage. The creek was dark-brown colored and looked like leachate. Process buildings, foul-looking ponds, and sparsely-covered tailings flanked both sides of the trail. I was familiar with Kellogg from my work on heavily contaminated mining sites in southeast Idaho and Kellogg is well-known for the mining and smelting impacts on the landscape, humans, and environment. Kellogg was named after a prospector's donkey, which allegedly wandered off and was found atop an unusual outcrop that led to the Bunker Hill Mine discovery. Biological lead from the smelter contaminated the town because no pollution controls were in place, affecting many of the town residents. By the mid-1970s, the average blood lead concentration in children was three to five times the national average. EPA and the state of Idaho directed the cleanup of over 6,000 residential and public properties in the area and replaced the contaminated topsoil. By the year 2000, the closure of mining operations and soil replacements in Kellogg brought the lead levels in the children down to acceptable levels.

From Kellogg, I pedaled up the trail along the south side of the interstate through Osburn and under the Silver Mountain ski gondolas and several resort hotels packed with tourists. I continued through magnificent terrain with historic mining towns and emerald hillsides. The trail couldn't have been more delightful and void of other bikers. The course became steeper after I crossed back under I-90 into Wallace for food and supplies, following a river beneath a long bridge bypassing the town.

Allegedly, Wallace had the last traffic light before the completion of I-90. The site of an early silver boom in the 1890s, Wallace's boomtown pressure was in due course out of control, with frequent murders and periods of civil unrest, at a point requiring the U.S. Army to intervene with striking silver miners. In 1910, half of the town burned in one of the most massive fires in U.S. history, and much of the city was rebuilt in the current form of a "fire-retardant" classic brick style. My impression was that Wallace is a cool town with a modern hipster feel blended with a look of the "Old West." High-end coffee shops, boutique shops, and unique restaurants, bars, and breweries line the main streets. I wished I could have tried one or all of them for a cold one; I was craving a beer. The town is advertised as the *"Center of the Universe."* I guess in an infinite universe, everywhere is in the center. The question is, do they serve beer there?

Around 6:30 p.m. I was about a mile from Mullan when I spotted a *"Road Closed"* barrier just to the left of the trail leading up into the woods. I looked around, slipped under the gate, and pushed the bike up into a clearing in the pines where I found a lovely grassy meadow surrounded by thick cedar trees blanketed with moss. There was an old pile of bear poop near one end of the campsite. My body was starving from a long day's ride so I stuffed my face with beef jerky and nuts, Triscuits and squeeze cheez, and one quart of Recoverite. I hung up all my food in a dry bag at a location about 250 feet east of camp. It was a wonderful and eventful day. I felt terrific, having ridden 72 miles from prairie to mountainous bear country. I looked at a map of the U.S. and noted that I was on the North Fork of the Coeur d'Alene River at the most northern latitude of the ride, maybe ten percent of the way to Boston. It was exceedingly cold for late July and I crawled into the tent and drifted off to sleep to the somewhat annoying sounds of I-90 beyond my wooded enclosure. Despite my cleverly clandestine mountain meadow surroundings, it was far from peaceful. A text message came in from my wife "*I miss U.*"

[i] Limnologist - A scientist that studies freshwater bodies,

mostly ponds and lake environments.

[ii] Moraine - Drift, deposited chiefly by direct glacial action, having constructional topography independent of the surface on which the deposit lies.

[iii] Tuff - A fine-grained volcanic rock comprised of compacted volcanic materials.

[iv] Basalts - Dark, extrusive volcanic rocks made of calcium plagioclase feldspar and pyroxene.

[v] Stratigraphic sequence - A succession of sedimentary rock beds chronologically arranged with the older beds below and the younger beds above.

[vi] Tertiary - The older of two time periods representing the Cenozoic Era.

[vii] Pleistocene - Geologic epoch equivalent to the Ice Age, about 2.5 million years to around 12,000 years ago.

[viii] Scablands - Area in the Pacific Northwest where denudation has removed all of the soil to bedrock, and the rock surface is covered with its own coarse angular debris.

[ix] Catastrophism - The doctrine that sudden, short-lived, violent, catastrophic events outside of our present experience or knowledge have substantially modified the earth's crust.

[x] Lake Missoula - A glacial lake from about 13,000 to 15,000 years ago existing in the mountainous region of western Montana that was dammed by a glacier at the Idaho border on the Clark Fork River, that occasionally broke, causing repeated cataclysmic floods across eastern Washington that formed the Scablands.

[xi] Pothole Lake - A lake formed in a scoured river bed.

[xii] Erratic Boulder - A sizeable rock fragment that is different from the bedrock on which it lies, usually glacially transported, but also found to be carried by the Lake Missoula floods.

CHAPTER 5 - ROCKIES TO THE BLACK HILLS

July 29 - Lookout Pass to Tarkio, Montana

I awoke to the highway traffic rush in the dark and turned on a light to see my breath inside the tent. I had no earplugs and was starting to adjust to constant highway noise. I packed up and departed my secretive pine meadow around 6:45 a.m. It was time to warm up and make some mileage. It was a comfortable one-mile ride into Mullan through the cedars, which incrementally displaced the Douglas Firs with gained elevation. Mullan is a small mining town at the east end of the Trail of the Coeur d'Alenes, made up of colorful multi-colored bungalows and an active silver mine near the east end of town. I stopped at the post office to send off some mail and met a young man coming out of the door.

"How do I get out of town and over Lookout Pass?" I asked.

"Well, you can't take I-90. Bicycles are not allowed on I-90 due to the highway construction."

"Is there another way?"

"Yeah, you can ride to the east end of town up past the mine, pick up Willow Creek Road and climb up and over the highway on an old overpass," he said. "From there, you can follow the old railroad grade through the woods to Lookout Pass. That will take you into Montana," he said. Sounded straightforward enough but I would soon learn otherwise.

I found Willow Creek Road near the east end of town, curving to the right and then up, up, up, the hill into the pines. The climb was remarkably steep, and my legs buckled under the strain. The seemingly endless road climbed nearly 500 feet above town. Deer crossed the road ahead of me, and I listened to large animals on the move in the forest below. Slowly grinding this hill was like climbing an Olympic ski jump at less than one mile per hour. I had to focus on everything else but the pain of my straining muscles, including a faded Chevron billboard, which was overtaken by tightly spaced pines. This road must have been the original thoroughfare into the valley before I-90. Near the top of the hill, I passed an old gas station that was transformed into a residence. On display were old-time Coke coolers and washtubs planted with fresh geraniums. A garage displayed relic gas pumps and vintage Chevron and Texaco signs. The street signs were named Hemi and Mopar. I looked inside through the glass of the old garage and spied a bright orange 1970s Dodge Challenger in mint condition. I loved it. The owner must be a real fanatic for the Chrysler muscle cars.

I crossed an aging one-lane concrete bridge above I-90 and then entered the forest on a US Forest Service dirt road. I checked Google Maps and looked for road cuts or other features on the satellite photos. Anywhere I could see fill or ballast exposures might indicate that I was close to the old railroad grade. The cedars were thick, densely spaced, and brilliant green, the terrain ridiculously steep. A text alert from my wife stated, "*We moved the refrigerator and broke off the copper pipe that is gushing water, and we can't find the shutoff downstairs. The house is flooding.*" I had no service to respond. Oh well.

The further I ventured into the woods, the more I worried about whether I had made the right choice. My other option would have been to accept a shuttle ride over the summit from the Idaho Department of Transportation. I promised myself to ride to Boston without motor vehicle assistance. Then, I noticed a weathered telephone pole in the canyon below me, a sign that the Union Pacific Rail Trail was close by. The road conditions became dreadful with little to no road base, creating an un-rideable surface. I got off the bike and started to push it up the hill through the woods. An old pickup truck chugged up the road from behind and pulled next to me. The guy in the truck was about 30, wearing a big smile and conspicuously holding a red lighter in his right hand.

"Hey man, is there a bike trail up here somewhere?" I asked.

"Yeah, this connects to the bike rail trail just ahead, probably less than a quarter-mile. Throw your bike in the back and I'll give you a ride up there to the parking lot."

"No thanks, man, I'm riding across the country without any motor vehicle assistance. That's just a silly rule I made for myself when I started the ride in Seattle. That's why I came up this way."

"Well, you are close. I'll meet you at the trailhead," he said enthusiastically.

I pushed the bike up into an empty dirt parking lot and met up with my newfound friend, Danny. I instantly liked this guy. It was such a joy and relief to make human contact.

"I just dropped off my dog at a doggie daycare to go hiking up here," he said. I was amused because I enjoy hiking with my dogs. Still noting the lighter clutched in his right hand, I told him that I would be headed to South Dakota after Montana. He rummaged through his truck, pulled out some maps, and showed me a bicycle tour route he took through the Black Hills. While looking over South Dakota's maps, he mentioned that he and his wife follow the Dave Matthews Band for extended tours. He was newly settled in the Coeur d'Alene area. It felt so good to talk to someone on a more personal level with things in common.

"Hey man, since you have that lighter in your hand, are you going to burn one?" I asked.

He smiled and enthusiastically said, "Yeah, man, let's do it! By the way, there is the rail trail," as he pointed behind us. He pulled out a few different types of legally purchased high-end weed. After a few puffs, we were laughing like 16-year-olds who had just demolished a pint of whiskey from their parent's liquor cabinet. He was the first great company I had experienced in four days of grinding. We hung out, laughing for about 45 minutes, sharing stories of our common interests of music, the outdoors, biking, dogs, and hiking. It was a hilarious scene, two strangers amused by everything and nothing at the same time. I didn't want to leave my new buddy, but we reluctantly had to say our goodbyes. Off I pedaled up the North Pacific Trail towards Montana through a dark cedar forest in the best mood imaginable.

The North Pacific Trail was semi-decent packed gravel on a gentle rail grade through a heavily treed corridor, with a severe 40-percent slope to the north. It was hard to imagine how the mountainside could hold trees, let alone how they engineered this railroad cut. It was some of the most fun road biking I had ever done in off-road forest conditions. The day's temperature rose under an azure sky, offset by a light breeze near the pass. Tree shadows cooled my skin. After several miles of riding and a few rough stretches, the trail emerged at the Lookout Ski & Recreation Area, about 4,710 feet in elevation. I crossed from Pacific to Mountain Time at the Montana border, but time didn't seem to matter. Only distance mattered. Two states were now in the rearview mirror, albeit Idaho was a very short one, but sweet.

Lookout Ski & Recreation Area is one of the oldest ski resorts in the country. A sign in front of the lodge claims this to be one of three ski resorts in the country that straddles two states. I locked the bike and went into the bike shop, where the employees were busy renting mountain bikes to tourists. The man behind the counter in the bike shop was utterly lame in answering any questions about directions traveling east. Another guy working in bike rentals told me, "*There are no paved bike trails in Montana.*" I had doubts about this bold statement and was irritated by his attitude. Every worker in the shop was entirely unhelpful and I concluded that no one enjoyed working there. I rolled across the parking lot and talked to a guy working alone in the maintenance shop who told me that I should ride on I-90 to St Regis. He said it was pretty flat terrain going east compared with the Idaho side. I hopped onto I-90 at the Montana State Line. Quite contrary to the full description given to me, I blew down the interstate at giggle speed. It is hardly flat; in fact, the interstate was so steep that I pushed 47 mph on a precipitous 1,600-foot downhill rush to Haugan, Montana. The lane was clean of both trash and loose gravel.

Halfway down the canyon, however, I was overcome with thirst and looked for a place to take a break. There was no fencing barrier between the highway and the forest so I wandered a short way into the woods, pulled off my Camelbak, and settled on a rotten log against a dead tree to relax. In less than a minute, giant red carpenter ants were crawling up my shirt. Then, they were on my legs. Then inside my pants and socks. It played out like a science fiction horror movie.

"My God, I sat right on their nest!" I screamed at the top of my voice.

They stung hard and everywhere up my stomach, back, neck, face, and in my hair. I jumped up and pulled down my pants. Ants were everywhere. Off with everything, fast. Passing vehicles honked their horns as I slapped dozens of ants off of my naked body and shook out my clothes. I noted at least one driver's astonished expression as she slowed to crane her neck.

The day approached the high 90's when I stopped in to take a butt break at the "50,000 Silver Dollar". The place was a revolving stop for every tour bus in the West. I wandered through the bar, which displayed thousands of silver dollars and a 10-foot wooden statue of Abe Lincoln. I strolled past glass cases of Montana knives and western wear. Lunch was delicious with about a ½ gallon of ice tea and the amount of food I was inhaling increased considerably by the day. The calorie content was about three times what I would typically eat. As I finished lunch, I couldn't help noticing that I smelled pretty bad. Is that why no one was sitting nearby? I looked around to see if I was offending anyone and walked back out into the blazing sun.

It was about 17 miles to St Regis. The afternoon heat drained me so I pulled over at the St Regis River's confluence and the Clark Fork River for a refreshing dip. Just off I-90, I followed a dirt access road to the St. Regis River, where I located a deep hole and jumped in (with my clothes on this time). It was cold and an utterly invigorating experience. Upriver, I watched two young cow elk behind a fly fisherman casting his line, working his way towards me, seemingly unaware of the elk enjoying an afternoon drink. It was a genuine *A River Runs Through It* moment.

I rode into Saint Regis but Highway 135 was being chip sealed at that time. No more of that. *"Screw that, I'm not doing it,"* I thought. I stopped and conversed with a flagger, who sent me south off I-90 up Cold Creek Road. I began to climb, climb, climb, and then a gravel road?

"WTF," I yelled aloud. "This sucks." But the road mellowed out and I descended into the valley and followed old U.S. Highway 10 along the north side of the Clark Fork River on an excellent highway towards Superior and Riverbend. It is a beautiful ride along this stretch, past log houses and ranches with horses and million-dollar per acre properties for sale directly on the river.

"Good grief, this property is in the middle of nowhere, and they want a million dollars an acre?" I wondered.

There was little traffic on the Mullan East Road. I started to get tired so I took a frontage road exit and ended up near a 90-degree bend in the Clark Fork River at Tarkio in the Lolo National Forest. I pulled off the highway behind a Montana MDOT shed, went to the back of the parking lot, and wheeled the bike out into the lodgepole pines.

The Clark Fork's forest is neat and tidy with a smooth pine needle carpet and no underbrush. Two small white-tail deer greeted my arrival; one was a cute little spotted Bambi. Both immediately bolted from the campsite with high vertical leaps that appeared utterly unreal. Still in the bear country, I wandered from my camp looking for a tree to hang the food, with little luck considering the limited number of branches on lodgepoles. I located two trees that had partially fallen against each other, hoisted the bag, and tied it off. I was tired but felt pretty damn good after putting in my first 77 miles in Rocky Mountain on/off-road riding. The day's highlight was meeting Danny near Lookout Pass and having the sheer pleasure of navigating the old railroad grade into Montana. I was delighted.

It was about 9:45 p.m. and the sky was still light. I downed a quart of Recoverite and grabbed Montana's map, unfolding, unfolding, and unfolding it in the tent.

"Holy moly, Montana is freaking huge," I thought as I looked at the scale at the bottom of the map. *It's going to be a long haul across this state. How many days would that be?* I couldn't be sure. I also noticed my gear started to smell as bad as I did, collecting considerable amounts of dirt. Beyond the walls of the tent, the sweet-sounding rhythm of the Clark Fork River lulled me to sleep. Later, a deer wandered by my campsite and began snorting. Here we go again.

July 30 - Tarkio to Outside Ovando, Montana

I roused around 8 a.m. but couldn't wake up. My mind churned and I questioned what I was doing. July 30 was my son's fifth wedding anniversary.

"What the hell am I doing out here in unfamiliar territory on a bicycle? "Is this ride worth it? Or just a selfish, silly adventure without any serious thought? Why am I riding I-90 with all the Harleys and truck and car traffic and noise? Is this an adventure? Is this fun? Is this what I wanted, to be alone, far from home, risking everything, and for what purpose?"*

I packed slowly without caffeine and then found that my river bag had become hopelessly wedged 15 feet overhead between the two trees with no apparent way to retrieve it. I rambled down a steep grade towards the Clark Fork River and found a dead lodgepole long enough to reach the bag. After about five minutes of swinging the heavy bag with the pole, I flipped it over the top of the pinched trees and retrieved it. I pedaled back onto I-90 because I had no other choice, and then took the first exit onto Old Highway 10. The railroad crosses the river on a few trestles at dizzying heights above the river bottom.

The magnificent Clark Fork is Montana's largest river by flow volume, over 310 miles in length, and a significant tributary to the Columbia River. Above Tarkio, the Clark Fork River forms a tight river canyon through the Alberton Gorge. Somewhere in the canyon I came upon a small yellow submarine, entirely out of place, left in the woods by the river. I scratched my head at this one.

A strong tailwind gave the sensation that I was traveling in the direction of river flow but it was just the opposite, which confounded me. Few side roads connect between Tarkio and Huson so I kept hopping back onto I-90, which was clean riding for a change. The breakdown lane was practically as big and smooth as the traffic lane. At one point, I came upon a long bridge, quite high above the river. It was narrow with a short guardrail and no breakdown lane. One bump from a car would launch me 80 feet into shallow water. At a break in the traffic, I pedaled furiously across the bridge at full speed. My heart raced.

At last, an exit off of I-90 into Frenchtown brought great relief. I spotted a bakery stand and an older woman named Irene selling cookies, pies, and muffins. I had never before stopped to buy anything from a roadside bakery stand, and it is much easier to stop on a bike than a car.

"Some days I sell lots of goodies but on other days, I don't sell much at all," she said.

I did my part and bought two large cookies, one peanut butter, and one sugar-cinnamon. Delicious. Sugar-fueled, I followed Mullan Road out of Frenchtown. This road was undoubtedly part of Missoula's old highway to Coeur d'Alene and it is still treacherous, narrow and busy with high-speed drivers with urgent destinations. This route was much too dangerous for my comfort level but there I was, so I kept on pedaling and sweating bullets. A cop passed me much too closely, with the siren blaring.

I passed the former Smurfit-Stone Container Corporation mill south of Frenchtown. The enormous industrial facility was vacant and by observation, the candidate for an urgent environmental cleanup. More than 1,260 acres of diked and partially covered waste tailings, sloughs, and ponds surrounded me, some very close to the Clark Fork River. These waste ponds will not endure in geologic terms and will become part of the river if not removed.

Rural Montana slowly blended into suburban neighborhoods. I checked my navigation to estimate the proximity to Missoula, which was close. I picked up a paved bike trail and pedaled up and over a prominent glacial lake bench where, for the first time, I could see the big "M" on the mountainside for the University of Montana. The Indians allegedly named Missoula after their word for the Clark Fork River, which roughly translates to *"place of frozen water."* I could make out faint bathtub rings on the surrounding hillsides, wave-cut remnants from glacial Lake Missoula which submerged Missoula under about 950 feet of water. I wondered whether the indigenous people had a notion of the prehistoric geologic past events through their oral storytelling traditions.

I was ecstatic upon reaching the outskirts of town. I worked my way into Missoula, transitioning from a well-paved rural two-lane highway to busy city roads with heavy traffic. Where bike trails didn't exist, the riding lane was wide and clean. I was now back in city riding mode. While approaching downtown Missoula in the bike lane, a black Chevy half-ton with dark-tinted windows blared his horn right behind me. I was clearly in the bicycle lane as marked on the highway with the ubiquitous diamond and bicycle icon.

"Nice. I thought this was supposed to be a laid-back town."

As the truck passed me, someone gave me the finger out the window. Classy. I navigated to the Adventure Cycling headquarters, arriving in the heat of a late-July afternoon. Adventure Cycling is a non-profit biking association committed to advancing long-distance bike touring across the country. I felt like I might be in good company here and hoped to learn as much as possible without mentioning that I had embarked upon my ride with such little training. Okay, no training. I met a friendly older gentleman on his way out of the building. He took the bike from me and locked it in the bike corral.

"I'll put it with all of the other all-star bikes," he smiled.

I felt a little honored by his comment. I went inside their office, where they offered ice cream and free soda. Such enthusiasm here made me feel worthy of my effort! I felt like a celebrity. Questions from the staff ensued: "*You left Seattle 6 days ago? Did you bike all the way? Alone? What route? Did you have any problems?*"

I saw my bike locked in the corral where all of the workers kept their urban commuters and felt a little love in my heart for my bicycle at that moment, something that I had not experienced before. That bike was my only security and best friend.

One of my worries was how I would cross the Midwest and Eastern states. Unlike the West, the East has a substantially denser network of roads, towns, rivers, highways, and cities. There are many ways to get lost, or worse, end up on a major thruway where bikes are not allowed. Navigating by Google Maps was more easily accomplished in the West, with little traffic by comparison. But a map with marked bike routes would boost my confidence. I biked unplanned to Missoula but thought I'd better start preparing for the rest of the ride. I bought three bike trail maps for Indiana to New England, part of Adventure Cycling's "*Northern Tier Route.*" By purchasing these maps, I solidified my belief that I could make it to Boston.

In my mind, I couldn't even think about how to navigate across Massachusetts, the state where I grew up and went to school, but the Northern Tier didn't even pass through Massachusetts. I'd have to wing it. They took my picture and put the photo on a large bulletin board among many, many other bikers. I laughed at the picture, as well as the others. I hadn't looked in a mirror in a few days and I looked rough. But all bikers had one notable thing in common; we all looked happy in our pictures. They labeled my hometown as Seattle, Washington, but I didn't say anything.

I purchased a bike shirt with "*Transamerica*" printed on the front, a cross-country bike route race from Astoria, Oregon to Yorktown, Virginia. Between 2014 and 2017, 154 bikers attempted the cross country race, with less than 100 finishing the ride. The fastest rider completed the route in about 18 days. I was hardly worthy of these racers so I put the shirt away for later. As silly as that sounded, it gave me another reason to make it across the country.

Adventure Cycling, Missoula, Montana

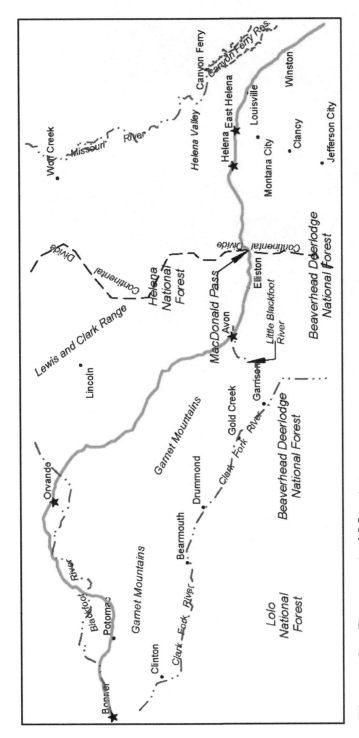

Figure 3 - Bonner to Winston

Adventure Cycling recommended Route 200 as the best bike route to Helena. As I headed for the door, they directed me to ride to East Missoula then turn north onto Highway 200 at Bonner. The other option would be more interstate. Riding across America shouldn't be all on the interstate. I needed some peace and back road scenery.

Route 200 was an excellent canyon ride on a highway heading north along the Blackfoot River, through woods and past ranches and irrigated fields. Beautiful forest and spectacular mountain views surrounded me. The lane was perfect riding—full, clean, and only a few rough spots. The ponderosa pines were elegant and the grass below the forests always seems so neat and naturally trimmed. Late afternoon was wearing on me but the surroundings enveloped me in incredible mountainous beauty. At one point, I stopped at a spacious field and counted more than 100 head of cow elk with the Garnet Mountains in the background. The view and sheer beauty reenergized my mind and body. It was an incredible display of western wildlife directly off of the highway. Cars kept whizzing by and I wondered if they even noticed.

I stopped for cold drinks at a gas station at the junction with Route 83 and the clerk told me there were reports of a few grizzly bear sightings up ahead in the canyon. I rode eight more miles and camped by a fishing boat launch and campground on the Blackfoot River. I set up the tent within 10 feet of the river and quickly doffed my clothing to take a dip. It was a joy to slip into the freshwater and wash off the road stench, sweat, and dirt. It is surprising how dirty I got riding a bike on dry pavement. I noted a lot of new, mysterious leg cuts as well.

The river was shallow and the mossy rocks much too slick to stand on so I eased my way out on my behind and up to my neck in swift, cold, crystal clear water. Drift boats with fishermen floated by and somehow managed to find the deepest spots. Fly rods swung from side to side, lines fluttering like ribbons in the air, glistening in fading sunlight, but no one seemed to note my still presence.

My adjacent campground neighbors were a couple from Alaska touring in a fifth-wheel trailer. Their "babies" were nine yappy Yorkshire Terriers penned in a small traveling kennel. Nine! I fixed a quick dinner of junk food, drank a liter of Recoverite, then packed all of my food and gear in assigned metal bear boxes about 50 feet away from the riverside camp.

At nightfall, I sat down on the riverbank and watched the full moon rise over the river. This moment was it. I was in my element. The air remained hot on the heels of a long and blistering summer day. I was getting eaten alive by mosquitoes but couldn't even get up for bug spray because I was too mesmerized by the surroundings and too tired to move. Two bald eagles glided past me downriver. This view and this feeling are what Montana is all about in my mind, outdoor heaven on Earth. I checked the mileage and noted 93 miles for the day. I looked at the Montana map in the tent, then checked my location on Google, zooming out to the country's extents to gauge my progress, roughly 13 percent of the way to Boston. I fell asleep lying on top of the sleeping bag and gear.

I awoke around midnight, expecting it was time to rise. I was excited to ride, but I realized I had only been asleep for an hour when I checked the time. I almost opened my cold coffee prematurely. I climbed into the bag and drifted off to river sounds echoing through the canyon.

July 31 - Continental Divide

At 6 o'clock, I looked out to a chilly morning and low-hanging fog over the river. I was a little sore and reached my rear to palpate open wounds. After a couple of ibuprofen, I donned my cold, wet, smelly clothes. I ate a quick breakfast of Pop-Tarts chased with a nasty powdered caffeinated beverage. I rolled out of camp, pedaling under unusually cool conditions. The cold air against my legs was a real eye-opener. My feet were cold and surprisingly, a little numb on the bottom. I rolled down Route 200 through classic western Montana scenery of long grassland valleys that stretched to faraway forested hills and mountains.

I passed through Ovando, Montana, noted on a sign to be the "*Jewel of the Blackfoot Valley.*" Ten more miles on a southeast course brought me to the picturesque Blackfoot Valley and the headwaters of the Blackfoot River. Fishing access was everywhere. My mind wandered back to the thoughts of a young boy who would have given anything to explore these waters with a rod and creel. To the left was the vast expanse of the Bob Marshall Wilderness, the second-largest wilderness area in the lower 48 states. I stopped at a sign detailing the story of Bob Marshall, the man. As a conservationist, he was considerably ahead of his time. Marshall secured much of the 5.5 million acres of wilderness in the 1930s before his premature death at age 38. He hiked the Adirondack Mountains of New York as a young man, served in the Forest Service and Bureau of Indian Affairs, and was a founding member of the Wilderness Society.

I continued pedaling long, straight stretches of rapidly deteriorating road. In many locations, the white line was missing, exposing me to near passing vehicles. I rolled past rustic and rural scenery, miles of fences, expansive ranches, barns, and scores of horses and miles of grassland valleys cut by barbed wire. I passed old stucco houses with worn-shingled roofs, broken windows, and cows standing on porches and in doorways. The idyllic scenery was dominated by massive, imposing peaks of the Garnet Mountains creating a backdrop in fading blue shades.

I stopped to photograph a "Meth Kills" billboard by one ranch. The sign depicted a basketball player with a knife in his back. The sign seemed out of place and I wasn't sure of the basketball player's significance or the number 32, or the knife.

"Is meth worse here than elsewhere in the country? Did it involve a big knife?" I wondered. At the junction of Highway 141, I turned right over the meandering Blackfoot River and headed south down Highway 141 for 33 miles to Avon. Route 141 is a great ride, combining long up and downhill stretches. I passed a large earthen dam forming Nevada Lake on the right. It was now getting hot, and a dip in the lake looked appealing but my legs wanted to keep going.

The breakdown lane was shrinking by the mile and in some locations, the asphalt degraded to gravel. I began to worry about my clearance to traffic combined with the blind hills. In a few places, the breakdown lane was absent altogether and the white line was painted on dirt. I kept a close watch behind but traffic was light. Ten miles past Nevada Lake, I passed a small summit. What a relief because I was bonking. I coasted for an exhilarating eight-mile downhill ride to Avon.

The road turns east onto Highway 12 at Avon. My next challenge would be the mighty Continental Divide and MacDonald Pass. The day was heating up when I reached the junction with Route 12, where I crossed the Little Blackfoot River on a rustic metal and wood suspension bridge. Sheltered by shady cottonwood trees, off came my sweaty and dirty clothes. I was losing my inhibitions, possibly due to my solitary existence and burgeoning sense of transience. I reveled in an afternoon dip in the clear, cold, fast-moving

Little Blackfoot River. These were the magnificent moments of the trip, celebrating in solitude while soaking in unspoiled water, with only the wild Montana surroundings. It fueled the fire inside me. It was heavenly, and words at that instant could not describe the joy in my heart.

Back on Highway 12, I noted a vast improvement in the riding lane and pavement quality. The Avon junction to McDonald Pass is an 11-mile ride with an elevation gain of over 1,800 feet. The road conditions were vastly improved but the steep grade combined with a scorching afternoon sun was challenging. I stopped at the general store in Blossburg Canyon, just below the pass and guzzled a king-sized Mt. Dew and then a large Gatorade while chatting with the clerk.

"It's quite an effort to bike over the pass. The climb starts just past the store," she said.

A group of Harleys with impressive paint jobs pulled into the station for fuel. The Sturgis, South Dakota bike rally was coming within the week, so on the current schedule, I might be passing through Sturgis at the same time as the rally. I engaged in small talk with some of the riders and their passengers. Leather certainly does something pleasant for the body; even the guys looked good. I mentioned that I was riding from Seattle, and they were surprised by the distance I had already traveled.

I got back on the bike, grinding up to MacDonald Pass past several mines. The area was a well-known route through the Rockies long before the completion of the highway. Captain Mullan of the U.S. Army pioneered a road close to the pass in 1850, following the original Indian trail while packing camels on their way to Walla Walla, Washington. Twenty years later brought the Northern Pacific Railroad and a variation of the road became a toll road in 1868. In September 1911, Cromwell Dixon flew a small plane over the Continental Divide near this point, earning a $10,000 prize. Sadly, he crashed and burned two days later in Spokane, flying the same plane. No good deed goes unpunished, I guess.

The climb to McDonald Pass was the most challenging uphill riding since Snoqualmie Pass. Up, up, up, I went, grinding it out, down to the lowest gear. Temperatures approached 95 degrees and the road grade was 10 percent in places. At this point, stopping would make starting up again nearly impossible. The guardrail impinged the riding lane and grinding it out became a grueling task, with burning hips and thighs. All I could see ahead was what appeared to be an endless climb followed by another corner. Finally, I saw microwave towers. These generally appear first to tell you that you're getting close to the highest point on the road. Frequent Harley riders passed me at high speeds while I moved at a snail's pace. At the pass, and I entered Lewis and Clark County. I felt strong, happy, confident and even began to tear up. I crossed the Cascade Range just days before and now I was soloing my way over the Continental Divide at 6,325 feet. I was thrilled.

I pulled off the highway onto a dirt road to the south into a herd of cattle and called my parents to wish them a happy 62nd anniversary. I did not have a cell signal the previous day and I knew they were probably worried. I joked with them while on the Continental Divide that it would be all downhill to Boston. Coincidently, it was my 22nd anniversary that day so I texted my wife, "Happy Anniversary." A reply soon came back that she received her anniversary card and a check I sent from the road.

"Is this check for me?" she asked.

"That's to cover all of the bills and our expenses for August," I replied.

After a half-hour, I resumed the steep grade down to Helena. I descended 13 miles, over 2,200 feet on a steep, winding road approaching 13 percent in places, at speeds of about 35 to 40 miles an hour. One big hairpin turn had me feeling low and stable over my right knee. Without hesitation, I took the full traffic lane because the breakdown lane was covered with loose gravel. I rolled into the state capitol to get food supplies for the night.

The history of the Helena Valley area goes back nearly 10,000 years. As recent as 300 years ago, the Blackfeet Indians settled the area. When gold was discovered in 1864, mass migrations of white men arrived to stake their claims and by 1888, dozens of millionaires walked the streets. Little did the miners know that the residents constructed the town on top of one of the most extensive gold placers[i] in American history before Helena became the capital of the Montana Territory.

"Keep going, you are doing great!" I told myself. I remembered telling my mom if I made it over Snoqualmie Pass in Washington, I would ride to Helena and reevaluate my physical condition and ambition level. I was riding high on adrenaline and

enthusiasm. I had no next-point in mind for reassessing my route, but I was happy. I pulled up onto the sidewalk behind a couple of twenty-something girls and asked for directions east out of town. The girls pointed me to a local road towards East Helena on Route 12.

The Helena landscape is very different from Missoula. Heading out of town east on Prospect Avenue, the city faded away and I noted no trees in any direction. The sun sank low in the sky, far below my four-finger rule. Prospective campsites were non-existent. It was late, and I knew I would have to find a location to crash soon. Late turned into dusk. I pulled off on a side gravel road over the railroad tracks and decided to crash in a low, grassy swale. I was tucked away mostly out of sight in a topographic depression against the railroad ballast. Crested wheatgrass provided the only cover. The site included four stacked wood pallets that served as my table.

A sun-setting sky faded to pale orange, then to deep lavender from the Earth's encroaching shadow above Helena's lights twinkling in the distance. I was over the Continental Divide, rode 97 miles for the day, and was utterly exhausted but euphoric. I made my second geographic goal. I felt sore but much stronger than when I started in Seattle. I put the food in the dry bag and moved it far from camp because skunks and other creatures were undoubtedly scavenging in the vicinity. Little did I know as I set up the tent, I picked one of the loudest places on Earth to camp.

August 1 - East Helena to Gallatin Manhattan Montana

I rose around 7 a.m. after little, if any, sleep. Trains roared past all night long like hurricane winds, blowing their horns far before the road crossing. The sonic intensity rivaled the end of an airport runway. Each train was extraordinarily long and each included three or more locomotive engines pulling from the front. As they sped past, their high-pitched, piercing sound intensified to a full crescendo at the end, where two or more engines appeared to be pushing backward. The ground shook beneath me like an earthquake when each train passed. I pulled my head inside the sleeping bag and plugged my ears.

By now, the routine of getting up and packing camp was completed by rote. During the first week of the trip, I couldn't remember item locations in the panniers. But at this point, I established a logical and organized packing system. I hit the road eastbound at 7:15 a.m. and followed a long uphill grade out of East Helena on

Route12/287. With a long vista to the southeast, I noted increasingly more white crosses beside straight road sections with few bends.
"What could have claimed people's lives here?" I wondered.

Montana's small white roadside crosses are easy to read on a bicycle. One, in particular, labeled *"Dad,"* caught my attention. I learned the highway cross placements began about 50 years ago to caution other drivers to slow down and drive sober. When the program started up in the 1970s, Montana had nearly double the national average for drunk driving deaths. The crosses reminded me that I might not be so safe from drivers around beer time and to be vigilant at all times.

Breakdown Lane Near Ovando, Montana

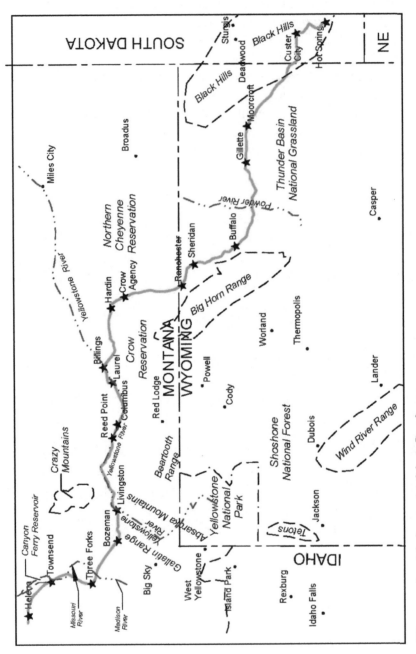

Figure 4 - Helena to Hot Springs

I stopped to shed my coat when I encountered the first long-distance rider of the trip. His name was Mark, he was from Ohio, and he had been bike touring for the previous four months. He just pedaled down from the North Cascades and through Glacier National Park and was headed to Yellowstone. It was so reassuring, enlightening, and comforting to meet another long-distance brethren. Someone who could understand my experience. I suggested that we ride together for the company, and he agreed. I cruised with Mark for about 19 miles, following long stretches with gorgeous views towards Canyon Ferry Reservoir. Keeping up with Mark was a real chore. Considering his four months of riding, I was no match for his hardened physical condition. He was close to 30 years my junior, thin and athletic, so I didn't feel too bad about lagging a tenth of a mile or more behind. On a long straight stretch, he pulled over to pee, and I waved as I passed by. Might as well carry on at our own speeds.

I pedaled hard, climbing a continuous grade for 13 miles to Winston. The countryside shifted from forested mountains to extensive prairie views with long vistas rather than winding roads through mountains and deserts. To the east, Canyon Ferry Reservoir dominated the view. This reservoir was formed on the Missouri River and is Montana's third-largest body of water. There were few if any trees around the lake. The lake submerged two towns and reached its ultimate height in July 1951, two years after the Bureau of Reclamation poured the concrete dam. They posthumously named the lake after an 1865 river ferry, which carried travelers across the Missouri River, now far beneath the canyon's flooded portion.

I pedaled into Townsend and bonked after 26 hard miles, stopping at a delightful donut shop for coffee. Relaxing in the heat of the morning sun, sipping coffee, and wolfing down two donuts, I saw Mark roll by on the main road at an incredible pace. That was the last I saw of the young devil on a touring rampage, Yellowstone-bound. I envied him and his free spirit, biking to some of the most beautiful places in America on an elegantly simple bicycle. I began to sense something inspirational and unspoken about the uniqueness and pure, liberating simplicity of this experience that maybe only solo cross-country bikers could relate to.

Freshly caffeinated, I jammed southbound to Toston. The road unraveled with increasingly treacherous riding conditions for 11 miles as the highway's shoulders retreated from the erosion of thin asphalt. This road desperately required highway crew attention but I made it to Toston and crossed the Missouri River. I was baking like a hot potato on two wheels. I needed to get my shirt and bandana wet and take a bath. The sweltering afternoon heat was approaching the high nineties, so I found a shady spot in the willow trees downriver from a large metal truss bridge. This grassy riverside location was the perfect place to strip down, do the laundry, wash up, and re-humanize.

The river bottom was rocky and slick with moss and not quite waist-deep about 50 feet from the bank. It probably wasn't wise to wade out much further alone. All around me, I noticed dozens of water snakes swimming upriver. Most of them were small, about a foot or more in length. They were dark in color, so I surmised that they were not rattlers, and the head shape suggested that these were not poisonous snakes. Then I noted several right next to me. They tended to go about their business swimming past me with heads barely out of the water. They had no interest in me, but they would dive below the surface when provoked.

The air intensified with the roar of more Harleys. A small group of bikers stopped above me on the truss bridge and waved. Birthday suit on full display, I turned to them and waved back and smiled. My inhibitions were gone and my focus was attending to my sunburned body, which I began to perceive as a battered and fried calorie-consuming machine. Getting clean and attending to my hand wounds, leg wounds, and butt cheeks with triple antibiotic ointment was a top priority—no need for infections. I've been there before. After a bath and washing clothes with biodegradable soap, a man pulled up in a car as I waded to shore. He jumped out and announced that he was an Army war vet who was *"disabled."* I didn't recognize his disability. He quickly donned all of his river gear and set up his fly rod in about five minutes, so perhaps it was PTSD. He told me that his job was teaching other veterans how to fly fish. The government was paying him for it because of his disability. Today, he was practicing.

"Fascinating job you have," I said as I put on riding shorts while he headed downriver to fish. With a bungee found on the road several miles back, I strapped the wet, freshly-cleaned clothes to the back of the dry bag and over the panniers. It was very Okie, with all of the laundry hanging off the bike behind me. I could feel the extra water weight as I pedaled south up Montana's Route 287.

This highway to hell was when the real work began. It was a long, steady, arduous 15-mile climb up a one to four percent grade into a hot blast furnace. It was now about 98 degrees, and my speed was reduced to under five mph. This was my first sensation of "*road despair*," which I defined as "the hopeless feeling when I could see infinitely far ahead to the horizon." Added to that misery were the muscle-aching pedal grade, minimal riding lane width, and no cloud cover. All of this bore down on my drive, energy, and mental strength, intensifying road despair by an order of magnitude.

"God, please show me a cloud or a bend in the road," I uttered out loud to the sky. The worst component on this road was that there was only one foot of breakdown lane outside of the white stripe because the line had crumbled away. In places, the highway department painted the white stripe on gravel. There were no rumble bars to warn me of drivers who might be coming up from behind. I was pedaling into a wind that was getting stronger and hotter by the moment, and I couldn't get at ease with the bike. Streams of traffic hurried by, increasingly closer to the bars at furious speeds, far exceeding my comfort level. Salty sunscreen and sweat trickled into my eyes. I had to shut them for seconds at a time and became blinded by stinging pain. There was nowhere to pull off the road. I felt motionless on an incline into the wind and uncomfortably close to what I considered insanity. I was spent.

At that moment, the right fingers pinched in the right shifter while changing gears, and I violently screamed. "Goddammit!!!!" "Goddammit!!!!" "Goddammit!!!!" "Goddammit!!!!"

My finger stung and bled profusely. I was losing it and reaching the edge of my physical strength. I was at the point of inconsolable aggravation when I inadvertently wiped blood in my eyes. "I hate this!" I screamed. I kept repeating it, shaking my head violently, as if this could change anything at all. I was a confused idiot with nowhere to ride. The line of truck traffic was frightful and getting worse. I was in a nightmare playing out in real-time. I was screwed.

"Where are all these trucks going?" I cried out even louder and began to pray. I just couldn't get comfortable on the bike. It was like one of those dreams where you are being chased but you can't run away because your feet are lodged in quicksand. I was starting to bonk in the heat and there was still nowhere to pull off the road. I was losing my mind. I could go no further and I knew it. I decided on a spot ahead to jump off the road by a ubiquitous highway reflector. But when I executed my move off the shoulder, the front tire sunk into soft, deep gravel.

"*Oh, shit!*" was all I remember. I went down hard, crashing backward with my left shoulder and head smashing into the pavement. I realized that my head and shoulders were crossing the white stripe into the traffic lane with semi-trucks approaching from behind. I was still clipped to the pedals and stuck in deep gravel. Adrenaline kicked in as I tried to inch-worm my way off of the road. But my head was still over the line, and I wasn't moving fast enough. It seemed like time slowed peculiarly as I caught a glimpse of a semi-truck tire merely inches away from my head in a soundless slow-motion framed against a cloudless sky.

"Oh my God!!!" I screamed as the semi-truck passed by, "That was a close one!" More trucks were coming, my legs and arms were bleeding. Completely shaken, I pulled all of the ways off of the road and unclipped. What a strange sight I must have been, alone in "*Nowhere,*" Montana on my side on the ground with a bike between my legs. Was I nuts? Was I losing control here? Yes, I was. I was indeed wiped out. But as I lay there, I focused on a sobering lesson; This ride was not a goof or lark across America. The trip could have dire consequences, including getting hurt or killed. I began to think about Griffin's words of caution back at the bike shop in Salt Lake "*it's not as easy as following a map*". I was shaken to the core as I stood up, dusted myself off, and wiped up the blood. More Harleys passed by and waved.

I continued down Highway 287, now my most hated stretch of road riding ever. It was the blazing hot dog days of summer; a semi-truck almost killed me, so what the hell else could go wrong? And now what? A new section of oil and chip seal surfaces added to an uphill grind's misery and an ongoing headwind. Heavy sweat stung my eyes, impeding my vision. I just couldn't build up momentum. I barely noticed that up ahead, blending in with the new light brown chip seal, was a diamondback rattlesnake, coiled in the lane between the stripe and the shoulder, ready to strike. Traffic kept me pinned to a path that was at most 14 inches wide and the snake took up most of that width. This had to be timed perfectly. As I passed the snake, I unclipped and lifted my legs high, rolling by his deadly fangs with inches to spare.

Fortunately, all he did was turn his head and watch me pass.

Up ahead, I perceived a slight bend in the road. *"Thank God, something other than a straight highway section,"* I smiled. The wind was now blowing across my right shoulder rather than head-on. A couple of clouds drifted in front of the sun, giving me a fraction of shade and a glimmer of hope that I could make it, wherever or whatever "it" was. I was physically taxed beyond any time in my life. Still bonking, I rode off the highway on dirt into a locust-infested field of weeds where I mixed Zip Fizz into a hot water bottle. It tasted terrible, but the effects kicked in immediately. There is nothing like a hot Zip Fizz on a summer afternoon. I gagged down the dregs, checked navigation, and noted that I was about five miles away from Three Forks.

On a steep hill just north of Three Forks, a dozen or so grazing wild horses stretched across an unfenced grassy hillside. It was a curious sight. Although their tails moved in the wind, I soon realized that these broncos were metal statues. I was mystified, mesmerized, and fascinated by this exhibition of life-sized ethereal artwork. There were no access roads and no signs or explanation. The dark broncos framed against the sky burned an unforgettable image into my soul. I felt an uplifting spiritual connection. This was one of the most stunning artworks I have ever observed, evoking a deeply felt, unexplainable emotional response.

I coasted steeply down Highway 287 to the outskirts of Three Forks, a town situated close to the confluence of the Gallatin, Madison, and Jefferson Rivers. Named by Meriwether Lewis in 1805, these three pristine fluvial highways are the purest of rivers forming the Missouri River's headwaters, the longest river in North America. This part of Montana is exquisite. I worked for two years not far from this location, mapping and prospecting Precambrian rocks in the Tobacco Root Mountains, discovering small uranium and thorium deposits outside of nearby Virginia City.

I rolled into civilization just before the junction with Interstate 90 at the Wheat Montana Farms and Bakery. I had to stop because their signs advertised the bakery for the past 50 or so miles, which was torture to my hunger pangs. My mind could only think about filling my stomach so I could start thinking about something else. The restaurant overflowed with tourists, locals, and hordes of Harley riders. The French dip sandwich was fabulous. With tremendous restraint, I consciously ate slowly and savored every bite.

I asked the workers in the bakery about the horse statues just north of town, but no one seemed aware of the roadside display. Did they really exist or had my road-weary haze concocted a mirage? The puzzled looks were just as astounding as the broncos themselves. I checked the camera to be sure I captured photos. *"What's with my head?"* I thought as I questioned reality. The harrowing events of the day pushed all of my senses to the limits. I later discovered from my mom that the horses were the creation of artist Jim Dolan of Belgrade, Montana, as a gift to the State of Montana for his love of the land and people and are known as the *"Bleu Horses"* (Blue Horses). I fumbled in the CamelBak and found another Zip Fizz, mixed it up, and drank slowly, savoring the moments off the bike and conversing with some locals.

I met a group of Harley riders outside of the restaurant on their way to the 2015 Sturgis Rally. They projected that approximately 750,000 Harley Davidson riders planned to attend Sturgis Rally for the 75th anniversary. They asked me about my biking plans. When I mentioned that I came from Seattle a week earlier, some drew back in amazement. One of them asked me if I had any "weed" on me, considering my town of origin.

"Ha. That's pretty funny, I'm afraid not," I said to the biker's disappointment. After getting my fill at the bakery, I pedaled onto I-90 to Three Forks. I exited after 3.5 miles, where I picked up nighttime supplies at a gas station. I rolled out of town and found a beautiful bike trail, which eventually petered out onto the gravel. Just out of town on Route 2, I jumped a guardrail and slid down a steep burr and poison ivy-covered embankment next to the Gallatin River. In this hidden sanctuary, I spotted a green grassy place to crash in thick cottonwoods and mosquitoes. Deer cracked and broke sticks in the willows just out of sight. Later that evening, the deer worked their way around the camp close to the tent. Before bedding down, I opened up Google Maps on the iPhone to assess my progress and also looked at a state map of Montana.

"Good grief, this is a big state," I thought. I was about 20 percent of the way to Boston and survived one of the most grueling, challenging, and dangerous days of my life. Solo. Treacherous road conditions. Searing temperatures and rattlesnakes on the highway. No support or backup plan and no idea where I would be going in the next

24 hours. A "ding" from the phone alerted me to a text from my wife. *"I'm being supportive here. I have no doubt you will finish. I sincerely hope you find the happiness you want. I'm really happy that you feel good. I love you. I also need another $3,000 to pay for the kitchen cabinet paint for last week."*

"I miss you too, but I'm trying not to think about that now. Some hours of the day require more from me than I thought I was capable of. I guess you can take the money out of the savings for the kid's college fund," I replied.

I tried to unwind after 83 hard-earned miles, but stressors at home were a considerable concern. Occasional train engines and horns rose above the Gallatin's soothing sounds as I drifted off to sleep. Two deer outside of the tent commenced their dialogue with me. I snorted back. The exchange went on for some time but I eventually drifted off into a deep sleep. Occasionally throughout the night, trains would pass by and interrupt my rest. I was now uniquely trained to the road, attuned to riding within a four-inch line, shadowing the interstate and railroad corridor. I felt confident navigating terrible road conditions, traffic, Harleys, and locating last-minute campsites.

August 2 - Gallatin River Montana to the Yellowstone River

I awoke to brisk air and foggy river dawn conditions. At the same time, a steady drip of condensation fell from the tent onto my forehead—another night of thundering trains and curious snorting deer walking about the camp. After securing everything on the bike, I realized that the back tire was flat.

"You dumbass. You should have checked that first," I thought. I noted a 1/4-inch tear in the back tire where the tube pushed through the sidewall. I had no spares, which I realized was a mistake. Coarse gravel frontage roads in Eastern Washington, chip seal, and old railroad grades in Idaho wore down the rubber past the wear bars. I placed a duct tape patch inside the tire to help the tire stay together.

I pushed 90 plus pounds of bike and gear up 70 feet on a 45-degree embankment over loose rocks, branches, and wet poison ivy, practically lifting the full weight of the bike. I cruised South Manhattan Road, riding cautiously on the patched tire towards Belgrade. There was little to no breakdown lane to ride on and infrequent traffic, so I rode the center of the road with little worry.

In desperate need of coffee, I stopped in Belgrade for breakfast at a busy cafe. A tattooed and pierced millennial waitress sporting blue and green hair took my order.

"Extra bacon, please."

I planned to get in one good restaurant meal a day. I'd fill the other two meals with grocery store food or obtain whatever I could in between at gas stations. Over breakfast, I phoned my daughter to help me send out monthly reports and invoices while I devoured breakfast in a loud, crowded cafe. Billing and monthly reports were overdue. I was far from the office and trying to convince myself that I could accomplish a feat that I outright knew I might not be able to finish. For years I worked as a hydrogeologist. My company became a never-ending drain on my personal life, consuming me to the point where the work itself defined me. Meeting constant deadlines was suffocating and I began to see myself as a robotic, tail-chasing dog. Escape from stress over the years incrementally became linked to the bicycle. I figured if any of my clients knew what I was doing, they might not be too impressed. I had no idea whether I could ride to Boston. Regardless, I had to keep the money flowing into the house and support my family, no matter what.

My Band-Aid tire fix held so I pedaled the frontage road towards Bozeman, discovering some pleasant and scenic bike trails along the way, complete with cute little truss bridges. I stopped at a bench to rest and reflect on a beautiful mountainous panorama under a clear blue sky. Bozeman is near the Gallatin Range, situated near the Rocky Mountains' eastern edge and one of Western Montana's larger metropolitan areas. The city was initially settled by and named after John Bozeman, who founded the town in 1864 along the Bozeman Trail. This route led from the Oregon Trail to the gold mining town of Virginia City.

After visiting four bike shops, I went to REI to get suitable tires. None of the other shops had any durable tires for the bike. It was already in the high 90's, so the first thing I did when I got to REI was drink about a gallon of cold water. I began to develop a water deficit. Water never tasted so delicious, but it didn't alleviate my thirst. Thirst dominated my thoughts, even though my stomach couldn't accept any more liquid. I picked up a new back tire, another spare tire for insurance, new riding pants, and a new flashing light.

I pedaled east out of town only to get another flat tire, so I headed back to REI for two more tire tubes and some GU. I pedaled out of town again in sweltering, cloudless heat. I had no idea where I was going or how to get out of Bozeman. The map didn't show an exact way, only interstate highway. I pulled up on another biker named John, casually dressed and riding a customized extended city-cruiser with oversized custom rack and panniers packed with lawn chairs. John was a retired fifth-grade teacher and passionate about bikes. I struggled to keep up with him. Moving along at a good clip, John guided me through Bozeman to East Main Street and pointed me in the direction of I-90. He said that this was the only route out of town. We parted ways as I followed Bozeman Trail Road to its end, crossed the railroad, and hopped onto I-90.

I pedaled hard over Bozeman Summit, a grueling 900-foot climb in six miles. This steep, strenuous section of the road was a nasty stretch. Though it seemed like the only option at the time, it is not recommended. The riding lane is narrow with a guardrail, and in a few places, it has two sets of rumble bars, leaving little room to ride. Unlike other clean Montana I-90 highway sections, this section was one littered road stretch. Metal and glass, Lite beer cans, Gatorade bottles filled with urine, broken beer bottles, angle iron, dirty diapers, clothing, fast food wrappers and bags, pieces of truck tires, broken up wood pallets and nails, all crammed into the narrow lane between the line and the guardrail.

"*Why is it always Lite beer?*" I wondered. "*There were never any bottles or cans of decent beer.*" Thirsty buggers, these Westerners, then pee in a Gatorade bottle and toss it out the window. After all, Montana's a big state, and it's all about making good travel time.

Up, up, up, I climbed as I strained and ground through my lowest gears towards Bozeman Pass. Following John's advice, I exited the interstate at Jackson Creek onto an excellent but steeply-graded frontage road. The side road attraction advertised, *"See Grizzly Bears."* The climb seemed endless as I ground to the lowest gear on five to six percent grades. I was sweating hard and thirsty and starting to cramp, but I couldn't stop because I knew that I couldn't begin riding again. There was nowhere to stop on the road and the traffic was too close for comfort. So it was literally "*do or die time.*" I wasn't afraid, just annoyed and strained to the limits of my physical strength. I stopped at the summit to douse my face and body with water, and in front of me, the splendor of the Absaroka Mountains unfolded into view. It was stunning. At that moment, my wife's text message notification showed her frustration for finding her passwords to the bank accounts.

"This is the problem. You leave all the responsibilities to me. You are running away from reality." The irony was that she possessed the password book, I couldn't ever remember passwords, and my reality never seemed more apparent. I sensed her frustration but wasn't in a position to help.

I stopped for photos and then clipped in and zoomed down the highway for about ten miles to the Livingston turnoff against a strong headwind. Ahead was Yellowstone Valley, a picturesque land interspersed with big ranches, lush green irrigated fields, large rolls of baled hay, and spectacular scenery. I took the first exit onto Highway 10 to the north into Livingston. It was dinnertime and I was famished.

Livingston is advertised on a giant billboard just outside of town as a place where *"Artists and Bull Riders Meet."* Livingston was the original gateway town to Yellowstone, America's first national park. I stopped at an outdoor restaurant to enjoy a juicy hamburger and a great side salad. Still suffering from incredible thirst, I mixed up five large glasses of ice water with Gatorade.

The restaurant patrons did not seem to notice my presence. Maybe I just smelled terrible or looked weird with all the biking gear and the bike leaning against the table. With my stomach overfilled from too much liquid and thoroughly exhausted from the heat, I mounted the trusty cycle and followed Highway 10 east through Livingston. The late-evening air became thick and red with haze and smoke. As I approached the east end of town, approximately 20 small fire trucks and an ambulance passed me headed west. I hoped everything was okay wherever they were headed.

About two miles east of town I came upon the Yellowstone River crossing near a radio station. I climbed over the guardrail and pushed the bike deep into the cottonwoods, past many goat heads and weeds. I found an excellent grassy site in the cloak of cottonwoods and willows by a sizeable dead cottonwood tree laying on the Yellowstone Riverbank. The scenery was exquisite, filtered through a wide riverside swath of large, dense foliage. The rugged Absaroka Mountains formed a backdrop of light gray scree fields garnishing lush green timbered slopes on the shoulders of jagged peaks. The exquisite scene gleamed in the last rays of sunlight.

The Absarokas are relatively young, primarily volcanic, and extend from Montana into Wyoming, with many peaks reaching over

12,000 feet in elevation. Fish intermittently broke the water's surface to catch low-flying insects. Although bushed and fatigued from the heat, I was mentally stoked. I checked my navigation and I was maybe about one-quarter of the way across the country. I zoomed out on the map to view the entire country. I was now starting to put a dent in America.

"Godspeed, John Brown," I muttered aloud. I didn't get a good count for the day, but maybe I put in 53 miles. "*Not good enough*," I thought, and I drifted off to sleep listening to the lullabies of fluvial harmony.

August 3 - Yellowstone River in Livingston, Montana to Park City, Montana

I rose at 5:30 a.m. feeling good, surprisingly awake, and without muscle pain. I camped within audible range of the Northern Pacific and Santa Fe Railroad, which occasionally sounded horns in the distance. I broke camp leisurely and was closely watched by a curious white-tail deer at close range. I played hide-and-seek with her for a while and was intrigued by her tame demeanor. Most of the deer so far had been white-tails. I hadn't seen any mule deer since Washington.

I called my parents and lingered in conversation. Today's route was unknown, as usual, but generally followed the course of Lewis and Clark, the early explorers of this corridor between 1804 and 1806. My view to the horizon suggested that not much had changed since that expedition. Feeling strong following my morning jolt of caffeine, I put the pedal to the pavement. I was in an entirely joyous mood on a beautiful day, with big mountain passes in the proverbial rearview mirror and the craggy Absarokas to the south. I was no longer taking ibuprofen in the morning, and my legs were no longer cramped at night. I had virtually no muscle pain whatsoever. However, my butt had sores on the sores.

"What the hell," I said aloud, "Come on, Bike! Let's hit I-90 and ride with the Harleys! Who cares if it's loud. I need some miles." I became used to talking to myself and the bike to keep my vocal cords exercised. I planned to knock off as many early morning miles as possible ahead of the predicted heatwave.

By now, Harleys became more common as the Sturgis bike rally grew closer. The first gathering was an Indian Motorcycle Club in 1938 and today, hundreds of thousands of motorcycle riders attend the experience each year. Several caravans of motor homes pulling trailers with Harleys passed me. I laughed at pickups with Harleys pulling more Harleys on their trailers. They couldn't even ride to Sturgis on their motorcycles. I mentally scoffed in their direction; riding a motorcycle seemed so undemanding compared to traveling on skinny tires with 20 gears and a crank.

I checked the GPS to see how far I might have to travel to find food. I skimped on breakfast to beat the heat and jumped a Jersey barrier after about 20 miles and ducked behind a couple of seven-foot hay rolls to eat. I resolved not to bonk. I gobbled handfuls of Triscuits with tuna fish and squeeze cheese topping, wrapped in teriyaki beef jerky. This is a little weird and something that would be nasty to eat at home. But on the road, riding 10 to 11 hours per day, you might try anything. I put everything into my mouth until the tuna was gone. My mouth was so dry that I choked while eating the remainder of the tuna from the bag. I guzzled a couple of liters of Gatorade, belched, and cycled back onto I-90 once again with a vengeance. I pulled 18 to 22 miles per hour on the highway. It was a pretty clean riding section, too, after that disgraceful trash-laden climb over Bozeman Pass.

About 40 miles into the day, the east headwind became quite intense. I pulled into Big Timber for my second breakfast in a run-down roadside cafe with scores of leathered Harley riders. I was exceedingly thirsty and desperately required coffee and water faster than it could arrive. I gorged on a 2000-plus calorie breakfast and two liters of ice water.

Two men were seated at the next table, speaking in severe and loud tones. One man's voice dominated and gave me the impression of a darkly disturbed individual. In short, he had some feud going on with his next-door neighbor and described how he intended to kill him later that day. He said that his neighbor threatened him the day before and then stated that he would go back with his gun and put a few 44 rounds right in his chest and one in the forehead. Then, he looked up from his discussion directly at me, maybe to see if I overheard the conversation or perhaps see who was in the adjacent booth. I stared intently at the cuts on my hands, already intentionally placed between his face and mine.

"Jeez, they can probably hear this moron five tables away," I thought. This guy may or may not be a killer, but my gut told me that

he was and that I should get out quickly and forget that last piece of toast.

"Check, please!" I yelled at the waitress.

I had no idea where to ride from Big Timber except keep heading east. I had no earbuds, no earplugs, no iPhone music; just the sound of road noise. I chatted with the waitress about the conditions of the local frontage roads going east. Considering the agony experienced on frontage roads in Eastern Washington, any knowledge of continuous off-interstate roads heading east would be desirable. The waitress was local and knowledgeable about the back roads. Her directions sent me down to the post office first to mail home all unnecessary weight. I followed her advice and traveled on Old U.S. Highway 10. This lovely section of pleasant hills, cottonwood trees, and creeks parallels the Yellowstone River. I was headed into badlands and towards the prairie.

I crossed under I-90 at Greycliff, not surprisingly named by Lewis and Clark after the gray cliffs, following the road east with little traffic. The riding conditions were excellent along this pleasant stretch. Still, it was oppressively hot with headwinds of 15 to 20 miles an hour, slowing me down to three miles an hour when I noted a sign marking the Greycliff Prairie Dog Town State Park. I rode into the park to investigate. Signs remind visitors not to feed the prairie dogs. Ironically, while walking around their burrows, I noted that they were feeding on each other. Prairie dog skulls laid atop many of the burrow locations. All around me, a minute-by-minute game of "pop goes the weasel" played out.

"Cheep, Cheep, Cheep!" they taunted me from all directions. The whole park amused me. Prairie dogs, darling cute as they may be, are considered a nuisance once they colonize into a community. I left the park and resumed peddling east into the wind. I tried shifting my body into a compact position to reduce wind resistance for long distances at a time but found that it was too hard on my back. In as many miles as I had already traveled, I still was not in riding shape.

I came to a big bend in the Yellowstone River where I noted a historical marker sign. I like these roadside historical markers because they provide good reasons for rest while getting the surroundings' historical perspective. This particular stop was the site of the Thomas Group pioneer grave. In 1866, William Thomas and his son and the prairie schooner driver were ambushed and killed by Indians.

Emigrants coming along later discovered the bodies and buried them in a mass grave. Seventy-one years later (1937), the enthusiastic nephew of William Thomas traveled west by automobile to find his grave, closely following the old "John" Bozeman Trail. He successfully located the mass grave, which is now encircled by river-smoothed rock. I looked around in all directions. It wasn't hard to imagine the scene in 1866 mirrored in front of me. If you ignored the road, the contiguous panorama resembled an old western movie set.

For some reason, I became overwhelmed with emotion and tears. Alone with the ghosts of the Thomas Group, I felt palpably excised from my present-day reality. The world around me was becoming more unreal with each day and every passing mile. With nothing but the blue sky above, a beckoning horizon line, and a destination, I pushed hard into the wind. Occasionally, the Yellowstone River popped into view to the north. I continued pedaling through Quebec and into a small community of fewer than 100 residents named Reeds Point. The settlement is a classic western town. *"Reed Point Welcomes Ewe"* read the sign on the side of a building. Another banner across the street advertised the big sheep roundup on September 15. Not one car could be seen on the road, not one person in the town along Main Street. *"Was this a ghost town?"* I felt far removed in a hamlet seemingly impervious to the noise of the outside world and instantly accepted as one who was also eschewing civilization.

I stopped to look over two prominent large, classic but defunct Montana grain elevator buildings with painted advertising, now fading to unrecognizable words. There was something about these buildings that demonstrated personality and uniqueness. Many Montana towns still have these old crib-style grain elevators, most built between the 1890s and the Great Depression. The unique construction represents ancient farming practices, now replaced by the more familiar massive round corrugated metal silos that modernized the agricultural West. Contemporary elevator structures are located in larger towns and cities in centralized locations to serve more farms. As a result, small American towns like this lost their businesses and people moved away, but the relic grain elevators remained.

My attention turned to a graying, small western bar across the street called the Waterhole Saloon. It appeared defunct; maybe it had not been open in years. Suddenly, the front door swung open and out walked a young man talking on an iPhone. *"Maybe I'm not so isolated from the modern world*," I thought.

I parked the bike by the wooden sidewalk in front of the bar and locked it to a horse hitching post. I entered through the heavy wooden door into a dark barroom replete with western nostalgia. Behind the bar was an oil painting of a young, topless woman poured out onto a couch in white bikini panties, prominently displayed between guns, liquor bottles, and cow skulls. The bartender, maybe 75 years in age, was both the owner and the young woman in the painting. She told me that she had the picture painted when she was 24 years old. She poured me a Mountain Dew on ice, the drink I had been craving for the last 10 miles.

I introduced myself to the 35-year-old guy sitting next to me, the same young man who I saw outside on his phone just moments before. He was having a second whiskey at 2:30 in the afternoon with his lunch. He introduced himself as A.J., a "jack-of-all-trades" type who recently moved back to his hometown of Reeds Point to raise his kids in an "unspoiled community." Five minutes later, his kids came running into the bar, playing games and laughing. A.J. ordered another drink as four barking dogs pushed open the door and ran in after the kids. I followed his lead and ordered another Mountain Dew.

I was getting pretty jacked up on caffeine. The bottle of Patron behind the bar seemed to look directly at me, but a tiny voice in my head said, *"No tequila for you, my friend."* Feeling the urge to press on, I downed my soda while A.J. provided me with road directions heading east. The plan was to get back onto I-90 and get off at Springtime Road about eight miles later at Stillwater. From there, I would ride towards Columbus on Old Highway 10. I was now about halfway across Montana, with the Rocky Mountains clearly in the rearview mirror.

Old Highway 10 proved to be far better and more scenic riding than the interstate. The Yellowstone River corridor through this area was enchantingly lovely. The river dominated the scenery, meandering, braiding, and coursing slowly over cobble rocks derived from the Rockies and I had panoramic views all the while. I drank it all in and savored every mile. Just outside Columbus, I came upon an attractive and well-dressed woman in her forties, accompanied by a dog, walking a connecting road to the Yellowstone River. Her name was Cindy, and her dog was named Red (he was a red heeler). I perceived she was somewhat of a lost soul. Her conversational segue was confusing as if she was experiencing passing random moments of an acid flashback. She spoke about the loss of her other dog a few weeks before and then she started to choke up. She leaned against me unexpectedly; I leaned forward on the bike towards her.

"Someone could use a hug now, right?" I said, smiling. She offered a warm, tight embrace. She smelled nice, and with her body pressed up against mine, I couldn't deny that it felt genuinely fantastic to hold someone.

"Do you want to spend the night at my house on the Yellowstone River?" she asked. It was a tempting offer. Nevertheless, the gold ring on my left hand meant something more to me.

I politely declined the offer. I wished her well and then cycled off towards Columbus, a stagecoach stop along the Yellowstone River in the late 1800s. I rolled into town, greeted by the funniest, most uniquely decorated garden I'd ever seen, with crazy signs and cute animal cutouts placed between the planted vegetables. I stopped to take pictures and chuckled. The homeowner emerged from his house and greeted me with two bottles of ice-cold water.

"Do you want to spend the night at my house?" he asked as I guzzled one bottle. Wow, two offers in one day. I wish I could have, but I wanted to get a few more miles behind me and try to break one hundred miles for the day.

In downtown Columbus, I rolled up on three women holding large protest signs supporting their husbands who worked at the Stillwater Mine. This mine that produces palladium and platinum is located south of Columbus in the Custer National Forest and is one of the few platinum mines in North America. I took a few selfies with the protesters before departing downtown, climbed a small mesa that provided a welcomed windbreak, and noted a ring forming around the sun formed by sunlight refracting through hexagonal-shaped ice crystals at very high altitudes. This can mean storms are on their way.

I stopped to get evening supplies at a convenience store and pedaled down Old U.S. Route 10 towards Park City to look for a campsite in waning sunlight. I finally bedded down by a windbreak near a swampy canal surrounded by Russian olive trees and tamarisk in between large spoil piles in what appeared to be the site of future residential development. This camp spot had the worst mosquitoes I had experienced since leaving Seattle, biting me mercilessly while setting up the tent. Later on that evening, strong, ominous winds roared but I itched my way to sleep, hoping I hadn't picked up West Nile Virus. This site was certainly not a great spot nor private and I was reasonably sure a few locals spotted me.

August 4 - Park City, Montana to Hardin, Montana

I was wide awake at 5:30 a.m. It was a windy night with large gusts buffeting the tent and occasionally waking me. *"Where was that wind when all those mosquitoes were eating me alive for dinner?"* I broke camp and took to the road, riding east past Park City and Laurel on Old Highway 10. A brisk tailwind pushed me along with little effort. Laurel is known as having the most significant train yard between Saint Paul, Minnesota, and Pasco, Washington. I stopped and viewed the tracks from an overpass.

I stopped at the Owl Cafe for breakfast, sitting at the bar to blend in with locals, needing some local socialization and information about navigating through eastern Montana. I explained to the man next to me that my riding plans included pedaling through Billings, then to Hardin, and through to the town of Crow Agency on the Crow Indian Reservation. Beyond that, I planned to travel farther east through remote cities of Lame Deer, Ashland, and then into the no-man's-land around Broadus, Montana. Without hesitation, he emphatically told me not to venture out Route 212 through the Crow and Cheyenne Indian Reservations. He recommended that I stay in a hotel for safety. Indeed, it was a lonely and desolate stretch of road with little or no services or help between towns and possibly nowhere to get water. I was entering a geographic area in which I had little knowledge or experience. I was riding on the western edge of grassland prairie. My imagination ran rampant and the adrenaline level may have been at an all-time high. I like challenges, but this route may be more in the realm of foolishness.

After breakfast, I dropped about 300 feet in 10 miles on frontage roads advancing east towards Billings. With a strong tailwind, I was traveling comfortably at 18 to 25 miles an hour. Billings is the largest metropolitan area in Montana and the biggest city in the region, but not an aesthetically appealing town. Billings was founded as a railroad town and named after the president of the Northern Pacific Railroad. I just wanted to get through traffic as quickly as possible. I bypassed downtown following First Avenue

North through some sketchy neighborhoods, passed a large refinery, and turned onto Highway 87, crossing the Yellowstone River for the last time. The lane crossing the bridge was in good condition and clean, but the low Jersey barrier and a long drop to the river hastened my pace.

My current plan was to shave some mileage and maybe some time by taking Route 87 to Hardin. This route climbs 850 feet in about seven miles around hairpin turns towards a towering mesa of shale and sandstone. There was little room to ride on this stretch, but there was also no traffic. The scenery and views were terrific but the ride was a downright grunt considering grade and the bike weight. I stopped at the mesa crest and looked back down to Billings with great relief; the sky to the west was hazy with gray rain clouds. I just escaped getting soaked.

I blasted down a 600-foot hill in just over four miles, which was both steep and exhilarating. Stopping at Pryor Creek near the bottom to rest on concrete rubble slabs, I noticed wild hops growing abundantly in the bushes. I picked a few buds to smell that familiar aroma, which made me feel closer to home. My hops would go unpicked this year. I slammed a Gatorade and headed out into the prairie on a lonesome road.

The scenery was notably different. Rounded landforms weathered from Cretaceous-age[ii] Niobrara Shale. Ahead, the prairie hills were draped in well-manicured grass and perforated with an uncountable number of prairie dog burrows, meanders of every inflection sinuously twisting into tortuous ribbons cutting an incredibly remote valley painted in yellows, greens, and browns. It appeared the perfect environment for prairie dogs. Popping up along the roadsides for miles, they scolded me and cheeped warnings to their neighbors. I returned their calls for fun. At times, I saw dozens of them running simultaneously. On one stretch, I provoked a herd of cows with my imitation bull call, which started a stampede. Oops. At one point, I noted cows spread out as far as the eye could discern, getting smaller and smaller until they became diminished specks like dust on an old photograph. By all measures, this area was a region seldom seen by anyone except local ranchers. This route was one beautifully lonely stretch and the wind pushed me effortlessly at 25 to 30 miles an hour. I was in a great mood and rode much of this stretch standing on the pedals.

I was close to bonking and stopped eight miles outside of Hardin to eat. A rancher and his son pulled up next to me in a Ford pickup truck to see if I was okay. I told them I was headed to South Dakota, then pointed to a distant range far to the southeast.

"Are those the Black Hills?" I asked. They both looked surprised by my question. They chuckled at my geographic naivety.

"I can assure you that the Black Hills are much farther away than that, several hundred miles at least. Are you lost?"

They had a point. A solo biker asking stupid questions about locations far from my position. I pedaled towards Hardin on a strong tailwind as the sun turned into a fiery red ball filtered through the smoke from distant fires. I stopped at O's Bakery and Cafe Diner and ordered a burger and salad.

"I don't recommend riding a bike out Highway 212. There were two murders on that road just a few days ago. They still don't know who did it," said the waitress. She strongly recommended I head south to Sheridan, Wyoming. A Crow Indian family at a table across the room overhead our conversation and concurred with her assessment. I later found her story accurate. The killer was later apprehended near Meeteetse, Wyoming after I left Hardin. According to the Native News:

"CROW AGENCY, MONTANA— The FBI confirmed Wednesday, July 29, 2015, that a husband and wife were killed in cold blood and their daughter was injured by gunfire on the Crow Indian Reservation."

This tragic incident began when a woman stopped to help a man stranded on the road who told her that he was out of gas. She drove home to get her husband and daughter. When they returned, the man brandished a gun, shot the couple, and then shot the daughter. The bullet grazed the daughter's head, and when she took off, he shot her in the back. The daughter somehow survived and was taken to the hospital, where she was reportedly incoherent. An awful story.

Based on their recommendations, I decided I would pedal south to Sheridan, avoid the Cheyenne Reservation, and bolt through Crow country in the morning. I pedaled to the west side of town to look for a hotel because I had gone ten days without a shower or a bed and had no clean clothes. I registered in the hotel and hauled the gear and bike up steep stairs to my room. The hotel was packed with Harley riders, all assembled and conversing in loud voices in the parking lot.

I took a half-hour-long shower, cleaning my clothes in the tub with my feet as an agitator. A stream of dirt flowed from me and the clothes in dark rivulets to the drain. Despite the comfy bed, the place was a dump. Shower and sink faucets leaked, the toilet didn't flush, glasses and towels were dirty, and the walls were paper thin.

When I got out of the shower, I noticed that my foot bottoms were numb. I couldn't feel the carpet in my bare feet. Concerning, but I chalked it up to long miles. I had ridden 80 miles to Hardin, but lay restless in bed. It seemed some of the bikers fell asleep in their rooms with their T.V.s turned on full volume. No doubt these guys were going deaf from riding those machines with their radios cranked to drown out the engine noise. After 10 days, I wished for a cold beer. I lay in bed, thinking about the next day, and eventually drifted off to sleep. I was awakened a few hours later, dazed and confused, when my friend Ben called. I thought the phone was the alarm and fumbled to turn it off but there wasn't an alarm. Ben told me that he needed to borrow my P.A. system at home for a weekend gig. I updated him on my progress as T.V. volumes blared in the room next door.

August 5th - Hardin, Montana to Banner, Wyoming

A night in the hotel room did not provide quality sleep and I wondered whether it was even worth it. Except for loud trains, camping out was quieter and cheaper but the room allowed me to wash clothes and charge the bike lights and phone. I stole one of the toilet paper rolls and the tiny bar of soap, packed up, and bolted from the room at 6:30 a.m. The toilet never flushed, so that was now their problem.

"Yes, we are living dangerously now," I chuckled. "Better camp out until I run out of laundry again."

It was a chilly morning so I donned my jacket and blew out of town on Old Route 87 next to I-90 on Frontage Road, crossing the Bighorn and Little Bighorn Rivers headed towards the Indian Reservation. A deep red sunrise pierced a blanket of fog and ash fallout drifted through the air. Late summer was becoming the time of year when opportunistic infernos consumed the West. These blazes seemed more frequent and widespread every year. In the distance I could make out farmlands in the Little Bighorn Valley and occasional oxbow ponds[i] through the fog. It seemed like I was dragging and couldn't keep my speed. The crank or something else on the bike started making all kinds of racket and I couldn't figure out where it was coming from. My legs were sore and struggling and the loss of feeling in my feet was disconcerting. The constant tapping of a buckle on the back of my leg was becoming painful even though it hardly touched my bike shorts. Everything irritated me.

At the town of Crow Agency, something seemed amiss. This town seemed somehow different from everything experienced on the journey. I noticed some other odd behaviors, including individuals driving or walking around, essentially half-dressed. A minivan drove past me with open side doors and young passengers dragging feet on the road, staring at me as if they had never seen a bicycle. Indians were parked everywhere, under overpasses, on the roadside, and on side streets with no apparent reason for being there.

"*Just keep pedaling and get out of here!*" I thought as I rode past a street called Left Hand Lane and laughed. Curiously, I began to take notice of the smallest of things. I passed by another small ranch with a bloated, deceased horse sprawled at the end of a driveway. No doubt this very tragic incident was the unfortunate result of an auto-equine collision. But why had it been laying there long enough to swell like the Goodyear blimp?

A series of frontage roads routed me past the town dump and the center of town and shuttered buildings. This was not the first reservation I'd ever visited; still, the most noteworthy difference was the astonishing number of loose dogs. I rode past house after house with unrestrained canines barking from unfenced yards. There were countless variations of Chihuahuas and Border Collies and at one point, a giant white American pit bull lunged after me. I stopped and confronted my would-be attacker face to face. I quickly dropped the bike as he approached me in an intimidating manner, then he pressed against me with all his weight.

Crow Indian Reservation, Montana

"Do not be frightened, do not show fear," I thought as I sensed the power of his rippling muscles leaning against my body. But this handsome un-neutered boy was not after blood. He began kissing me with his exceedingly sloppy wet muzzle, and I rubbed the inside of his ears. He was adorable, and it was genuinely a unique new-friend experience for the journey. His affection made me miss my dog at home. I rubbed his tummy and his back and gave him big hugs for at least 15 minutes. I didn't want to leave him, and he wouldn't let me go

either. It was like a bond of love at first sight. I don't care for the pit bull breed, but this sweet pup made a case for changing my mind.

The frontage road roughly paralleled the meandering Little Bighorn River. I rode past the site of the Battle of Little Bighorn and through the town of Garryowen. This town was the site of Sitting Bull's camp just before the battle that would define General George Custer's dead-end career. About three miles past Garryowen, I picked up Old Highway 87. As I passed through Lodge Grass, the clouds burned off and I began to weaken from lack of food. I pushed upward for about 58 miles, from 2,900 feet elevation through a rural tree-lined river valley to about 4,100 feet in wide-open grasslands near the Wyoming border. The Bighorn Range appeared ahead, dominating the skyline. The north end of the Bighorn Mountains is a noteworthy northward plunging anticline[ii] exposing ancient Paleozoic rocks. The rocks dip sharply to the northeast beneath the much younger Wasatch Formation. The Wasatch Formation, formed from mudstones and sandstones, is exposed across much of central Wyoming and weathers into semi-arid rolling grassland overlying some of the world's most massive coal beds.

An enormous forest fire raged in the Bighorn foothills, sending up an imposing vertical column of smoke into already hazy skies. Finally, the Wyoming border sign appeared ahead and a huge relief came over me. Five days to cross Montana from Lookout Pass. Entering "*Wild Wonderful Wyoming*." With Montana behind me, I began to believe that I could make it to Boston.

I pedaled over the pass near Parkman, Wyoming, at an elevation of 4,350 feet and then descended a series of long hills into Ranchester. On the right, I spotted a crowded bar and a parking lot jammed with pickup trucks. I locked up the bike, went inside, and sat at the bar, desperate for an ice-cold Mountain Dew. The joint was a fun place where everyone was on a first-name basis. Picture portraits prominently displayed on the walls around the barroom identified local patrons, some of which were sitting at the bar. After a few minutes, two tall Crow Indians walked in and purchased two liters of vodka. They asked for two Styrofoam cups and a bottle of soda water. The bartender called one of them out by name; then, she instructed them to be on their best behavior as they walked out the door. Alcohol is typically not allowed for sale on the Indian reservation, but that doesn't stop them from jumping the border to get some hooch.

I finished the sodas, said my farewells, and rode down State Highway 345 into the Powder River Valley, closer to the massive fire on the mountainside. I stopped for a snack when I met a guy named Dave Fischer, riding out to his mailbox on a 4-wheeler. Dave introduced himself as a retired history professor at Sheridan State College. When I mentioned Salt Lake, he said he built race cars using snowmobile engines for speed competition on the Utah Salt Flats. He pulled the Sheridan Newspaper from his mailbox and the front-page story was about the current forest fire.

After a pleasant chat, trading email addresses and getting directions to Sheridan, we bid farewell. Sheridan, I noted, was named after General Philip Sheridan, a cavalry officer in the Civil War. He fought against the Sioux, Cheyenne, and Crow Indian tribes and advocated for the buffalos' extermination. I rode the I-90 shoulder to the Port of Entry, then cut over I-90 and headed into town on a beautiful, wide riding lane.

I stopped to change a flat and then called the bike shop back in Salt Lake because the bike continued to make a mysterious grinding noise when I cranked the pedals. A Wyoming Highway Patrol officer stopped across the road and rolled down her window.

"Do you want a ride into town?" she asked.

"No, I'm doing a solo cross-country ride and can't accept any rides. I'm good!"

In Sheridan, I stopped to pick up food and supplies. I bought beer and two minis of tequila to celebrate riding from Montana to Wyoming. This was the first alcohol purchase since Seattle, and while I felt some guilt, the vow of non-consumption met little resistance. I wanted to party. I was on my way to 100 miles for the day! I rode Big Horn Avenue south out of town towards the town of Story. The moon was up, I was closing in on a "century" for the day, and I had to stop soon. I was worn out by every measure. I pulled up a hill and into a field with a half-dozen seven-foot diameter straw bale rolls and set up the tent between them. Just after settling into camp, a Wyoming Fish and Game officer (aka, fish cop) pulled up on the road in front of me with his lights flashing. He got out of his truck, resolutely put on his hat, and walked with intent directly towards me. He was armed. He was a classic-looking western officer with a Stetson hat, bolo tie with an elk ivory cabochon, large silver belt buckle, immaculate cowboy boots, and a sizably perfect Tom Selleck mustache. He walked to the bike, grabbed it with both hands, looked it over carefully, and then informed me that I was trespassing on the Barbosa Ranch, private property.

"I'm sorry, I'll take down my tent and move down the road. I didn't know this was private, I'm sorry. You see, in Idaho and Montana, you have to mark your private property with "no trespassing" signs, or orange markers or posts every 300 feet," I said.

"Not in Wyoming. You don't have to post anything, and you are trespassing, my friend," he advised me, looking me directly in the eyes.

Down came my camp in minutes and I packed up the bike and rode down Meade Creek Road towards Story. After about a mile down the road, the same officer pulled up behind me and turned on his lights and siren, which about startled me into cardiac arrest. I pulled over to the side of the road, and he pulled up alongside, rolled down his window.

"I just spoke with the ranch owners and you now have permission to go camp back at the Barbosa Ranch, just leave a clean campsite," he said.

Relieved by the news, I smiled, gave him a "thumbs up," turned around, and headed back up to reset camp between the straw bales, brushing off the frustration of having to set up camp twice in the same spot. I called my parents for the daily check-in. The fish cop returned once again to check on me. As he walked back to my location, I handed the phone to him so the officer could speak directly with my parents. At this point, there seemed to be something concerning about his shadowing behavior. I overheard them chuckling over my bike trip and how far I had pedaled. He handed me back the phone, tipped his hat, smiled, and departed. Finally.

Soon, dark clouds blew in from the west and I hunkered down for a violent night of weather. An ominous thunderstorm overtook the Bighorn Mountains and white-hot lightning and echoing thunder ramped up. The wind intensified and I was glad to be tucked in between giant bales of hay. I checked the Google Earth map and noted that the following day would put me past Gillette, Wyoming. In just a few more days, I would be in South Dakota.

I texted my wife and kids, "*I did 104 miles today. I've lost weight, and I'm getting strong. I'm camped at the Barbosa Ranch and had a run-in with a fish cop.*"

"Sounds like you're doing well, goodnight."
Continuous rolls of thunder echoed off the mountains and intense blinding lightning flashed through the tent walls as the storm moved directly overhead. The phone rang from home. I didn't answer. With all the problems I'd experienced over the past few days, I was concerned that they might be worried. The moment of a violent storm was not a good time to talk and could result in a panic on their end, imploring me to come home. My focus was on keeping my head straight while riding in unfamiliar territory. For a few minutes, the storm lingered immediately above the camp as the tent strained under the weight of heavy hailstones. I was again grateful to be sandwiched between the giant rolls of hay.

After the past few days of close calls, it became much clearer that life could unexpectedly turn dire on the road. Because of this, I couldn't handle being upset for any reason. Celebrating my first century of the trip, I downed a mini bottle of tequila and a giant Budweiser.

August 6th - Outside Banner, Wyoming to Rozet, Wyoming
I awoke at 5:15 a.m. under a bright red sunrise. Everything was soaked. I rallied out of the tent and slammed a can of cold Starbucks coffee, multitasking my way to readiness. I needed to shorten up the pit stops, get more miles than the previous day, and keep on track, whatever "track" was.

"Wait, this is curious. Am I on a schedule? What is so pressing to think that I am on a schedule?" I wondered. Maybe I was about 1/3 of the way across the country, but I knew there were many more unknowns ahead. I could now see the miles melting away day by day, and I grew increasingly encouraged.

I was out of camp by 6:30 a.m. and pedaled strenuously uphill to Banner and past the boarded-up general store. Then I realized that the next village, Story, was at nearly 5,000 feet elevation, with an uphill climb of 700 feet in three miles. I stopped near the top of a 12 percent grade to a view area where construction workers performed road work. One of the truck workers had a belly so large it fell out of his shirt and lay down over his knees. My goodness, things that you see on the road.

I turned left and was now riding through beautiful pine trees and clear running streams, about 1,000 feet above the Sheridan Basin.

A text arrived from home.

"There is a family of mice living in your office."

Great. Hot and sweaty, I stopped at a spot with private creek access. I dropped the bike and shorts and slipped into the shallow mountain creek with a bar of soap, lingering for 20 minutes in solitude. After the bath, I coasted downhill for five miles, losing 450 feet, and then pedaled onto I-90 for about 15 miles to Buffalo. I had a stiff tailwind off of the Bighorns, miles were going down quickly, and the day was still young.

"I rode a century yesterday. I can do more today," I muttered aloud. The freeway section was pretty clean and I cruised at speeds up to 28 miles an hour. I rode past Lake de Smet, named after a legendary Jesuit priest. The lake is rumored to have a prehistoric monster living at great depths, something akin to the Loch Ness Monster. I dropped off I-90 and rode into Buffalo, stopping at McDonald's, where I filled the Camelbak and my bottles with ice and water. I drank as much water as my stomach would hold. This day's ride was going to be a severe endeavor. I was headed east into a desolate Wyoming desert. There is no other way to bike across Wyoming. Either you have to ride on the interstate or sprout wings. Lacking feathers, I submitted to the logical choice of riding I-90. Today was forecast to be sweltering heat with a sprinkling of more heat, with pavement radiating heat from the ground with even greater intensity. There were no clouds above and it was a brutal uphill slog under the bluest, windless sky.

About 10 miles outside of Buffalo, I caught up to a biker on a long uphill stretch and we were soon riding side by side in the breakdown lane. He went by Cameron, bearded, tall and slender, probably mid-thirties. Cameron had been on the road for over two months. He flew his bike and gear from his hometown in Phoenix to Anchorage and was headed to Argentina.

"Wow, my little adventure is pretty insignificant compared with yours!" I said, panting, gasping for breath as we climbed. Cameron's bike quest was something I could never have even imagined before leaving Seattle. I was riding in the company of a great adventurer—a guy with ambitions for really living life and exploring the world at bike speed. Success was not defined by the status quo. This guy knew something that most of us may never realize, that there was more out there beyond the humdrum expectations of society.

We enthusiastically chatted for about 10 minutes, pedaling in a standing position, while semi-trucks passed only feet away. I realized we did not know each other's riding habits, so what we were doing was a little precarious. I bid Cameron farewell and took the lead. His destination was Gillette but I was determined to take it further, another century for the day.

Up, up, up, I climbed, grinding over the blazing-hot pavement. Two major hills proved challenging before dropping elevation to the Powder River. This muddy, slow-moving drainage is probably the most notable feature on this stretch. From the river, I climbed over 800 feet in the next 20 miles. The heat was overwhelming and I-90 twisted unremittingly through grassy hills and over dry washes, always climbing, it seemed but I knew it couldn't go uphill forever. Cell towers are generally placed near passes. This highway, however, was cruel and relentless. In the vast Wyoming desert, cell towers are placed on ridges with only higher elevations behind them.

"Good Lord in Heaven," I yelled out, "how far uphill could this highway possibly go?" My ass was killing me — nothing but an endless sea of grassy hills meeting a distant horizon.

After a while, I came upon highway construction near the bottom of a dry wash. The highway department shut down one side of the interstate, sending east-bounders onto the divided westbound lane. This restricted interstate travel to one lane in each direction with no breakdown lane. That meant it would be impossible to pedal the two-lane stretch of interstate on the bike. On the other hand, riding behind the barricades on the closed eastbound section could be an excellent opportunity to have the highway all to myself.

I hopped to the other side of the orange barrels and began riding on an empty interstate. It was a remarkable experience and exceedingly quiet. After a few miles, I passed by three crews constructing large fill sections to raise the road grade. The pavement was gone and the dirt was uncompacted, so I pushed the bike through the workers, startled by my arrival.

"We were told to stop any vehicles and report unauthorized trespassers to the Highway Patrol," said the construction worker. "We didn't expect anyone to show up on a bicycle, so we will allow you to pass on through. Just keep away from the big equipment."

A water truck rolled by and intentionally sprayed me. Usually, I would be angry by that kind of construction site horseplay, but a good soaking felt good in the heat. I stopped to chat with the foreman. He told me that they were placing fills in a low area to raise the highway. The crews were completing bridgework and wiring up rebar cages to pour caissons for bridge supports at other locations. They were all startled to see me on the highway and acted a bit confused. I just smiled and waved hello. At one place, I walked the bike across a partially constructed bridge on metal beams because I had no other choice. It was a precarious balancing act with the bike. Another supervisor stopped me and asked me what I was doing on the closed interstate. I told him that I was biking from Seattle to Boston. He didn't think I had any chance of making it past the construction zone.

"This is a big country; you have a long way to go to Boston," he uttered with a dismissive tone, a snicker, and a shaking of his head.

"No shit!!??" I said, "that must be why my butt hurts!"

My Dad told me not to be a wise guy. There it is. I know it is a big country. Why did he have to remind me like that? I was struggling enough as it was. This section of interstate sucked. The supervisor did not detain me, probably presuming that anyone stupid enough to be out there pedaling alone deserved whatever fate lay ahead. Off I rode on the single highway to find more uphill, more up, up, twist, then twist the other way, then more uphill. I alternated between standing and sitting on raw saddle sores with cuss words in-between, voicing loud utterances of disapproval of the endless Wyoming desert.

"How high do these freaking prairies go!?" I yelled out to an infinite landscape. I was delirious from sun exposure. In the scintillating heat of the afternoon, I took an exit and rode beneath the overpass. Piled underneath the freeway were many hundreds of partially used one-gallon paint cans, stacked 8 feet high. Someone had a lot of hazardous waste to get rid of in a hurry. After hydrating, I reluctantly left the shaded overpass and braved my way back up onto the interstate, making Gillette around dinnertime.

I filled up with more empty fast-food calories and ice water, then pedaled east on Wyoming Highway 51 towards Rozet. I felt strong, more so than at any previous time. It was my favorite time of day to be outdoors. I rode past miles of coal railcars, by far the longest trains I have ever seen. I passed by Wyodak, the location of one of the world's largest coal seams, and pedaled into Rozet, stopped at the Rozet Bar, locked up the bike, and entered through a rustic wooden door covered with Wanted posters and Old West nostalgia.

A text message from home flashed, "*You are a rockstar. Keep it up!"* I was relieved to see a positive message from home that didn't involve some small disaster or need for unforeseen capital expenses.

A gregarious fellow named Kirby sitting next to me bought me a beer and a shot of tequila. The young blonde tending bar looked like she couldn't be more than 21 years of age but Kirby said she already had six kids. "That can't be, I remarked. "She must have started having babies at the age of 14."

Norma, the woman who owned the bar (and most of the town), said that I was welcome to camp behind the building next to the bar. However, as I left the bar, she warned me that it might be a little noisy at night because I was close to the Rozet Main Street crossing and trains would be hauling coal all night. Good hell, she wasn't kidding. The night was interrupted by the loudest train horns I had ever heard. I packed toilet paper in my ears to lessen the horn sound and drifted off to shallow sleep. But toilet paper earplugs didn't help much as trains awakened me once or twice an hour.

August 7th - Rozet Bar to Custer City, South Dakota

The instant ent that sunlight splashed onto the tent netting, I sprang into multitasking mode. No coffee this morning, just nasty powdered caffeinated mix, which barely did the job. I packed up the bike behind the bar and rode onto State Highway 51 with enthusiasm. Today I would make some real mileage.

The road conditions were ideal with smooth pavement, a full breakdown lane, little traffic, and a quiet start to the day on the high prairie. I had a strong tailwind, which helped tremendously, cruising at 20 mph or more with little effort. I picked up Highway 16 in Moorcroft, Wyoming and stopped at a small, country-style grocery store for supplies, gagged down coffee, mixed up Gatorade, and wolfed down some nasty pre-packaged pastry. I didn't care too much about what I was eating; I was only looking at calorie amounts on the package to address my fuel requirements.

Southeast of Moorcroft on State Highway 16 was an absolute joy with no traffic. At times I rode to the oncoming side of the two-lane highway for better views or just for fun. Sagebrush and antelope appeared on both sides of the road. Occasional idled oil pumps appeared as well and the soil was getting darker, almost blackish. I assumed it was shale but it was black as coal and standing water in the drainages looked tainted with salts. After 20 miles, the climb ended near Upton. The terrain took on a unique expression as clusters of pines swallowed the prairie, morphing into a tidy forest. I couldn't imagine why the landscape was so abruptly different, given the same approximate elevation.

Just before reaching the town of Upton, I was greeted with a large white water tower proclaiming Upton to be the "*Best Town on Earth.*" Really? The most magnificent city on the planet? I had a good chuckle at this slogan. I stopped at a miniature western town named "Old Town," a re-creation of the old "Iron Town" as it was called for the nearby creek's flavor. I stopped for pictures in front of the Sod House, the House of Ill Repute, and the Jail House. A sign at the front of the town discussed General Custer and his historical significance in the area.

At the convenience store in Upton, I grabbed some peanuts and Mountain Dew and asked if it were true that their town was the "Best Town on Earth," but the girls inside the store shrugged and laughed about it. I later found out this slogan was as old as the town itself. The town moniker came into being because 30 percent of the town structures were saloons after the time of Prohibition. Suddenly the slogan made sense.

The pines were a welcome sight after so many miles without a tree but in the summer heatwaves, everything looked tinder dry. Another 14 miles brought me into the Osage Oil Field. Although the pumpers went on for miles, I only saw one of the pumps working. There were hundreds of pump jacks, some of the smallest oil pumpers I'd ever seen. I passed an old rusted cable tool[iii] drill rig permanently retired on a well.

Down the road, I stopped in a ghost town called Oil City to photograph some of the most ancient cable tool drilling rigs I'd ever seen. A large metal drill derrick stood sentinel on the hill directly above. Oil City appeared to be the last vestige of an earlier glorified automotive travel era, overgrown and forgotten. Lost in thought, mysterious biting flies started attacking my legs. It was time to hit the road. Above me, a prominent 22-degree halo formed around the sun, predicting a weather change. Another 14 miles down Highway 16 brought me to Newcastle, the last of the eastern Wyoming outposts. The city had an impressive oil refinery with no ownership name that I could see. Uptown was attractive but noisy and overrun, with Sturgis bikers rolling in full-swing. Harley-Davidsons and bikers clad in leather filled the streets.

I stopped at Decker's Grocery Store for a sandwich, chips, and drinks and sat on a wooden bench outside to eat lunch. One of the employees, a native American Crow, came out to join me. The last map I had was for Montana so I didn't know where to go at this point. She brought a South Dakota map from inside the store. I loaded up on fluids as she explained South Dakota roads to me. The Black Hills have sharp curves, steep hills, and narrow canyons. She mentioned many buffalo on the roads, so I should be careful on the bike because buffalo are unpredictable. They are typically gentle creatures until they're not. The distinctive, fast tail waggle in a vertical position is the key to understanding when you are pushing a buffalo's patience. You certainly can't outrun them, and I have personally witnessed their aggressive capabilities in action in the Tetons.

I thanked the woman for her directions and bid her farewell, pedaling up through town past an elegant city hall building and many lovely homes. Road conditions were exceptional. Only nine more miles of comfortable riding and 200 feet of climbing lay ahead to the South Dakota border. The excitement was palpable as I picked up speed out of town. South Dakota and the Black Hills were unknown to me at this point. The Black Hills was an area that I had only read about in books. I vaguely understood the region's geology, mulling through reference papers related to my earlier exploration geology career. The gaping void in my geography of the U.S. was supplemented by roadside signs explaining historical conquests and adversarial relationships between the Indians and the U.S. Government.

I rode past Camp Jenny, an original Black Hills base camp, and then past the Cheyenne to Deadwood Trail, which was heavily traveled by gold seekers from 1874 to 1878. This trail was the site of a momentous gold rush as prospectors fled from Colorado and Montana by the thousands. By 1880, the area was the most densely populated part of the Dakota Territory. Another road sign described the Indian's relationship with the Black Hills dating back for thousands of years, their struggle between each other, and the Anglo invasion into the long-held Indian territory. To Native American Indians, the area was known as *Paha Sapa*, or *sacred center of the world*. These hills were prized by the Lakota Tribe, who defeated the Cheyenne in 1776. The Lakota took over the Black Hills territory but only used the region for sacred rituals and walkabouts. Paha Sapa was a place to adventure, hunt, and seek higher consciousness, but not a place to inhabit. The U.S. government signed the Fort Laramie Treaty of 1868, giving the Paha Sapa exclusively to the Lakota tribe and barring the whites from settlement or trespass into the Black Hills forever. As it happened, two scientists with the Custer expedition discovered gold in 1874 and prospectors invaded Paha Sapa in a gold rush frenzy. The Great Sioux War of 1876 (the Black Hills War) ensued in a series of battles over two years between the Lakota Sioux alliance with the Northern Cheyenne pitted against the United States Calvary. The U.S. Government defeated the Sioux, broke their written promise, and took ownership of the Black Hills. The U.S. Government then reassigned the Lakota Sioux to other reservations in western South Dakota.

I began to realize that the road was emotionally affecting me in ways that I didn't anticipate even days before. I felt a great sadness for the tribes and the broken promises made by the U.S. Government. I wondered if I would still feel the same way if I was traveling in a car. Travel on the bike was the perfect speed to experience history. Up ahead, I spotted a large sign that elevated my spirits with joy. An intense adrenaline-boosting rush overtook me. It was the South Dakota state line. *"South Dakota—Great Faces, Great Places."* I approached the sign with increasing speed and an incredibly overwhelming feeling of joy that is hard to express in words. Wyoming was scratched off and I felt strong. The broad smile on the selfies told the story. I rode up in front of the sign and leaned the bike against it.

South Dakota was beautiful and not what I expected. I was fascinated by the geologic structures laid bare by erosion. Up ahead were large monoclines[iv] on the left and right, exposing older Permian to Pennsylvanian-aged[v] formations (deep ocean rocks). My mind instantly tries to envision geology on a regional scale. The Black Hills look like an oval bulls-eye-shaped dome, with rock beds dipping away from the center. The highest point in the Black Hills (Harney Peak, 7,242 feet) is located near the center of the range and is the tallest mountain east of the Rocky Mountains. The Black Hills are a dome structure[vi] raised like a boil in the western plains around 60 million years ago. The Black Hills expose geologic history that spans from some of the oldest to some of the youngest rock formations on Earth. The oldest Pre-Cambrian-aged[vii] pegmatite[viii] and metamorphic rocks represent the range's central core. World-class cave-forming Paleozoic limestone[ix] forms the next outer ring. Even younger rocks are exposed on the outer part of the regional ring beyond the limestone[x].

I clipped back in the pedals and rode another six miles with 650 feet of climbing, which brought me to the Black Hills National Forest boundary. The trees were such a welcomed relief in the heat. I pushed the bike right up onto the sign. It was probably not the best manners, but after all, what was anybody going to do to me? I was beginning to think of myself as an invincible animal on a bicycle. I was a bold, crazy man, the guy you see out on the highway occasionally and wonder, "*What is that idiot doing on this road?*"

Two Harley riders from Boston, Massachusetts approached and pulled up next to me to take pictures with their bikes. Sturgis was just days away and they were excited to be close to their destination. I snapped pictures for them in front of the Black Hills sign with the bike still leaning in the background.

Highway 16, also known as the Mount Rushmore Road, is a beautiful forested ride with lovely grassy meadows and abundant roadside wildflowers. It was a constant grade of climbing but not quite equal to the endurance required for the Washington and Montana passes. At about mile number nine, the fun began to run out. The woman back at Deckers wasn't kidding about these hills. I was approaching eight percent grades, similar to McDonald's Pass in Montana. Up, up, up, I pedaled, grinding it out in the heat. I was starting to bonk, so I pulled over, grabbed some shots of GU, and watered up. I noticed that as soon as I got into South Dakota, the breakdown lane was not so suitable for riding. While the road was smooth concrete, I rode the breakdown lane on the old crappy pavement.

"Oh man," what a freaking climb," I screamed.

At times I wandered onto the smoother road when it was safe but despite the hill, I was feeling pretty strong. With two days of centuries back to back, I was gunning for a hat-trick. I stopped near the hilltop to give thanks in prayer to God for getting me to that point. I stopped in a clearing and overlooked a denuded 80,000-acre area, destroyed by the Jasper Fire in the year 2000. I didn't notice much new growth but the site afforded long views of the Black Hills.

Finally, after 12 miles and 1,200 feet of climbing, I went around a large switchback and reached the summit. I passed many signs warning that the road ahead contained a single narrow lane with no shoulder. Hundreds of cars blasted by me with only inches to spare. A speed trap over the road posted vehicle speeds. Each vehicle exceeded the speed limit by 20 to 30 mph and few slowed down despite the flashing "SLOW DOWN!!!" warning.

The warning signs were correct because there were no shoulders. I began to sweat profusely and felt nauseous. This road section was not a place to my liking. I sprinted for another hundred feet with no shoulder and waited my turn for a break in the traffic. My emotions snapped from overly confident an hour before to utterly terrified. The line of vehicles seemed endless. It was the tourist season in the Black Hills. For the first time since leaving Seattle, I thought that maybe this was the end of the trip. To this point, it was a great ride. My eyes teared up. I felt invincible at times, challenged at other times. Still, I kept pushing on, never quitting, grinding it out, inured by whatever obstacle or manifested pain, inching my way towards Boston. I told my mom I could do this. Shannon told me she believed that I could pull this off. But maybe this was it. I was done. I'd ridden high passes in the west, traveled dangerous interstate, almost been crushed by a semi-truck, and pushed tens of miles on loose gravel in the heat.

"Wait! I told myself before I left that I would rather die than not do this." I dropped my head and exhaled slowly. Turning back would have meant defeat. Turning back would have meant facing a life of saying that I tried to achieve a childhood dream but couldn't pull it off. Turning back would be quitting. And I was not a quitter. Besides, turning back to where? Where would I go? I had nowhere to go, maybe back to a business that no longer existed.

"I am going to Boston, damn it!!" I screamed at the cars as they passed by. So I waited, and I waited and waited. Car after car after RV blew past me by less than inches. Despite the electronic sign flashing to slow down to 35 mph, no one obeyed the warning.

Suddenly, a stroke of luck. A group of Harley Davidson riders approached at slow speed. With adrenaline pumping, it was now or never. I jetted out onto the road and cranked as fast as I could to catch them. Two more Harley riders pulled up slowly behind me. We dropped into the canyon riding in perfect formation. It was a steep and sinuous, narrow two-lane road through trees and cliffs with incredible views to the south. At one point, I had Harleys on both sides and behind me, providing the perfect traffic buffer. My knee was so low in the turns that I thought I was going to scrape the pavement. One of them looked at me and smiled, and it seemed like a strange bonding moment between two-wheeled riders. It was illogical, exhilarating, and weirdly amusing all at once.

"Too fast, too fast, too fast, brake, brake," I thought as I leaned into the hairpin turn at the bottom at speeds nearing 40 miles per hour. Suddenly the highway climbed at a 12 percent grade. I quickly moved to the right and dropped out of formation, letting them go ahead of me. There was about a one-foot strip on the right side and I pedaled up that lane with only inches to spare between a guardrail and the highway. I pulled up the hill and came upon the entrance to Jewel Cave National Monument. Parked at the entrance and downing cans of beers were my motorcycle escorts from Chicago on their way to Sturgis. They joked with me and told me that I was crazy to be out there alone, riding the canyon on a bicycle.

"You knucklehead, are you nuts riding out there like that in that canyon?" one exclaimed.

"Get away from me, man, you are crazy," said another one of the bikers, backing away from me with his hands up.

They were right. That was probably the most insane road stretch that I had ever pedaled. I sat on one of their motorcycles, and they took turns sitting on the bicycle, laughing and taking pictures of each other. These were 700-pound Harleys with wide-ass cushy seats compared with my 90 plus pounds of a bike, gear, and a skinny touring saddle. We couldn't be any more different, yet we shared a bond of adventure on two-wheelers.

After they finished their beers, the bikers roared off into the Black Hills while I coasted down the access road to Jewel Cave, only to find the park ranger had just shut down tours for the day. He treated me to a one-on-one talk about the cave and the geology as we hiked back up to his car. The cave was discovered in 1900 by the Michaud family, who felt puffs of cold air coming from a small hole in the canyon. The entrance was too small for human entry, so the Michauds blew up an opening to find a cave lined with calcite crystals[xi]. Soon after its discovery in 1908, it was designated by Theodore Roosevelt as a National Monument. It was the third-longest cave in the world, with about 200 miles of mapped passageways.

Newcastle, Wyoming

I cranked hard, heading towards Custer City on Route 16. I was approaching 98 miles for the day and my thirst was overwhelming. I pulled into a KOA campground and spied a soda machine by the waterslide. The waterslide was staffed by a rude lady who gave me a hard time about the bike sticking six inches into the water slide stairwell. I apologized for the "terrible inconvenience," as she put up a chain and a Closed sign across the entrance and walked away.

"*Seriously? Had a bad day, lady? Why pick on me?*" I thought.

It was late and I needed to find a place to camp. Staying at the KOA is not camping. I noted a Forest Service road about a 1/4 mile back down the hill so I turned around and found an open gate on the north side. I slipped past the entrance and rolled the bike down a rough dirt road into the woods. Off with the lights, orange vest, the red jacket. I found a perfect site by large, randomly-stacked piles of cut trees that provided cover from nearby houses and the highway. I was finally in a place without highway noise and trains. Peculiarly, there were no mosquitoes. I did not have a cell phone signal to check the National Weather Service; however, the 22-degree halo around the sun earlier in the day didn't mean break out the tanning butter. I spread the fly on the tent before bed and battened down the hatches. Rain fell gently through the night. I pedaled 99 miles for the day, one mile shy of three consecutive centuries.

[i] Placer - An alluvial sand and gravel deposit containing gold or other precious minerals that can be washed from the formation.

[ii] Cretaceous - The third and latest Mesozoic Era period, approximately 146 million to 66 million years ago.

[i] Oxbow Pond - A crescent-shaped pond formed in an abandoned river bed that has been cut off from the main river course.

[ii] Plunging Anticline - An upwardly convex folded strata of rock where the fold's axis lies at a relatively steep angle to the horizontal.

[iii] Cable Tool Rig - A percussive drill rig that makes a hole using a heavy tool bit suspended on a cable that is lifted and dropped, breaking the formation. The broken rock is bailed out with another tool lowered on a cable.

[iv] Monocline - A one-limbed flexure of geologic strata.

[v] Pennsylvanian-Permian age - Sixth and seventh periods of the Paleozoic Era, approximately 250 to 323 million years.

[vi] Dome Structure - A roughly symmetrical upfold with geologic beds dipping more or less equally from a point.

[vii] Pre-Cambrian Age - All rocks formed before the Cambrian Period, or older than about 540 million years ago.

[viii] Pegmatite - Coarse-grained igneous dikes of various compositions that cross-cut large intrusive bodies of larger intrusive rocks that are finer-grained.

[ix] Paleozoic - Rocks deposited during an era of geologic time between the Precambrian and Mesozoic Eras that includes the Cambrian through the Permian 540 million to about 250 million years

ago.

[x] Limestone - A bedded sedimentary rock that is comprised mostly of calcium carbonate.

[xi] Calcite Crystals - Hexagonal-shaped calcium carbonate mineral, formed by dissolution of limestone and reprecipitated, reformed in crystalline structure in limestone openings.

CHAPTER 6 - THE PLAINS

August 8th - Custer City, South Dakota to White Rock, Nebraska

By morning, everything was soaking wet. I packed up without coffee, which didn't help my mood. But the day rapidly brightened as I pushed the bike from the woods and set off to Custer City, South Dakota, about three miles to the east on Route 16. The temperature was perfect, about 75 degrees and sunny. I rode past granitic rock pinnacles, spires, and cliffs peeking out above the trees between residences along the way.

Custer City was a cheesy town, complete with a Flintstones theme park campground, advertisements for daily magic shows, t-shirt shops, and Old West gun dueling reenactments. I like Fred Flintstone as much as the next guy but this was too much so I blew out of town as quickly as I could fill my water bottles. Climbing south on Highway 89/385, I pedaled past a gun shop advertising a special on target shooting with a 50-caliber machine gun and firing a grenade launcher.

"Nothing cheesy about that," I smiled and stopped for a selfie, thinking it might be fun to do it just once. Maybe not.

The ride south out of town was sublime, a New England-esque scene of lovely homes in the pines with tidy yards, interspersed between natural parks. When the sun broke out of the clouds, it brought instantaneous heat. At Pringle Junction, I turned left and followed Route 385 down the canyon, picking up more speed as I approached Wind Cave National Park. I rolled into the park to the sounds of a bazillion chirping prairie dogs, small fuzzy heads poking from hundreds of burrows.

I pedaled over to the ranger station and locked up the bike. Wind Cave National Park has an extensive cave system formed within the Madison Limestone (also known as the Pahasapa Limestone). Theodore Roosevelt declared Wind Cave America's seventh National Park in 1903 and it was the first cave in the U.S. to achieve National Park status. The cave system is over 140 miles in length, the sixth-longest in the world, and the wind from which the cave derives its name results from air pressure differentials between the cave interior and outdoor ambient conditions. In fact, wind speeds can reach 70 mph at the cave entrance.

I walked through the entire visitors center and took in as much as I could about the history and geology, remounted my bike, and cruised south from the last shaded hollow into the rolling prairie. Emerald green prairie grasses bent in a gentle wind as darker pines overlooked low hills on the eastern horizon and I stopped at another extensive prairie dog colony for a closer look and to take pictures. Standing tall at the edges of their mounded burrows, they would call to me and then hide as I approached while their neighbors surfaced behind me and chirped for my attention. I repeatedly turned and stalked in the opposite direction, carrying on the silly game for 10 minutes before I realized I would not get any good close-up photos.

"What am I doing, chasing rodents? Get moving," I thought.

I pedaled down Route 385 into Hot Springs. The springs flow from the north side of town down the canyon town through the city, and elegant setting with Main Street building facades comprised of pinkish-brown sandstone. It seemed like an attractive place to explore at greater length, with none of Custer City's tackiness.

I stopped at the information center and conversed with an elderly gentleman surrounded by hundreds of brightly-colored visitor pamphlets. I recounted my story, now recited a dozen times since Seattle. Out of the blue, he compared my bike ride with the 1970s movie *"Easy Rider,"* a late 1960s movie about two Harley Davidson riders crossing the country from the West Coast. They get killed by gun-toting rednecks in a pickup truck.

"I hope it doesn't end up for you in the same way," he said.

"I'm not on a motorcycle, and why would someone want to kill me?" I didn't make the connection.

He gave me somewhat of a strange look that was weird and chilling. Why did he say it in that manner? An awkward silence ensued while I perused the brochures. He directed me to the grocery store but first, I stopped at the bank to get $100 cash and checked the balance. Little did I know, this would be the last cash I would get (from a bank) for the remainder of the trip. I still had 60 percent of the country left to cycle.

I pedaled down to the grocery store for a deli sandwich and large Mountain Dew and then rolled out behind the store in the shade to eat. A store employee taking a smoke break gave me a thumbs up on the bike ride and kudos for my effort. It reminded me of all the positive reinforcement I had received since Wyoming, which always lifted my spirits and heightened my enthusiasm. He gave me verbal directions on how to get to the Nebraska border, which seemed an eternity away.

Before leaving Hot Springs, I stopped at a park along the bike path to check out the clear-running creek originating from the springs. I plunged headfirst into the warm, swift-running, waist-deep stream in my riding clothes and lost my bandana. I couldn't feel the gravel creek bottom, and the loss of feeling in my feet became more concerning. I savored the last few moments in the thermal waters, unaware this refreshing swim would be my last outdoor clean water bath for the trip.

At the junction with Route 18/385, I turned southeast on a busier concrete divided highway. The lane was smooth, wide, and comfortable cruising as I pedaled south into bonafide grassland prairie towards Nebraska. After several miles, I looked back to appreciate a sweeping view of the Black Hills. Nothing but Nebraska and the Midwest states lay ahead of me as the country landscape changed and unfolded its beauty right in front of me, morphing into endless grassy plains and sky. The grandeur of the Cascades, Rockies, and Black Hills became a rear-view mirror, fading memory of images.

The grind to the Nebraska border was 31 miles with a 500-foot climb into the wind. I languished at six-mile-per-hour drudgery in 96-degree heat with cramping legs. I struggled over long, low hills and endless expanses of oscillating grasslands to the Route 385 junction and terrible riding conditions—a coarse, red gravel chipseal road with a hot headwind pushed against my upper body like an NFL linebacker.

"Oh man," I thought, *"Where is my juice now? Am I starting to bonk? I just ate lunch. What's the matter with me?"*

I pulled into a gas station and fishing tackle shop in Oelrichs. It was brutally hot with increasing humidity, which made the ride feel even more wretched. Utterly spent, I went inside the store and sat in a plastic chair next to the air conditioner with a large Mountain Dew, candy bar, and licorice. Caffeine and sugar. Something here had to work. I dreaded getting back on the bike; I was experimenting with my body in a way never tried in my entire life and I began to perceive my body as a separate entity that guided my consciousness like a puppet. My body was the machine, my mind made decisions, and the body responded, "*OK, I'll do it as long as I can hold out.*" Long periods of exercise followed by junk food. Not a recommended way to ride, but this day I needed something to keep pushing up the grade into the heat and headwind.

The store clerk said it was 13 miles to Nebraska, and all uphill. After a brutal ride, the lights of the Stateline Casino sparkled in the distance, an oasis in a remote prairie grassland far, far from anywhere. I locked up the bike alongside several cars, pickups, and Harleys and went inside, craving a Mountain Dew, but they only had Coke. I was so parched that I didn't care. There were a few Harley bikers, but their frequency was noticeably beginning to decline.

A scantily-dressed young woman sitting by me at the bar overheard my conversation with the bartender about my bike trip. I expressed my need for coffee first thing in the morning to get rolling. She looked a little creepy, for lack of a better word—pale blonde hair, missing a few teeth, a petite frame meagerly covered with lacy underwear exposed through torn Daisy Duke cutoffs and a loosely-fitting blouse. Her face was once undoubtedly attractive but now wore the fatigue and scars of what might have been a long-term drug habit. I noticed her slip out the back door as I finished up a second icy cold Coke, bid the bartender farewell, and exited the dark, cool, replenishing confines of the casino walls.

Outside, the same young woman from the bar approached me and said she would make me a percolated pot of coffee to go. She must have missed the part inside where I mentioned how I wanted coffee first thing in the morning. She was delightful, and her smile disarming. I told her to skip the coffee because I had to leave but thanked her for her kindness and said, "God bless you!" She repeated back the same to me and waved goodbye.

I rode up to the large green Nebraska State Line sign, stopped to bask in the late afternoon rays of the sun, and took a few selfies with the bike and the Nebraska sign behind me. *"Nebraska, The Good Life."* I loved the state welcoming sign and the acknowledged meaning behind the slogan while relaxing for a few minutes to appreciate where I was and how far I had come under pedal power.

Outside Chadron, Nebraska

I coasted the bike downhill for miles to the White River bridge, where there was no water, only a dry ephemeral river wash. I pulled off the road and into a field of wild sunflowers and camped behind huge, old, moldy hay bales. About a half-mile north was a ranch house and farther out I saw heavy dark gray cumulus clouds and lightning. To the west, a golden sunset radiated behind low hills. Just then, my mom called and mentioned reports of tornados to the north of my location. Making matters worse, the mosquitoes were awful, which surprised me, considering I camped next to a dry wash. Traffic was heavy throughout the night as I scribbled in my journal. Distant flashes of lightning lit the tent walls.

August 9th - Chadron, Nebraska to Cody, Nebraska

It was an uncomfortable night. I tossed, turned, and sweated. I wasn't used to the heat and humidity and the bugs were intense outside the tent. A few mosquitos found their way inside and bit me. Something smelled a bit nasty as well, and it wasn't me. I was up quickly, downed powdered caffeine, and discovered the horrendous stink throughout the night was from dead deer mice around and beneath the tent.

"Great. Deer mice. Hantavirus."

I rolled out of camp early, leaving the deer mice stench behind, and cruised down Route 385 under cloudy conditions into Chadron, Nebraska for a fast-food breakfast, loading up on fat calories and filling my Camelbak with ice. At 3,400 feet, Chadron was still reasonably high in elevation, with a prominent skyline of tree-covered bluffs south of Chadron dominating the scenery. I pedaled east out of town on Route 20, dubbed the "Bridges to Buttes Highway."

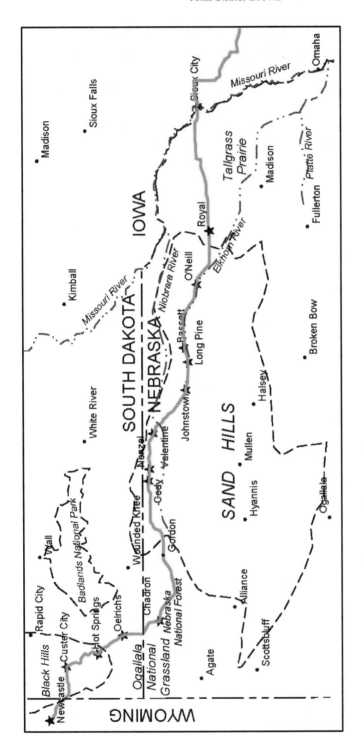

Figure 5 - Newcastle to Sioux City

Highway 20 was great touring on the bike, with a full, clean breakdown lane. The main complaint was the presence of ubiquitous pavement cracks across the entire state. Not small cracks either. These gaping wounds were spaced about every 50 to 100 feet, some being over two inches or greater in width, creating a constant annoying jolt to the bike. I headed south about 18 miles to Hay Springs, climbing into state forest land, traveling through red pines and 50-foot cliffs, then into woods. *Bluffs in Nebraska? Woods?* I stopped at a rest area in the "*forest.*" The sign warned about encroaching pine trees, which they designated as being unnatural as well as dangerous. Therefore, the dendrophobic Nebraska Game and Parks Commission decided that it would be best to harvest the trees to prevent crown fires, insect endemics, and disease. I laughed aloud. This place could benefit from a few more trees.

I did not expect to find this type of lovely scenery in Nebraska. Geological outcrops included Tertiary-aged bluffs of sandstone and mudstone; some of the country's younger sedimentary formations. I stopped in the Rushville grocery store for supplies and a young cashier in the store asked me about my bike tour on the way out. I recalled some of the more unusual incidents and she told of her own prospects of a cross-country adventure. "I'm planning on riding my horse across the country one day," she said. *Could you even do that?* I wondered. She made me laugh. I think she was serious, too; I loved the fact she showed such great ambition and spirit.

I pedaled east on Route 20 through Clinton and then to Gordon, always going uphill, it seemed, but in fact, I was heading downhill most of the time at less than one percent grade. These towns are so small that you might not notice them in a car but riding from town to town on Route 20 was fantastic. This was the perfect speed to see Nebraska. The lane was wide and the traffic was virtually non-existent. I became entranced by a deep blue sky and emerald green trees separated by endless expanses of hayfields in various stages of growth and harvest, bracketed further by battalions of cottonwood trees on the horizon. There is a surreal feeling to the landscape here that is hard to describe without experiencing it, especially from the saddle of a bike.

I kept a faster cadence thanks to an advantageous crosswind from the northwest, my improving physical condition, and more forgiving riding terrain. I noticed that if I angulated my body to the wind, like a tacking sail, the wind increased my speed, slightly pushing the bike. I had been toying with the idea since Montana. If it was a dead-on headwind, then it was like sailing "in irons" where the sail flaps, and I'd go nowhere with great effort. But with the wind at my back, I was on a "run" and clocked speeds nearing 30 miles an hour with only moderate pedaling effort. However, the enjoyable speed was hampered by continuous, full-body hammering from the endless two-beat clunks over the cracks, amplified further through the saddle and bars. The rack and panniers rattled as if ready to fall off the bike—as if my ass wasn't sore enough already, this was brutal punctuation. When there were no cars around, I took to the road lane for smoother cruising to alleviate the pain.

Beneath this landscape lies the Ogallala Aquifer, one of the world's largest groundwater aquifers, occupying nearly the entirety of Nebraska's underground. It is one of the country's most unique and irreplaceable natural groundwater resources, extending approximately 175,000 square miles from South Dakota to Texas. This precious store of water is ancient, dating to the Pleistocene era, and it is currently being depleted at an alarming rate to sustain agriculture and insatiable human thirst.

Somewhere around Gordon, I passed a most unusual display of yard art. Dozens of bells of all shapes and sizes were prominently displayed in someone's front yard, scattered about in the shade of mature cottonwood trees. Most of the bells appeared in working order. I spent about 20 minutes walking around, amazed by this unique campanology of museum-worthy instruments. I ran my hand over many of the curved, smooth textures. Cicadas whined loudly above me in the trees while a gentle warm wind swept through the verdant canopy overhead. I very much wanted to meet the owner of this unusual collection, so I walked to the front door to ask questions, but oddly, there was no doorbell. Oh, the irony. I knocked, but no one came to the door.

About ten miles east of Gordon, the scenery went from relatively flat, irrigated farmland to low, undulating, undisturbed hills of grass. The Bridges to Buttes Highway waved ahead of me like a ribbon in the wind to the horizon as I arrived at a vast and unique geologic region of the country known as the Sand Hills. The road became a roller coaster of up and down pitches over ancient dunes, climbing over 150-foot crests and plunging into interdune hollows.

The Sand Hills region is about 20,000 square miles, encompassing about one-quarter of Nebraska. Interestingly, some of the dunes became nomadic several times during the last 15,000 years—when the plains' climate became too dry, the dunes lost their vegetative cover and roamed freely with the wind. For the most part, however, the dunes became stabilized by prairie grasses—wetlands and ponds formed in the interdunes, extensively disseminated among the central Sand Hills. Lakes and wetlands then began where dunes migrated into ancient stream channels and dammed pre-existing streams.

I stood up, pedaling hard on downhill stretches, which carried my speed uphill over windward slopes, dune after dune. Emerald green interdune valleys with azure ponds reflected a piercing sapphire-colored sky. Near Merriman, I stopped next to a fenceline to make friends with two handsome chestnut thoroughbreds. I received an affectionate wet, and organic-flavored kiss on my cheek. Later, I stopped in at a rundown bar for two Mountain Dews on ice, which I began to crave every day about this time. Alas, they didn't have any ice, but I didn't care because, with a little caffeine boost, I could push on to Cody as long as I still had a tailwind.

A text came in from my wife at home.

"How are you?"

"108 miles so far today."

"Wow, you are hardcore."

It felt good to get a message from home that didn't contain bad news and I took to Route 20 with newfound enthusiasm. Around 8:00 p.m. at mile 110, I was rapidly approaching the end of my daily endurance. I rode into Cody to camp in the city park. Cody charged $15 per person per night and Nebraska hospitality includes camping in town greens. Cody Park was a wonderful place to camp, complete with picnic tables, potable water, freshly mowed, lush, green grass, and a shower. The shower wasn't spotless but I relished every minute of hot water.

After I set up camp, another biker rolled into the park, named David Lindsay. He hailed from a small town in Ohio, was riding without a helmet, and wore sneakers. His bike had flat pedals. David said he had disabilities, as he was losing his eyesight, and said he didn't have too many years before it would diminish to the point of complete blindness. He jumped up and crouched on the picnic table as he wolfed down Little Debbie Snack Cakes for dinner. He was a total trip, starting with his proclamation that he would not pay a fee for camping in the park "*out of principle.*" He rolled a cigarette while I deposited money into the box.

"Hell, most of them are free camping!" he moaned as he puffed away.

I was dog tired and had my fill of David. I zipped up the tent and drifted off to sleep with a head full of rolling dunes and prairies, endless skies, and hay bales evenly placed to the horizon. Lights from the nearby baseball game lit the sky and a cheering crowd at the nearby field broke the quiet of the night. I rode more than a century of surprisingly scenic Nebraska beauty and it felt great.

August 10th - Cody, Nebraska to Bassett, Nebraska

I awoke at 5:30 a.m. and everything inside the tent was saturated. The Nebraska morning brought in the heaviest fog and early dew I had experienced in many years. I couldn't believe how atmospheric conditions had changed so drastically between Chadron and Cody. I would have to start covering things up at night because the air would only get damper farther east. The mosquitoes were terrible and a few made it into the tent again but I finally had the first good night's sleep in a long time. I emerged from my nylon shelter into the foggy morning to see David already awake and getting set to depart camp. But first he rolled another cigarette. Unusual, I thought, that a biker would be smoking so many cigarettes. His minimalism was a complete departure from the typical touring biker and I double-checked to see if it wasn't tobacco he was smoking. While rolling another, David imparted some advice about biking across Iowa.

The Sand Hills

"Iowa has no breakdown lanes. There is nowhere to ride on Iowa roads that aren't right in traffic. It's dangerous. It is nothing like the conditions that you have experienced so far on your trip," David explained. "And don't even think about riding anywhere north of Kankakee or you will be riding in heavy Chicago traffic. That could pretty much end your trip."

"Oh, bullshit," I said to him with a smile. "And Montana has no bike trails. And it's flat to St. Regis from Lookout Pass. Yeah, I had heard all these stories back in the West. How do you know the conditions I have been riding since Seattle?" I said.

"I've been there," he said.

Unfazed by my quick dismissal of his advice, David headed west to Wyoming. Little did I know at the time that he was dead-on about Iowa and how arrogant I was to dis his recommendations. I drank the last of my nasty powdered caffeine and headed out of town on Route 20. Without real coffee, I was always lagging and semi-awake and the air was so foggy outside of town that it was basically like a morning on the beach. I couldn't see more than 50 feet down the road and my riding glasses were fogging up. Occasional deer peered out from grassy draws, motionless and staring at the passing two-wheeled apparition.

Then the fog abruptly lifted, exposing a Sand Hills landscape that looked like miles of golf course littered with sand traps that had spilled out onto the greens. Another three deer, one with a large velvet rack, watched me from a draw between some dunes as I rode past the tiny town of Nenzel and then dropped elevation to Kilgore. The rough road breaks in the breakdown lane persisted, jarring my prostate with every thud. A couple of miles east of Kilgore, I passed into the Central Time Zone and lost one hour of riding time. Up ahead, a biker touring on a recumbent bike and over-loaded with gear approached, sporting a bright orange shirt and flip-flops. I flagged him down to chat and he told me his name was Michael. He was remarkably tall but riding a relatively small and unusual recumbent touring bike. The bike was streamlined and tricked out with full suspension and a tiny front tire. The bike was so unique I wondered where he could ever get replacement tires or parts. His bike looked pretty worn down at this point, and his bike and gear were filthy. A magneto ran a charging station on the front of his bike to keep all of his lights and phone charged. Michael was from Denmark and had traveled Europe, Turkey, China, New Zealand, and Australia on his recumbent. He took a cargo ship for about 90 Euros per day to cross the ocean and said the sea voyage was dull but worth getting to America with his bike and gear. I asked him if I could take his picture.

"Sure for $5 a picture," he said as he held out his hand for payment.

"Funny guy...not," I thought. Michael was headed back west to

Yellowstone. I asked him about riding conditions on the Cowboy Trail, sub-paralleling the Bridges to Buttes Highway. He told me not to bother with it because it was loose gravel and it would only slow me down compared with Route 20. We said our goodbyes and I contemplated his round-the-world adventures. I was meeting bikers with ambitions that amounted to nothing more than working to save enough money for the sole purpose of exploring the world on a bicycle. I knew at that moment that I loved this adventure more than I ever could have imagined. I felt complete satisfaction because I was both mobile and exploring the country at the bike's speed. Living in the moment was all that mattered. It was a liberating and joyous feeling.

I continued pedaling past Kilgore, then Crookston with some small climbs and down long hills, venturing into the town of Valentine. I headed south on the east side of town on Highway 83 and stopped at a scenic sweeping overlook of the Niobrara River. The view of two large bridges with a long climb up the opposite side on a broad curve was spectacular. Something about that view of the two bridges over the canyon on the plains captured my imagination; the panorama was far different from any scene I would have expected in Nebraska.

About five miles south of Valentine, I picked up Route 20 again and rode past the tiny town of Wood Lake. I was heading out of the Sand Hills into a grassland prairie where endless groves of large, majestic cottonwoods cast dark shadows. The constant high-pitched drone of cicadas replaced the roars of Harley-Davidsons which was getting on my nerves. Cicadas have a loud metallic whine and sometimes they sing in unison, but today they were out of sync and piercingly loud.

I approached Johnstown, population 63, which is in Brown County, and chuckled over the coincidence with my name. As I pedaled into town, a three-legged red heeler chased me relentlessly. As usual, protocol dictated that I stop and call him out in a shameful tone of voice. He stopped and looked at me like the crazy man that I was on two wheels. With a missing leg, no doubt he had been run over on Route 20 before. He turned around and headed home with his tail between his legs.

The late afternoon sun pushed the heat well into the 90s so I parked the bike in front of the local bar and went in for a soda. A few cowboys with Stetson hats and spurs and a potty-mouthed barkeep were playing cards and drinking Coors Light and watching *How I Met*

Your Mother on the TV. They asked me about my trip so I recounted that I was riding from Seattle to Boston. One of the cowboys looked over at me and asked if I could ride a quarter horse.

"Hell yes, I can. I just rode that bike from Seattle," I blurted out, smiling, not even sure if I was accepting a dare, a bet, or just making conversation. He stopped playing cards and headed outside across the street, where he led a horse from a trailer. I followed the cowboy outside with the others, not sure of where this was going. Sure enough, he asked me to mount up.

Johnstown, Nebraska

The horse's name was Curly. I couldn't tell if Curly was a gentle horse so I made introductions with him in a soft voice and patted his neck to be sure I didn't spook him. He seemed kind enough but there was a wild look in his eye that caused me a bit of alarm. I put on my bicycle helmet, placed the cleats into his stirrup, grabbed the horn, and mounted Curly amidst the creaks and squeaks of a well-worn western leather saddle on a sweaty horse. In my mind was the memory of my last ride on my sister's horse in New Hampshire, where the horse cleaned me off on a low-hanging tree branch.

That was the old me. The new me just rode to Johnstown, Nebraska, I thought. With a big smile, I grabbed the reins, kicked hard with the cleats, and bolted off to the north down Main Street in a canter. Only three people on Main Street, a Lycra-clad guy in bicycle cleats, and a horse named Curly witnessed this ridiculous display of cross-training. I pretended to be in charge because that was what Curly expected, but I was scared to death. We turned at the end of the street and to show more moxie I shouted, "Pick it up, Curly!" I gave him a kick with the bike shoes and Curly bolted back to the bar. While this was genuinely fun, it was also frightening, but the smile never left my face. This riding was the shit, and I loved it. I never expected to do something this spontaneous. Ahead of me, I noticed the cowboys laughing and taking pictures with my camera. I turned around and took another lap down through Johnstown, and then cantered back to the cowboys, dismounted and handed Curly's reins back to his owner. We all had fun and I knew in my heart that Nebraskans were some of the best-natured folk I met on tour; probably among the most pleasant people I have met in the United States. A palpable, laid-back attitude persisted here. I thanked the cowboys and the bartender for the drinks and the experience. I mounted the trusty bike I had decided to nickname "SeaBos" (for Seattle to Boston) and blew out of town with the biggest grin on my face I'd had in decades.

It was ten miles from Johnstown to Ainsworth. Towns like these were almost always visible from a distance, with a telltale visage—a bright blue water tower tank with the town name painted in large letters facing a direction that welcomed you into town. Ainsworth was a bigger town, with charming homes nestled among well-manicured trees. I was now in prairie land, heavily watered by massive pivot irrigating systems. Each pivot irrigates a circular diameter of about a half-mile and I marked my miles by each pivot's width. My butt became sorer by every mile and I developed a routine to increase my stamina: Twenty pumps on the crank, then coast until my speed dropped to 18 miles per hour. Then crank again. I was now traveling for miles only in the standing position but my sore rear end thanked me for it.

Outside of Ainsworth I saw a silver pickup truck off the road into the woods. It had freshly broken-off several small trees, missing a large cottonwood tree by inches. I approached the truck cautiously, noting the paint buckets and lunch pail in the back. The wreck appeared to be recent, my heart began to race, and I braced myself for the sight of a bloody body in the front seat. But no one was inside and I breathed a sigh of relief. It looked like a drunk driver may have left this one behind the night before.

After another eight miles I reached the town of Long Pine. The pines were mostly on the smaller side, many with the appearance of Christmas trees clinging to the hillsides of a shallow canyon cut by Long Pine Creek. The pines seemed oddly out of place with the prairie country and once I passed through town, they quickly disappeared. I was back to pedaling through the prairie with hay bales and rolls scattered randomly toward the horizon. From Long Pine, it was nearly nine miles to Bassett and I rode into the Rock County Fairgrounds with a body that was close to complete exhaustion. I probably pushed a little bit too far for the day, notching well over 100 miles, and I needed a place to crash. The fairgrounds had showers, water, picnic tables, and plenty of freshly mowed spaces for camping. I pulled the bike up to the men's room next to a massive RV, unloaded some gear, and sat down to mix some Gatorade. A blonde on a Giant road bicycle (similar to mine) blasted past me, missing by mere feet. Not noting my presence, she popped off the bike and hurried up the steps into the RV. Moments later, she emerged out of the front door.

I walked over to say hello and she introduced herself as Julie. She said she was camping in the fairgrounds and supporting her kids, who participated in a rodeo the previous day. She brought the motor home to the fairgrounds so they would have a place to change between events. She rambled at length about her kids, rodeo, and life in Nebraska. Julie (or Jules) was an attractive woman I was instantly drawn to because of her infectious spunk and high-pitched articulation combined with energy and personality.

"I divorced five years ago because my husband ran off with a younger woman, leaving me to raise five rodeo kids pretty much on my own," she said.

Jules had a positive outlook on life and presented her thoughts with a cute laugh and a lovely voice. It was an accent that I didn't recognize from anywhere in the past—a Sand Hills dialect. "Wow! I have never met a real-life cowgirl before," I told her. I was intrigued by this rodeo lifestyle, which was foreign to me. We talked for a while and then parted as I was off to take a shower. "The shower smells like horse shit," she said with a smile. "The smell in the showers is from the rodeo, but it's worth it for the water pressure and endless hot water!"

She was right; the men's room was dark and malodorous like an unclean horse stall. But despite the nasty, slimy floor, slime on the shower walls, and the pervasive odor, the copious flow of hot water and free soap was indeed paradise. Outside, I washed off my feet with a hose and then set up camp next to Julie's RV. I changed clothes, shaved, and then went over to knock on her door. Jules opened the door and invited me inside with a big smile. The daughter of a water well-digger, she was a lively and entertaining Nebraska cowgirl who liked motorcycles and worked as a nurse at the local hospital. She was exceptionally proud of her kid's achievements in rodeo events, as well, despite some mishaps including a few broken bones. Rodeo is something I know little about and learned it is a serious sports event, one that can seriously injure kids and adults alike. The animals are big enough to kill you, and some riders don't make it out of the ring on their feet. My kids played team sports while her kids rode and roped huge, powerful animals. I was really starting to like Nebraska and its friendly, hometown-proud people.

When I first pulled into the fairgrounds, a passing woman mentioned because it was Monday that it was "hamburger night" at the Corral Bar. So I asked Jules to join me in town for dinner. She graciously accepted, we hopped onto our bikes, and she led me through the back streets of Bassett to the bar. A heavy wooden door opened to a traditional, dimly lit smattering of tables and booths. We sidled straight to the bartender and I ordered a tequila shot and a beer. Jules ordered Coors Light with tomato juice. "Red beer," she called it, her favorite. The barmaid brought me a tequila shot that looked to be nearly four ounces and I stared at the glass in total disbelief, thinking, *"I'm not in Utah anymore!"* Jules offered me a taste of the "red beer" and once I got past the color, it didn't taste all that bad. We laughed and I gobbled one of the best hamburgers of my life. I didn't even think about being on a bike ride at that point. I was with a newfound friend, sharing a love for kids, riding bikes, the outdoors, writing, poetry, music, and drinking. As an outsider to Nebraska culture, I felt right at home in a place I had never envisioned.

After an excellent meal, we stepped outside into a night of warm winds and a starlit canopy backed up by chirping crickets and a chorus of resonating cicadas. I was apprehensive because I knew from past "experiences" that I shouldn't drink and ride a bicycle. It seems that every time I did, something terrible happened. The most recent episode occurred in Mill Creek Canyon with my son Andrew, which resulted in separated ribs. Then there was a broken left arm in Liberty Park in Salt Lake. With that in mind, I asked Jules to go slowly and we carefully made our way back to our camp.

I took my journal into her RV to enter the day's events while she fixed herself a large glass of wine. I crossed the Central/Mountain time zone boundary earlier in the day and put in over 100 miles, so I was pretty much dog tired. Lady Antebellum played on the CD player and we chatted until about midnight, until I could hardly keep my eyes open and focused. Jules offered me to spend the night on the couch rather than sleeping on the ground in the tent. I thanked her but declined, hugged her goodnight, and returned to my tent to settle on soft, freshly cut, Nebraska grass. I tried to drift off to sleep but I could hear Jules in the RV gabbing away on her phone.

"It's like, 1:30 in the morning, Jules! Aren't you going to bed?" I yelled at the RV. I drifted off before sleep to visions of a vast Nebraska sky, the foggy Sand Hills, and a rolling Bridges to Buttes two-lane highway.

August 11th - Bassett, Nebraska to Royal, Nebraska

I was not sure what the time was when my groggy mind grasped that morning was well underway. It was late. I felt the effect of the tequila tumbler and beers from the night before. I popped out of the tent and saw Jules looking at me from the RV's bedroom window.

"I'm ready with coffee and breakfast. Come on in!"

"I'm up! I'll be right there," I beamed.

I quickly packed up the bike, excited for the prospect of hot coffee. I bounced up the stairs into the RV and watched Jules fix toast with Nutella and pour coffee from a giant freshly-brewed pot. She had all of her writings, stories, and other musings out on the table as if she was caught up in a frenzied multitasking midstream of thought. There were stories of patriotism, lists of unusual cocktails, records of every human medical ailment with humorous diagnoses. Jules wrote stories covering matters which evoked patriotic emotion, including a story of a young girl singing the Star-Spangled Banner in a stadium. Jules was a real American from the Heartland, a patriot, and that got me thinking about getting an American flag for the bike since I was crossing the country. If nothing else, it might give me greater visibility.

We consumed a pot of coffee over the discussion of her prose. I didn't want to go but I had many miles left to pedal across Nebraska and this precious moment would have to pass. I kissed her on the cheek and invited her to friend me on Facebook.

"Goodbye, Jules!" I yelled back to her as she waved. I rolled out of Bassett, heading east, steadily but gently downhill for 20 miles to Stuart. I could see that I was leaving the Sand Hills behind and moving well into the flats. About 10 miles beyond Stuart, I rode into Atkinson, a charming farming community of well-kept homes with nicely maintained yards. I stopped in for a Subway sandwich and talked to the locals while waiting in line to order. These hard-working Nebraskans are the true worker bees of America, each performing specific roles that integrate into a much larger collective community to feed America. There appeared to be a healthy interdependent relationship between ranchers, farmers, the guy who supplies the water and mechanical support, fertilizer suppliers, transporters, fencing cowboys, and much more. It takes a village of individual talents to pull off this much agriculture in such a vast expanse of land.

"So everybody has to get along," said the man next to me in line. "Nobody gets too excited about anything around here." Nebraskans were some of the most helpful people I'd ever met in the country. Their state motto should read *"Nebraska, friendliest people on the planet."*

As the day heated up, the cicadas became more pervasive, continuously in-and-out-of-synch, and increasingly annoying. I rolled into O'Neill, the Irish capital of Nebraska, and stopped at a Radio Shack to pick up an AM/FM digital radio. I couldn't take the never-ending swell of cicada droning. Once back on the road and plugged into the AM/FM, I found little to listen to except static. The only signal for miles was an AM station carrying local news and weather info. The rest was an endless loop rundown of all the agricultural commodities that changed by fractions of a penny throughout the day, but it beat the whine of the cicadas.

I spent the afternoon exploring and wandering from the gravel Cowboy Trail to the Bridges to Buttes Highway. The Cowboy Trail is a delightful way to pedal across Nebraska and see some beautiful parts of the state. This multi-use rail-trail runs generally east to west through northern Nebraska, following a graded gravel surface and nicely-constructed footbridges utilizing the abandoned Chicago and North Western Railway corridor. When I rode this section, the trail was completed for the most part between Valentine and Norfolk, about 190 miles, making it the longest rails-to-trails conversion in the United States.

The trail is incredibly secluded from the road at most locations between towns, flanked by thick Russian olive and cottonwood trees, and frequent bridge crossings are a marvel of construction. The weathered gray wooden bridge decks cut on an angle added to the visual enhancements of the ride. Some of those crossings spanned substantial lengths and I stopped on one of them to watch pillows of lazy yellowish-brown sediment moving downriver through lush green grasses and cottonwoods. Considering the vastness of the area and the complete absence of a population between towns, it wasn't too surprising I didn't see another soul riding the entire stretch.

The heat and heavy buzz of cicadas filled the air and occasionally, small biting flies stung my arms and face to sample my blood but cottonwood shade blessed the rest of the afternoon ride. Stands of wild hemp appeared near the trail. I recognized the flower, the leaves, the patterned leaf points, a form of marijuana—ditch weed. I have never seen this in the wild. Even though hemp bears the familiar narrow, five-fingered leaves similar to marijuana, it contains virtually none of the psychoactive components. Some of the plants were over six feet tall with juvenile buds, which smelled just like pot. I wondered if these plants might not be the hemp plants cultivated by our forefathers. Some of the plants appeared cross-pollinated with cannabis; I noted at least three different morphologies. It was everywhere, growing in people's front yards and in fields of hay and corn.

A text came in from home.

"Hi, how are you? I haven't heard from you in a long time."

"Yes, I was thinking of you last night, but I lost an hour to Central Time. I rode a quarter horse through Johnstown to everyone's amusement."

"I miss you and think about you all the time."

I made a dogleg due-east turn on Route 20 and crossed the Elkhorn River towards Orchard, noting that the scenery was again changing to flat, heavily irrigated farmland. Massive pivots lay ahead as far as I could see. I pedaled into the town of Orchard in the late afternoon sweltering heat and my head suffering from a droning cicada cacophony. I stopped at the town park to take a long, cool shower at the shower facilities, a welcome gift for a man on a bike. I soaked my shirt before leaving the men's room, and then pedaled to Royal, about eight miles to the east, passing extensive agricultural facilities and silos. Royal touted themselves as a "*Small Town With A Big Heart.*" I wandered side streets and set up camp in the town's central park, alone. Immediately to the west was a field with a few Buffalo and Watusi cows sporting gigantic horns. I walked over to visit them and called my older brother Matt to wish him a happy 60th birthday.

August 12th - Royal, Nebraska to Sioux City, Iowa-Halfway!

The night blessed me with uninterrupted, restful sleep and I woke up around 5:00 a.m. to the neighbors starting their trucks to head to work. Busy bees, these Nebraskans; agriculture in perpetual motion before sunup.

My bike's panniers had started to disintegrate and the outer pouch needed some sewing. I packed up the gear best I could and talked a bit with a man named Lloyd, who lived in a house adjacent to the park. He owned the two buffalo and the two Watusi cows in the field by the park. Lloyd and his brother raised both buffalo from calves and considered them their pets.

I said goodbye to Lloyd and rolled out of town with a hell of a cross-tailwind pushing me. Road conditions were right, although the asphalt breaks continued to rattle my teeth. Listening to the new radio relaxed me somewhat and I picked up a couple of other stations. Still, only country music played the airwaves here, and the occasional agricultural commodities prices came on every hour. I wondered who was listening. Me, I guess. Now there was plenty of hardcore country music to listen to between soybean prices.

Suddenly, all I could think about was food. This desire was not the regular hunger pains one might experience after a day of not eating; I was like a bear after a winter of hibernation and I needed food quickly. I rode into Plainview for caffeine and supplies and needed a grocery store, not a gas station. My appearance was pretty rough, unshaven and dirty from the road. I loaded up with grub and talked with an older woman outside of the store while enjoying a deli ham, salami, and cheese sub with pickles and chips, cookies, and two quarts of Gatorade. I told her I was riding from Seattle, Washington, and she couldn't believe I had come this far. Neither could I.

After lunch I rode about two blocks and had a flat tire. What a pain in the butt. It was nearly always the back tire, which required unloading all of the stuff. I changed the tube in the shade and after passing Randolph, the road went from relatively decent paving entirely to shit. It was bad. Not only was the breakdown lane wholly broken up, but Highway 20 had eight-inch holes which became quite dangerous. The breakdown lane also had gravel and was missing pavement, a real hazard rolling over 25 miles per hour. Between Belton and Laurel were some of the worst road conditions I had encountered on the ride. I alternated between cursing out loud at the highway or singing along with the radio. The scenery didn't offer much reprieve; it was exceedingly flat and I could see long, long distances ahead in all directions.

About 45 miles from the Missouri River, I was close enough to Sioux City that I started to make out rock and roll music through radio static. It was Led Zeppelin! I never thought I'd be so happy to hear an overplayed classic rock song. I turned north in Laurel with a full tailwind for about four miles before turning back to the east. The road became increasingly hilly with surprisingly steep elevation changes of 150 to 200 feet and occasionally, loose canines chased me on the highway. I loved stopping and sternly commanding them to sit. They usually did, but in a disgruntled way. Eventually, they would get up and leave, wanting nothing to do with me.

When I reached Jackson, I came to a bluff overlooking the Missouri River basin. I stopped for a picture and then coasted down the hills at high speed on crappy highway pavement. The highway divided just east of Jackson when I bonked, so I pulled over to cut up an orange. I was amazed at the amount of energy it provided and I was back rolling in no time.

Continuing east on Route 20, I intersected Highway 75, a dangerous road with significant city traffic, unlike I had ever seen on a bicycle, with merging vehicles and cloverleaf intersections. It was a whole new riding game. I exited onto Dakota Avenue, a busy city street heading north straight through South Sioux City and the Missouri River came into view after a little more than two miles.

"Oh, my God!" "Oh, my God!" "Oh my God!" I yelled aloud, "I am freaking halfway across the country!!!!"

I popped out of the clips and jumped up and down with

complete joy: elation, euphoria, ecstasy, all at the same time. Dopamine gushed in a way unknown to me and I loved it. I stopped for pictures in the middle of the bridge over the river and became extraordinarily emotional. I was about halfway to Boston. Tears began to flow. All my feelings mixed into a slurry and I sensed a new mood emerging, a sense of fearlessness. Without a doubt, I had reached the bardo of my existence. I crossed the mighty 300-foot-wide Missouri, the same river where I bathed in Montana in waist-deep water with the black snakes. I made it to Iowa, and Nebraska was one more conquered state.

Iowa is the only state whose east and west state lines are defined by significant rivers and Sioux City is the last navigable point upriver where big cargo ships can travel. The city is located geographically at the edge of the Tallgrass Prairie. In this area, thousands of years of soil deposition formed around 10,000 years ago from retreating continental glaciers. The glaciers scraped the Canadian earth surface clean down to bedrock and left America blanketed with thick deposits of Canadian soils and loess (wind-deposited silt) derived from those scraped-up earthen materials. These soils are responsible for Iowa's incredible fertility, North America's "Mesopotamia." This region holds some of the thickest, most fertile lands in North America. For thousands of years, this area was roamed and naturally fertilized by wild buffalo, wolves, coyotes, and elk. The soils were then worked and tilled by prairie dogs. Rampant human and cattle population growth wiped out the buffalo, prairie dogs, the rest of the native animals as modern agriculture overtook the land.

I rolled into the Stony Creek Hotel on the north side of the Missouri River and rode the elevator with my bike to a nice, second-floor room with a big bed and a hot shower. I pushed the bike into the room and giggled the entire time as I threw my clothes into the shower with some shampoo and hot water and washed them with my feet. My legs bled streams of dirt. All the wet clothes were then strung across the room on two beds to dry. After cleaning up, I called my parents to relieve their worries, as I did every night. I told them that I had never been as focused on any task in my life. I thought that maybe this was the first time I ever felt alive. It was a euphoria I had never experienced.

It was time to celebrate for making it halfway, thank God for some incredible help and only a few close calls. Other than almost having my head squashed in Montana, I had no accidents and just a few falls. But my feet were completely numb. I pulled the panniers from the bike, rolled it past the front desk, and cruised to the Firehouse Bar. I now looked at my bike in a new way. SeaBos had become a reliable companion and carried me a far distance. I felt a relationship with my bike in a way I had never before felt and anthropomorphized the rudimentary steel and rubber-wheeled machine.

I rode through well-lit Sioux City streets with my lights flashing, surprised by the leg power I felt without the panniers. I ripped through town, passing cars and feeling sporty. The Firehouse Bar was a hectic indoor/outdoor tavern, full of activity and loud people. I rolled SeaBos through their wooden gate and leaned him up against a nearby fence. Bright Christmas-style lights, copiously strung above tables, added to the ambiance. I pulled up to the bar, since every table was occupied, and asked for ice water.

The barmaid, Sarah, had a darling personality, a sizeable curly mop of blond hair, big brown smiling eyes, and white hot pants, exposing legs that shouldn't be admired to the point of being noticed, but I had no doubt that was a common occurrence. She nodded her head at me and then looked at the bike. I told her I was halfway from Seattle to Boston and showed her the map. She smiled, stepped back behind the bar and brought a free Diet Coke and bottled water with ice, and marked up a special water bottle for the accomplishment. She wrote, "*August 12th - Sioux City - halfway from Seattle to Boston.*" I drank my water and took a few selfies with her. Sarah said that I should come back to Iowa and ride *RAGBRAI*. I didn't understand quite what she said or what I heard, but I kept thinking, *ragbray? rugbee? ragbry? What the ...?* I mused at the word but didn't think much more about it.

After a few minutes, I took reluctant notice of the loudmouth sitting to my right. He was hitting on the barmaid ever since I showed up and was extremely annoying to me as well. He seemed especially impressed by the sound of his voice and his big pile of cash on the bar. He made a few inappropriate remarks to me about the bartender, then started telling me he was recently divorced. He said that he just found himself a new girlfriend and he liked her a lot, so he recently got engaged. As if a stranger, such as me, could give a hoot about this blowhard or his girlfriend.

"She's very hot, and she's completely dependent upon me," he said. "She's also about the smartest woman I have ever met." To pretend I was even the slightest bit interested, I hesitantly asked him what she did for a living.

"She's a stripper," he replied. OK, I know what you are thinking. Maybe you've heard this conversation framed as a joke. I told him that I was married and had a wife at home in Salt Lake City.

"Oh yeah, what does she do for a living?" he asked.

"My wife is an elementary school teacher," I replied.

He immediately cut me off and fired back in a disdainful tone, "Well, she couldn't be very smart. Teachers are about the dumbest women out there."

Fuck him. I took great offense to his comment. Who the hell was he to tell me my wife, who sacrificed so much of her time educating children, was stupid when he's acting like a loudmouthed ass, engaged to a stripper he met just a month before? My wife is stupid? She most certainly was not; she held two college degrees. I had about enough of this idiot and was beyond annoyed. My hands started to shake in anger. I should have decked him without thinking, but I exercised restraint to avoid jail time. Typically, I have a short fuse, fight or flight. It shocked me that I didn't put him on the ground but the time was late and it was time to head back to the hotel, which was costing me by the hour. I guzzled my Coke, said goodbye to Sarah and rolled SeaBos out the gate from the Firehouse Bar. I was halfway across North America and I was on an incredible high. I headed down through lonely streets at nearly traffic speed, with bike lights flashing. *Any drunk driver should see me on the street,* I thought.

It felt strange not to have the panniers on the bike and I was cruising faster than usual. I sped into the hotel lobby, took the elevator up to the room, laid down, and enjoyed my second-night stay in a hotel. I was tired but I had trouble falling to sleep in a bed. I kept looking over at SeaBos, leaning against the wall.

"My God, what an incredible country you have carried me through, SeaBos!" I said happily to my bike. "Sleep well!"

It was a great day and I put in 98 well-earned miles. In my mind, I envisioned my ride through Nebraska, a beautiful landscape of endless fields and pivots, Sand Hills dunes and cows, ponded pockets of water with reflections bluer than the most transparent azure sky. Nebraska is neither West nor Midwest; it is a high plain geographic grassland all of its own. Populated two-to-the-mile by hard-working

131

honest-to-God beautiful people in a place which many in the country woefully dismiss as "flyover country." You unbelievers keep flying over; I pedaled every mile of it and I call it "bike-over country." I slept with a smile, but only for four hours. I loved Nebraska.

The Bell House

The Eponymous Cycle Path

CHAPTER 7 – IOWA

August 13th - Sioux City, Iowa to Denison, Iowa

After not nearly enough rest, I sat up in bed, wishing for a couple more hours of sleep. But I was eager to explore Iowa so I went downstairs to a hot breakfast of eggs, bacon, cereal, and coffee. I filled my stomach to the limit. I had learned to eat in stages to glean the most calories, like topping off a gas tank before a big trip. With each day, my body felt more like a machine than a human. I packed up my stuff, reattached the panniers, and headed out. Too bad in a way; such a comfortable room and only four hours of quality sleep.

I pedaled the Highway 20 business route out of town through neighborhoods with tall hemp plants growing in nearly every front yard. After running out of back roads, I joined Route 20 in a state of shock and disbelief. There was no breakdown lane here at all, not even two inches of buffer. Maybe some rumble bar but that was it. I remembered Dave Lindsay's advice back in Cody, *"Iowa has no breakdown lanes."* He wasn't kidding.

I panicked. I was unprepared and beside myself in a cold sweat. *Could I even continue across Iowa at this point?* Not since South Dakota did I ever seriously doubt my abilities to navigate the U.S., but now I was faced with new challenges. A completely new level of difficulty had me stymied. I went into a convenience store on the corner and questioned the clerk about the absence of the breakdown lane, where she confirmed my worst fear. There was nowhere to ride a bike on the road. What now?

Highway 20 was a two-lane divided highway with heavy traffic and legions of roaring semi-trucks. I stopped at a road construction site and talked to the crew about any ideas where I could ride. They recommended I follow Route 20 east to Moville and then go south and pick up Route 141 east because it was less busy. I followed their lead but it was a scary ride to Moville; the deadliest part of the entire journey so far. I turned off Route 20 and eventually hooked up on Moville Blacktop Road, heading south with great relief. The road had no breakdown lane and was hilly with some steep grades, but far less traffic. After about 10 miles, I passed through a town appropriately named Climbing Hill. No doubt in my mind where the town name originated—I climbed 600 feet over just a handful of hills. I previously thought that Iowa was flat, but my legs felt otherwise.

Relentless Iowa Hills

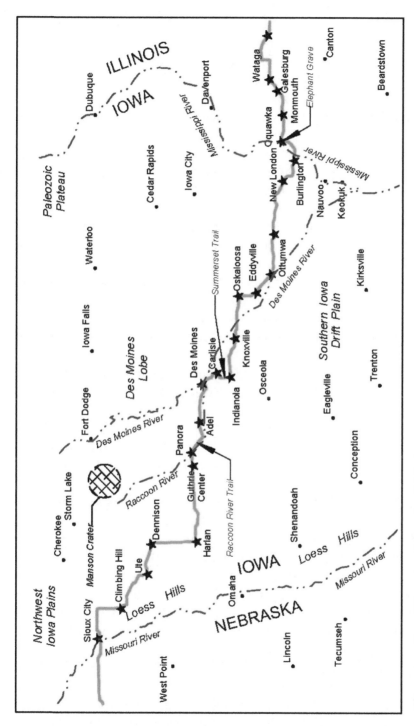

Figure 6 - Sioux City to Wataga

This terrain was nothing like Nebraska; most of the side roads off the main route were gravel and unrideable. Four new challenges presented themselves: poor road conditions (no riding lane), ridiculously high humidity, many steep hill grades exceeding eight percent, and a pungent, unpleasant odor emanating from everywhere. The route eventually met up with Route 141 in the Loess[i] Hills. These hills are formed of enormously thick (up to 200 feet) deposits of brown silt laid down by wind after the glaciers' retreat. The Loess Hills stretch for about 200 miles to the south of Sioux City and form the Missouri River Basin floodplain's edge.

Corn stretched on for miles before me, as did the endless crops of soy. Iowa is the biggest corn-producing state in the U.S. corn belt, grown on over 13 million acres. There was a persistent stench from the corn, which I didn't smell in Nebraska. To me, it stunk a lot like human waste, and indeed, I think it was, based on a confirmation from at least one local. I pedaled into Smithland, climbing steep hills at about four to five miles per hour, and then descending at 35 miles per hour.

I certainly didn't expect it but Iowa was the biggest challenge yet. The road became a roller coaster ride of endless hills. Doubts brewed, circled, roiled in my mind. Bouts of panic ensued as I grunted up hills and around blind corners on Route 141, sans breakdown lane. What a difference one day can make; 24 hours earlier I felt fearless for riding halfway across the country. Nebraska was too easy and I got soft.

Keep your mind on the road, stupid. One earbud in, one out, I cranked across narrow bridges with passing transport trucks. Everybody was driving way too fast as I followed Route 141 to Mapleton. In April 2011, a swarm of EF-3 tornados wiped out 60 percent of the town, fortunately with no lives lost. I continued straight south on Route 141 to a big easterly bend at Ute. I stopped before the town for a selfie picture in front of the town sign, made in large concrete letters welcoming me to "U T E." I burst into laughter as nothing here was even remotely similar to Utah. I read that they named the town after the Ute Indians, a branch of the Shoshone Tribe.

As I rolled into a gas station in Charter Oak for supplies, I met up with a group of young kids on bikes. The boys were genuinely cute and curious about my bike and gear. Another one of their friends, possibly a 10-year-old, pulled up to the gas pump on a four-wheeler.

"He just rode here from the *State of Seattle!*" they told their friend.

They were very intrigued with my bike, in particular why the tires were so thin. I told them that it was a touring bike, and the skinny tires allowed me to ride at higher speeds. I took a selfie with the kids, bid them farewell, and rolled out of Charter Oak towards Denison. It was cool to have a temporary fan club in town.

The Charter Oak Gang

Denison felt different from much of the rest of the country I passed through. Mainly, it smelled bad thanks to the fertilizer plant nearby. On a positive note, Donna Reed, the Hollywood actress, was from Denison. I adored her as a kid as she was my first TV boyhood crush. I stopped for ice water and a Subway sandwich and asked a woman at the next table about local places to camp, but she said there was not much camping in the area. I'd have to search for a renegade place.

Reenergized after loading up the Camelbak with ice and inhaling my foot-long tuna sandwich, it was time to get out of Denison and away from the pervasive, overwhelming smell of fertilizer. Maybe that was the reason the corn was over 10 feet tall here. I headed back to the highway and south out of town, climbing on Route 51. Well beyond spent, I searched desperately for a place to crash. I rode into a wide area of hardwoods and spied a coarsely graveled road up a hill into the woods. The woods were exceedingly dense, literally impenetrable. I pushed the bike up and found the only flat spot I could as darkness fell quickly. I called my mom, and then my friend Charlie back in Salt Lake City. It was good to hear his voice; he was quite upbeat and full of encouragement.

It was exceedingly hot and sweaty inside the tent so I cracked the fly, noticing faint flashes of light all about. I unzipped the fly, and to my surprise, a myriad of fireflies drifted lightly in the windless woods like my own collection of stars. As I wrote in the journal late into the night, a few trucks drove by the tent slowly but didn't stop. Investigating the drifting nomad? I turned out the light and heard unfamiliar noises from the woods that gave me the chills. I did not recognize any of the sounds. I've camped in many different environments around the country, from the White Mountains to the Cascades to the southwest desert canyons. By comparison, this hardwood forest environment resembled nothing that I had ever experienced. Creepy.

August 14th - Denison, Iowa to Panora, Iowa

I was up at 5:15—another sopping wet, humid morning with dew dripping off the fly onto my forehead. I said a few extra prayers for safety before hitting the road. Each morning I started the day with two prayers before riding. First, I would recite the Lord's Prayer that my Dad taught me, followed by an adlib road safety prayer, followed by crossing my chest. I am not even Catholic but what the hell, it couldn't hurt. I thought I'd cover all the bases. I wanted to pack up quickly and get out before the neighbors were off to work. Apparently, I had been discovered by a few of them in the night. Below me, through the jungle of trees, I could hear the rush of fast-moving trucks and cars. I did not want to get back on that road and I hated Iowa at this point. I was scared, and my advice to bikers is to avoid riding this section of Iowa alone.

I started at a fast downhill clip but my right shoe smacked something behind me in the panniers. I looked back and realized that a water bottle was protruding through a large hole in the fabric. I pulled over quickly to make repairs in a farmer's driveway just as he was leaving and waving from his beat-up Ford truck. I have no mad sewing skills and the panniers looked like Frankenstein's forehead with all of the ugly, coarse stitching. Not pretty, but it worked. Good advice from Griffin back at the bike shop in Salt Lake. Bring a sewing kit. I didn't know why at first, but now I was glad I followed his advice.

This stretch of Iowa was hard riding for the grades alone, notwithstanding the absence of a riding lane, blind-corners, and a repetitive and endless wave of hills. South of Defiance, I picked up Old County Road 59. At some point on Route 59, I noted a crop duster working the cornfields on both sides of the road, systematically flying at high speed over the road from east to west. The plane would climb, go into a stall on each turn, then shift his position and return, dropping his load of chemicals just feet above the fields. I was cranking on a heady downhill pace of about 25 miles an hour. I didn't want to be anywhere near the plane, so I decided to accelerate to avoid contact with the aircraft's pesticide drop. The pilot must have seen me on the road and adjusted his course because immediately to my left, the plane stalled, turned, and I sensed intent on a strafing run. I approached 40 miles per hour on a steep downhill and within seconds of his turn, the plane bore down on me in a steep dive. Locked and loaded. Sure that the aircraft would hit me, I dropped to the handlebars, laying flat on the bike. Just like the near-miss semi-truck incident in Montana, time slowed down just enough for me to take in every frightening detail. In a surreal cartoonish way, the crop duster looked like the giant whirling blade of a food blender headed for a collision with my head. The aircraft passed so closely over me that the bike shuddered and wobbled from the turbulence. I momentarily struggled for control. The wings, propeller, and landing gear missed me by mere feet. It was utterly frightening and exhilarating. What an ass.

I picked up Route 44 in Harlan and turned east on a highway dubbed the "Western Skies Scenic Byway." Same as before, the route was one hill after another, with some approaching 10 percent grade on 50-to 175-foot climbs. Up and down repetitiveness of hill after hill after hill on an unnerving highway. I wasn't enjoying myself. There was a small breakdown lane in places but it was 18 inches wide and all rumble bar from the stripe to the edge of the pavement. It was completely dangerous, exposed, lunatic fringe crazy biking, ridiculous risk-taking at its finest. I thought that I must be nuts for doing this. I would never have considered this kind of riding before the trip.

In Hamlin I stopped in at Darrell's Place, a local café with exceedingly good food. This place was fabulous and so were the people. I drank two pitchers of ice water to wash down a giant bacon cheeseburger with sweet potato fries and a root beer float. I felt somewhat dazed after the ice cream but oh, so satisfied. With such a full belly, I concentrated on moving slowly to keep it all down. It wouldn't do to regurgitate lunch all over SeaBos.

After lunch, I slowly wandered out of the heavenly air-conditioned restaurant into oppressive heat and humidity, blinded by the intensity of the sun. Still, somehow I mustered the strength to pedal east on Route 44 for 21 miles to Guthrie Center, and then continued east for about seven miles to Panora. In Panora, I turned off Route 44 and intersected with the Raccoon River Trail by a food drive-in. I had no prior knowledge of this trail and was overjoyed to get off the road. There was a small permit traveling fee of $2, so I unloaded all my change, possibly $6 in pennies, nickels, and dimes, just to lose the weight. I sealed a pound of coins in the envelope and dropped it in the fee safe, hearing the coins all fall out on their way down.

The Raccoon River Trail

The Raccoon River Valley Trail is paved and constructed on an old railroad grade right-of-way built in the 1870s to carry rail traffic between Des Moines and the Great Lakes. This trail is a real gem, wandering through farming countryside and a range of landscapes from suburban neighborhoods to heavily wooded stretches shading the path, past prairie, and small communities. I can't say enough about how wonderful this break from road riding was after so many deadly road choices since Sioux City. Finally, there was something to like about riding in Iowa. A text came in from home:

"Where are you, and how are you?"

"Hot and sweaty and headed for Des Moines. Thank God I

finally found a bike trail!"

The Raccoon River is the western tributary to the Des Moines River, which I had been following since Panora. The river has three branches, with the longest nearly 200 miles in length. Large floods in 1993 wreaked havoc, flooding the Raccoon River and shutting off Des Moines' water supply. About six miles down the Raccoon River Trail I found a great campsite in a wild marijuana stand by a field of fly-covered cows. I was exhausted; Iowa had kicked my ass for the day.

That night I called my buddy "TBone" from inside the tent and told him that I was on an adventure far from home. He said he was worried about me and after several minutes of good-natured harassment, I realized he thought I was riding across the country on a motorcycle.

"Tbone, I'm on a bicycle," I said.

As crickets chirped, there was dead silence on the phone for about five seconds, and then Tbone broke into hysterical laughter. He said he was anxious about my safety and frame of mind and should be back home taking care of business. He had his point, but I knew it was too late for that kind of advice. Things were rough at home before I left. I tried to explain these things to him, but he wouldn't have it. I felt that no one could understand me at this point as my perception of reality was genuinely evolving.

As ground fog approached the fields, the sun grew into an ever-larger scarlet candy red sphere seeking the horizon. I sipped a 20-ounce Budweiser, downed a mini bottle of tequila, and relaxed as the sun went about its business.

So much for no alcohol consumption on this trip. Another text from home:

"Where are the keys to the gun safe?" she asked.

"It's locked away in a secret place."

"Is it in the house? I need to get into it...Hello?? Why are you stopping me from getting into the gun safe? Just let me know where the key is!"

"Sorry, I can't do that," I uttered aloud. Now I was genuinely concerned about her frame of mind. There was no sense in thinking about home now. A phone call could be very unpleasant at this point.

The heavy red sky could no longer hold up the sun as it slid into heatwaves behind the blank stares of nearby fly-covered cows, while mist and fog crept ever closer towards the tent. There would be a heavy dew tonight. I was so tired of Iowa; I just wanted to leave and never come back. "*Iowa, let me go, goddammit!!*" I put in 89 well-earned miles for the day and pondered my new challenges at home as I drifted off to sleep.

August 15th - Panora, Iowa to Indianola, Iowa

At 5:15 a.m., I was eager to go. Barely light. Feet still completely numb. Everything around me was soaked from the heaviest dew I had ever experienced. I sat up and snatched my can of coffee, always placed within an easy reach just outside the tent, and waited for that morning's caffeine buzz to kick in. Unzipping the fly, I arose to the world in a thick patch of six-foot marijuana bushes in early flowering. I still couldn't believe what I was seeing and rubbed the sleep from my eyes. Outside, I took care of business as usual. Suddenly, a horde of bikers blew by, yakking away, not seeing me or the tent.

On bikes! Wow, a pretty enthusiastic early morning crowd here. I packed up camp and headed down a most unique bike trail. This bike path is no Trail of the Coeur d'Alenes by any stretch but the pleasant, shady tree groves formed a natural tunnel over the trail and occasional views of endless farmlands could be seen beyond the canopy in either direction. How incredibly fortunate I was to have located this trail by complete serendipity amongst the ridiculous disjointed web of county back roads and unrideable Iowa state highways. I felt euphoric.

"Seattle to Boston!" I gleefully yelled to oncoming squadrons of bikers. I was feeling so good I stopped and called my mom to update her on my progress. "I'm more than halfway to Boston, Mom!" I rolled into Adel and stopped at a restaurant called Amber J's for a desperately-needed second cup of coffee. I was the only patron in the restaurant. Small signs about the cafe displayed verses of New Testament scripture. The restaurant's logo was an angel with large wings in the middle of the "Amber J's" name. The owners told me that their restaurant was new and had only been in business for two weeks. So far, they had few customers.

"You should promote your restaurant as a bike-friendly cafe. That might bring in more customers," I suggested while enjoying a much-appreciated cup of coffee. It was then that I learned they named the restaurant after the owner's daughter, Amber. Her father said, "One morning last winter, she woke up not feeling well, sick with a fever. Within five days, it became worse. She went into the hospital and died." His voice broke and he turned and walked away. Overcome with an unexpected surge of sadness, I put on my glasses to hide tears welling up in my eyes.

"It was Amber's dream for her dad to open a coffee shop so he quit his job and started this place to honor Amber," said Grandma, as she refilled my coffee. I immediately thought about my own daughter.

"Keep it together," I thought as I fought back the tears. The bike ride's stresses seemed to amplify my emotional responses to everything and sadness seemed more resonant and profound than usual. I bought another coffee and took some selfies with the proprietors. As I was about to leave, Grandma handed me what later proved to be the best blueberry muffin I'd ever tasted. I wondered whether meeting them and hearing their story held a deeper meaning or if it was a solely random chance at that moment in my life. Or if it meant anything at all. Was I supposed to learn something? My mind worked overtime as I delved deeper into alternative explanations to daily life.

I pedaled back on the trail, crossed a bike bridge over the Middle Fork of the Raccoon River, and headed towards Waukee and Clive, again pedaling into the countryside and farmlands. In Waukee, I turned onto the Clive Greenbelt Trail System that followed the river to Clive. In Clive, I cycled past industrial complexes, businesses, brickyards, and residential neighborhoods on a beautiful cycle path adjacent to a four-lane highway. The trees approaching Des Moines are large, stately oaks dividing grassy parks and meadows and this section of trail was by far the most lovely place I'd pedaled in Iowa. I crossed more bridges and then rode through even more extensive groves of outstandingly stunning oaks and elm and locust trees crowding a muddy-banked, meandering river.

In West Des Moines, the trail was posted with a "closed" sign. I felt trapped and had no idea where I was or which way to go at that point. I needed a map of the state and an idea of where I was going next. I went back to a park where I found a hose bib around a squared-off gravel drain and stripped naked. It was scorching and humid and I didn't care if anyone looked at the white parts of my body. I could see and feel my body starting to change size and shape to a leaner, wirier figure. I washed up as much as I could without being obscene.

I donned clean clothes just as a guy on a bike named Steve showed up out of nowhere."Steve, are there any bike shops nearby? I need a map of bike-friendly roads in Iowa heading east."

"Follow me, buddy!" he said. Steve escorted me at high speed across West Des Moines to a store called Bike World. When we arrived, he introduced me to the owners. I picked up extra tubes and some maps detailing the safest bike routes, and filled the water bottles and CamelBak from their fountain. The staff were incredibly supportive, showing which roads were the best to ride, both out of Des Moines and across Iowa. I also learned about Iowa's big RAGBRAI ride, which takes place every year. RAGBRAI stands for the Register's Annual Great Bike Ride Across Iowa.

OK, now I get it. That's what Sarah was talking about back at the bar in Sioux City. The ride takes about seven days, ending on the last Saturday of July each year. The Des Moines Register Newspaper first conceived the RAGBRAI ride in 1973 and they tout this non-competitive ride as the most extensive in the world. Riders begin on Iowa's western border (this location changes year by year) and ride to the eastern border, stopping in towns across the state to socialize and camp or stay with host families. Riders dip their back tires in the Missouri River and then the front tire gets wet in the Mississippi River. I headed back to the trail and worked my way in and out of Des Moines on the River Trail.

The Des Moines River is a western tributary river to the Mississippi. It is over 500 miles in length and flows from southern Minnesota southeasterly to its confluence with the Raccoon River in Des Moines. The Des Moines River flooded Des Moines in 1993, requiring residents to evacuate much of the town. The river today appeared extraordinarily muddy and I had to wonder if this overbank mud was a leftover from those floods. Several bridges on the river still had monstrous heaps of driftwood jammed up against the abutments.

Some sections of the trail meandered through deep woods, while other parts followed a most beautiful greenway ride along the river. At one point I passed the mother of all marijuana plants in the woods. The plant was 10 to 12 feet tall, with a three-inch diameter stalk. I stopped and leaned my heavy bike up against the plant to get a selfie with SeaBos. A young couple on bikes stopped to ask me what I was doing. I told them that this was the largest pot plant I had ever seen. They seemed to be as shocked by this plant as I was and started photographing me, the plant, and the bike parked against it, unaware that it was hemp.

"Better cut some and take it with you," said the man.

"No, I'm not doing that," I replied. "No sense getting in trouble for carrying ditch weed. If that's what it really is." From here, the trail was incredibly delightful and led me past the remarkable gold-domed capitol building near the Raccoon and Des Moines Rivers' confluence. The capitol building has a European-style design, far different from a typical single-domed building. It took 15 years to build and has an exterior cut from Pleistocene glacial erratic boulders found in Iowa. It is the only capitol building in the country with five separated domes, with the center dome constructed of brilliant gold. I stopped for pictures along the trail by the river.

And then, the trail just ended. What the hell? I was forced back onto the city streets into heavy traffic. The Iowa Fair was in full swing, and Hillary Clinton was in town. People I met along the way encouraged me to go, but a political show wasn't on the agenda. I was headed as quickly as possible out of Iowa; I was not there to slap bugs and look at fly-covered cows. By the time I rode into East Des Moines, I was beyond thirsty and ready to get supplies for the evening, so I stopped at a convenience store.

"What's up, brother man?" I enquired to the clerk as I threw the unhealthy booty of junk food onto the counter. He looked at me in disbelief, cocked his head, obviously guessing from my clothing that I was not a local. "Are you shitting me? You are in East Des Moines, Iowa, my friend. Not one fucking thing goes on around here. Not a fucking thing," he said routinely, looking down with a dejected expression as he rang me up. "How soon till I can move here?" I chuckled to the clerk. "I'll take two mini bottles of tequila, please."

The East Des Moines route ended on a dirt county road that I followed to the southeast side of town. The hordes of bugs were incredibly thick and when I stopped to change my shorts, I was instantly attacked by hundreds of mosquitoes on my butt. I needed to look at the map and see where I was going, but there were so many mosquitoes that I couldn't stop. This continuous swarm was the worst mosquitos I'd encountered in years. We don't have much in the way of bugs in Utah and I felt like I was being sucked dry. Little did I know that it would get worse.

A man walking his dog told me to take the Summerset Trail to

Indianola and I found the trail in Carlisle and headed south. The trail is an abandoned railroad line between Carlisle and Indianola alongside wetlands and the Middle River. The sun neared the horizon and I gazed at a great sunset view reflecting over rippled water turning gold through a cloud-filtered sky. Next to the trail was an elevated wooden observation platform above the marsh. I climbed to the top and snapped pictures of the sunset above idyllic wetlands and lakes. The air looked as if it was thick with smoke, somewhat like the western skies during the fire season. The sun was setting and I still had ten miles of Summerset Trail left to ride.

I rolled into Indianola in the dark, looking for a hotel. It was unsafe to ride with heavy traffic in the street so I had to hang on uneven and broken sidewalks. After stopping at a few hotels, I found out that everything in town was booked months in advance due to the state fair. I rode to the Indianola fairgrounds because one of the hotel clerks said there was camping available but I arrived to find a stock car race in full swing. The air reverberated with a deafening thunder of un-muffled horsepower and the fairgrounds was an absolute zoo of spectators and vendors. I turned around in complete frustration and headed back into town and then east towards Knoxville in total darkness. I figured I would ride until I could find a place to slip into the shadows at any point on the roadside and lie down. It was late, and I was dog-tired. Even a ditch would do for the night.

About 1.5 miles east out of town, I found a turnoff to a large baseball field complex. I rode into the parking lot and found a lighted men's restroom, which was open, warm, and clean. I washed up in the sink and wrote in my journal. I rolled SeaBos over to the southeast corner of the field in the darkness up against a transformer box where I wouldn't be seen and far from the lights. I knew that I would have to be increasingly prudent about camping as I progressed eastward. The new plan was that of disappearing quickly after dark on the outskirts of towns.

I set up the tent and settled in for the night. The grass was already wet from dew so I knew it would be another very soggy night. I put in 81 miles for the day, and I was too tired to do much else. My air mattress deflated slowly as I drifted off, but I was too tired to do anything about it.

August 16th - Indianola, Iowa to Ottumwa, Iowa

I roused at 5:15 a.m. The soggy air hung wet and heavy, cloaking every surface. I was soaking wet and barely able to endure the smell of my clothes. I packed up all my stuff, soaking wet and twice as heavy as the night before. The hose bib outside the men's room allowed me a 6 a.m. cold bath. I threw away all of my underwear and excess dirty clothing in the trash, including shirts and extra socks. It was time to lighten the load.

I rode out of the baseball complex and took a right, riding State Route 92 past Ackworth, Sandyville, Pleasantville, and Marion. I rode 25 miles of smooth hills before arriving in Knoxville and stopped in for breakfast at Manny's Restaurant. The place was packed and the waitresses asked me if I attended the auto race held the night before at the Knoxville Raceway. After breakfast, I headed north for a few blocks to the track to check it out. This dirt oval race track opened in 1954 with stock cars. Eventually, the arena graduated to sprint cars, now dubbed The Sprint Car Capital of the World. Sprint cars weigh 1,500 pounds and put out 900 horsepower. With wings for downforce and steering, these cars bump around the track at ridiculously high speeds. I talked to a guard at the raceway's closed front gate and told him about my bike tour across America. Even though the sign in front of me read No Bikes Inside, the guard opened the gate for me. Some drivers were still packing up their gear and pushing their cars into trailers for the next race.

Rolling into the fairgrounds towards the stadium, I met a race car driver named Brian Brown. He was accompanied by his Barbie doll wife, lap dog, and kids packing suitcases into a truck. I stopped to do a selfie in front of them. She did not look pleased. As I approached the track gate entrance, another worker allowed me to ride SeaBos onto the track. The bleachers were empty. The silt track was peeling off in glossy, thin layers. I envisioned the thundering, testosterone-driven machines trying to outrun each other at bursts of 160 mph, plastering mud against the guard rails. I stopped to snap some pictures of SeaBos on the track.

I blew out of Knoxville on Old Highway 92 and rode about 27 miles to Oskaloosa, passing mile after mile of silos and cornfields and crossing the Des Moines River once more before the town. Oskaloosa was home to Daniel Boone's son, named after a Seminole Indian princess, and the center of coal mining in Iowa. It seemed that many of the cities that I visited had strikingly similar town squares. Oskaloosa blended in with the rest.

I turned south on Route 63, pedaling for what seemed like endless hills in high heat and humidity. I passed Eddyville and then pedaled another six miles south of town by Chillicothe near the Des Moines River. A sign on the right side of the road marked the burial place of Curtis King, the oldest man to serve in the Civil War. I stopped to rest and investigate his overgrown gravesite. Mr. King was inducted into the Union Army at age 80, served one year, then retired and died three months later. The site was a sanctuary, secreted away from the road by sumac foliage and pine trees and enveloped by a dense overgrowth of vines and weeds. I noted an apparent lack of visitors and wondered if anyone would stop here in a car. I rested the bike against a stone bench outside an iron-fenced enclosure amongst thick, uncut grass. I walked around to get a better look at the headstone, decorated with two American flags. I never intended the ride to provide history lessons but it is hard not to notice the past, either geology or history, on the ground at the speed of a bike. This experience can't be the same on anything but the bike. I had ridden past the site of the massacred Thomas Party in Montana, along the paths of Lewis and Clark, past by the battlefields of Indian/Calvalry wars in Wyoming, South Dakota, and past early settlements of Nebraska pioneers. I had now arrived in Iowa at the interred site of a remarkable man who fought in the Civil War. I wolfed down a Pop-Tart, Triscuits, and squeeze cheese with Gatorade to celebrate my reintroduction to the tribulations of war and Westward Expansion.

From Chillicothe, I turned off Route 63 onto Eddyville Road and headed southeast for about eight miles fighting a headwind to Ottumwa. Ottumwa is split in half by the Des Moines River and several bridges connect the city. Ottumwa is the home of the real-life Korean War veteran portrayed by fictional Corporal Radar O'Reilly in M*A*S*H*. The town is also no stranger to aspiring politicians to the White House. I changed my clothes with tremendous energy and headed out into town up a steep hill to a Pizza Hut, where I ordered a pepperoni pizza. I then rode down to a nearby convenience store and picked up beer. It was time for a hotel, beer, more pizza, and a hot tub.

Oh, this is heaven! Beer and pizza! I giggled to myself. I cautiously rode down a steep hill holding a pizza box in one hand with a beer in the bag hanging off the handlebars, amusing the front desk clerk. I enjoyed a cold brew in the hotel room and wolfed down pizza, marveling at the view out of the window. I could see large radio towers up on a high hill to the east, covered with a wake of turkey vultures who had previously been circling overhead at great heights. After dinner, I went down to the hot tub, hoping that the water jets would help me regain some of the feeling in my feet. The hot tub was a luxury and an excellent opportunity to stretch out and massage my leg muscles. One of the employees came over to ask questions about my trip.

"Why are you doing this? How long will it take you? When will you finish?" he asked. These were all excellent questions. I paused to consider each one and tried to come up with some substantive or inspired answers. I knew it was my childhood dream but after 23 days of riding, it became so much more than the seeds of a long-ago ambition. So my answer to "why" I was doing this adventure was, "why not!"

August 17th - Ottumwa, Iowa to Gladstone, Illinois

I awoke at 6 a.m. in a bed so incredibly comfortable that I didn't want to get up. Refreshed and exuberant, I was excited by the notion that this would be the last day in Iowa. I brewed some terrible coffee but didn't care about the taste because it was hot. I went downstairs to a massive continental breakfast and ate some of everything. I loaded up on yogurt, milk, eggs, and raisin bran muffins. I rested for ten minutes and followed up with more cold cereal and four more cups of coffee. I was so full I could hardly move and I again had to ride slowly to keep it all down. This binge-eating in stages to top off the tank was new to me.

I had to climb out of the river valley, which was so steep I had to push the bike up the hill from the hotel. Then I struggled to get around road construction. "Oh, help me, Lord, to get out of this town and get me out of Iowa. Please, God, I've had a butt-load of Iowa," I prayed aloud. I wanted out of Iowa more than anything I had wished for on the ride. I stopped in a convenience store for supplies and encountered a cute redhead named Tiffany, who painted Ottumwa as a low-income housing welfare town. The store was crowded and I became sandwiched between a couple of guys in their 70's in coverall shorts with long gray beards, filthy dirty ball caps, and a horrible, fetid odor. I actually found people who smelled worse than me. Oddly amused, I held my breath while waiting in line.

Finally out of Ottumwa, I hooked up with Highway 34 and pedaled smoothly, blessed with a pleasant tailwind. The route still had no riding lane, or the strip had rumble bars regularly spaced in the concrete between the road's edge and the line. Sixty miles out of town, I reached New London and mailed my wife her birthday card with a large check. I headed south out of town on a narrow county road towards Danville, where a semi-truck brushed by so close that I could feel the turbulence off the side of his tie-down shackles. To my left were semi tires mere inches away from the handlebars.

"Crap, that's too close, moron!!" I yelled at the top of my voice as adrenaline juiced my body. He very slowly passed, then moved more to the left, showing me that he crowded me on purpose. Occasionally, the road had a slim shoulder but there was nothing to ride on most of the time as the miles ticked down to Burlington and the Mississippi River. Thunder clouds formed all around as I pedaled into Burlington. There was not a lot to say about my last day in Iowa, except there were few hills and I pulled everything in tenth gear or higher. In Burlington, a convenience store clerk told me that Illinois had many paved roads, including mostly paved back roads as well, far more than Iowa.

We shall see.

Road conditions degraded across Burlington, with big chunks of missing road surface. SeaBos rattled in the back end and I thought possibly the back wheel was coming out of true. Poor SeaBos had worked so hard to please me. Iowa riding tested my mettle as well, leaving me depleted, expended, and drained. I kept thinking about the seven-day RAGBRAI bicycle ride across Iowa. It sounded like fun but I hoped they followed better roads. I crossed the state in four challenging days just to get the hell out of the state. While I thoroughly enjoyed the Raccoon River Trail from Panora through Des Moines, I was not impressed with Iowa as a whole. And the smell of the fertilized corn was, at times, nauseating. Maybe RAGBRAI could change my mind.

On Route 34 through Burlington, the eastbound lane was profusely strewn with trash and construction waste but at last, a breakdown lane. I came around a corner under an overpass and the bridge across the Mississippi River came into view—the hydrologic line dividing West from East. I became super-emotional and excited at the same time. I was finally leaving Iowa. The bridge across the Mississippi was dangerous, covered with chunks of concrete and metal, trash and broken pallets of wood and wire, making it nearly impossible to ride a straight line. This was one of the messiest bridges that I had encountered since Seattle. I was quite high above the river in addition to the treacherous riding lane, looking down at a short guard rail. It seemed like a hundred feet to the water. A red railroad drawbridge drew my attention to a massive river panorama to the south. Minutes later, I was across the bridge and into Illinois.

I pedaled into Gulfport, Illinois and became lost in a town of abandoned strip clubs and boarded-up, dilapidated buildings. I stopped a Harley rider and asked him how to get out of Gulfport. "I have no idea, man. I've never been here before," he said.

I had to wonder what he and I were doing there in the first place. Every direction out of town brought nothing but dead-ends, so I rode back to Highway 34. The road shoulder was gone entirely, it was getting dark, and it was too dangerous for me to continue much farther. I turned off 34 onto 900 East and headed north towards Gladstone, Illinois. After crossing the tracks, the road paralleled a canal. At some point along the canal just before sunset, I saw two young, heavy-set men, up to their necks in water. They were noodling the canal bottom, feeling around under old logs and submerged junk in the mud trying to locate and snag catfish with their bare hands.

"Hey, any campsites around here?" They climbed up onto the bank to greet me. Both of them were covered with swarming mosquitoes in less than a minute, forming a literal fur coating of mosquitoes on their arms and backs. Unbelievable. I raced to put on bug spray and then offered it to them.

"No thanks, buddy, they're not that bad tonight."

Dumbfounded, these were the worst mosquito conditions I had ever seen. I asked about their fishing method and one of them showed me pictures of his 45-pound noodled catfish on his phone. "Over the years, I've noodled freshwater eels that were over three feet in length," he said. The other guy didn't talk at all but laughed at everything told by his buddy. Then he picked up a fishing net hidden behind a culvert that held a massive 25-pound catfish they caught earlier. I bid farewell to my mosquito-coated friends and rode through a maze of cornfields. Corn was everywhere, just like Iowa, except the countryside was completely flat. And the Illinois cornfields had a different look; the hemp and weeds growing at the edge of the cornfields in Iowa were replaced here by a strip of mowed grass, giving a tidy appearance.

Periodically, I noted a recess of mowed grass extending back into the cornfields. I found one of these cul de sac paths into a cornfield around a corner, well hidden from the road, pushed the bike off through the grass and found a secluded place to camp in the corn. Unfortunately, I didn't realize until later there were metal rods everywhere in the grass, including underneath the tent, which made more holes in the air mattress. I laid down for the night, completely exhausted and covered with mosquito bites, but 99 miles closer to Boston.

A text message arrived from my wife:

"Where are you?"

"I just crossed the Mississippi River. I'm in Illinois."

"Huge accomplishment."

Thank you, I'm happier already, out of Iowa, what a tough place to ride a bike."

[i] Loess - A homogenous, non-stratified unindurated deposit consisting predominantly of silt with lesser clay or fine sand, typically windblown.

CHAPTER 8 - THE FLATLANDS

August 18th - Gladstone, Illinois to Victoria, Illinois

I sat straight up in a sweaty sleeping bag around 5:10 a.m. It was beginning to get light and I was uncomfortable with the half-buried metal bars sticking into the tent bottom. It rained off and on during the night, just enough to irritate me while packing up a wet tent and tarp. The panniers were beyond disappointing; genuinely crappy quality and falling apart. Deplorably disposable in design and I now needed a new sewing kit because I was down to the last roll of thread. I packed up, pushed SeaBos out of the cornfield, and headed north to Oquawka for breakfast and supplies.

On the way, I stopped at a historic roadside stop called the Henderson County Covered Bridge Park. The plaque said that Jacob Allaman built the bridge in 1864. In 1982, floods washed his bridge away down the river. Someone salvaged, restored, and returned the bridge to its original location on a raised foundation. I leaned the bike up against the red bridge and sat down to eat tuna fish on Triscuit crackers. I choked on the dryness of the combination and spat out the contents. A few minutes later, a pickup pulled into the parking lot. In the back of the truck was a wire cage trap with a five-pound opossum. I had never seen one other than in pictures. It bared giant teeth, made a drooling hissing noise, and flicked its rat-like tail. Not a visually pleasant creature but it clarified the mystery of the flattened roadkill I'd observed for the past 30 miles. I initially thought they might be raccoons, but apparently, this was a critter I had not seen before. These strange animals are marsupials, akin to the class of mammals found in Australia. Momma carries little beans around in her pouch for 80 days to develop. They can also play dead for extended periods. The man said that he trapped a family of them under his barn. He didn't like killing them, so he captures and releases them back into the wild at the park by the bridge.

I rode into town and stopped in at the Oquawka grocery store, complete with a small restaurant inside. Sitting alone at a table, I overheard a group of farmers in the next booth dressed. They wore customary workday-worn clothing and swapped jokes, laughing and drinking late-morning coffee. I noticed a number of them were notably missing teeth. The breakfast was delicious, exactly what I needed to refuel my body—bacon, eggs, and pancakes with lots of butter and syrup. I interjected into their conversation and asked their advice for riding across Illinois.

"Where did you ride from?" asked one of the farmers.

"I left Seattle around July 24th," I replied.

They had many questions, but they kept referring to my motorcycle, probably because my bike helmet somewhat resembled a cop motorcycle helmet. When they connected that I was riding a bicycle, they looked perplexed and didn't even know how to respond. They looked at each other with dumbfounded expressions. Probably not many cyclists pass through this remote hamlet. As told by the farmers, the town's main claim to fame is the grave of an elephant killed by lightning in the 1970s. The elephant grave was at the Oquawka town green. After breakfast, one of the farmers guided me through Oquawka on his four-wheeler to show me the elephant grave. Sure enough, there it was, the tomb of Norma Jean Elephant, struck down in her prime in 1972 when the circus came to Oquawka. The crew set up the evening performance and chained Norma Jean to a tree in the town square. Without any prior storm warnings, a bolt of lightning hit the tree, killing Norma Jean instantly. A town backhoe operator dug a large hole next to the pachyderm's body and a dozen townsfolk pushed her remains into the excavation. As a result of her unfortunate demise, the event never returned. Her death was a $10,000 loss and they couldn't afford a replacement. Norma Jean was their big attraction, and the circus went bankrupt.

The day warmed up and it was time to shed clothes and pump

up the tires. I pushed as hard as I could on the pump handle with no movement. My frustration exploded as my brand new Lezyne pump was deadheaded and couldn't produce air. I took it apart and put it back together. No luck. What the hell? New equipment, hardly used, now complete garbage. In addition to the panniers coming undone at the seams, now no pump. I was rafting without a life jacket.

Sufficiently peeved, I headed east out of Oquawka on Route 164, climbing gradually out of the Mississippi Valley, riding through massive agricultural areas towards Monmouth, the birthplace of Wyatt Earp. When I finally got a signal, I called REI to talk about the pump problem. By the time I finished, a young strapping bearded man had emerged from a nearby house and asked me if I needed help. He introduced himself as Justin Allaman, the great-great-grandson of Jacob Allaman, the bridge's constructor back in Henderson. Justin was a youth director at a local church and doubted that there was a bike shop in Monmouth.

"I can give you a ride to Galesburg. Just put your bike in the back of my truck," he said.

"No thanks, Justin, I've been unsupported so far. If I have to walk, then I'll walk."

I blew past Monmouth and headed directly to Galesburg, the birth and burial place of Carl Sandburg, a three-time Pulitzer prize winner. I rode into town on busy Highway 34 with a wide shoulder. The road was in poor condition, and some of the bridges had holes through the pavement where I could see the traffic below. I stopped at a bike shop in Galesburg, bought a pump, and then stopped at a sewing shop. One of the women gave me a small sewing kit for free. I grabbed a quick sandwich from a sub shop and rolled back out of town.

A steady rain began falling, so I put on my red Gore-Tex coat then headed up Highway 153 toward Henderson, following Route 167 to Wataga. Active thunderstorm cells brewed to the south and soon dumped fat raindrops that bounced off the street in beads and the sky turned an unusual shade of light-green. That's never good. I stopped at the Wataga Bar for refuge and a soda, hoping to wait out the storm. It was an amiable crowd, engaging in friendly conversation, passing the bad weather with a cold beer. It could have been anywhere in America. The TV screen behind the bar and every cell phone lying face up had the National Weather Service radar GIF in motion. Cumulonimbus supercells surrounded Wataga. The Weather Service called a "tornado watch." It was late afternoon and there was no sense in continuing in terrible weather. I had never been around tornadoes before, so I decided the best course was to hang there for a couple of hours until the severe weather passed.

"Listening to these warnings is like crying wolf to us. No one believes it. Then the actual tornado shows up," said one of the guys at the bar next to me.

That wasn't too comforting. No one seemed to get too excited about it. I guess a lot of times, the National Weather Service will post warnings but the tornados never materialize. I hoped that would be the case this time.

After a couple of hours, the rain had let up. I donned my Gore-Tex coat, turned on the headlight, and headed out of town on dark roads, pedaling east on Route 167 to Victoria but it was too dark and too dangerous to ride any farther. I found a propane facility and rode around the back behind some semi-truck trailers in wet, dark, and incredibly windy conditions. The surrounding cornfields made creepy, surreal, strange noises, like something from a Stephen King movie. There was a signal now for the phone, so I pinpointed my location and quickly set up the tent in hard rain and buttoned everything down to brace for a night of bad weather. I put in 66 miles for the day, which wasn't great, but considering the weather holdups, what else could I do? On a bike, you are entirely at the mercy of the weather. In a car, you adjust the temperature and turn on the windshield wipers, maybe change a CD. I knew I could have made more miles if I wasn't scared to death of encountering a tornado on the bike.

I wrote in my journal and laid back as the howling wind pushed hard against the tent. While drifting off to sleep, the lightning and thunder alarmed me. This storm was getting too close; a flash, then a horrific cannon of thunder. I prayed there would be no tornadoes coming in the dark, one that might roll one of the semi-trailers on top of the tent.

Now, what was that calculation? Was it from the lightning flash, count the seconds to the thunder, divide by 5, then you have miles to the storm?

At first, the pause was 12 seconds, silence, then a gap of 6 seconds, then 3 seconds. I grabbed the iPhone and opened the calculator, and it was about 1/2 mile away. The corn began to shake, producing an ominous sound like none I had ever heard. I was on the wrong side of the semi-trailers.

August 19th - Victoria, Illinois to Dwight, Illinois

I couldn't sleep. In the wee hours of the morning of August 19th, my tiny FM radio issued a tornado watch in the area lasting until 10 p.m. It was a dreadfully threatening night, as two major storm cells rolled by my campsite, drenching me through the fly. The wind bursts were extreme at times, but my little MSA tent held strong.

"What time is it?" I thought. I looked at my phone, and it was 2:15 a.m.

I could only think about getting up and riding with the possibility of a tornado anywhere in the dark. Anxiety kept me awake. On the nakedness of a bike, you eye up the closest refuge, wherever it might be, and take cover. Storms moved so quickly in Illinois. There are no mountains or hills to slow down winds; just flat corn country. Although I remained energized for the ride, I was increasingly anxious about navigating and riding the Eastern States. All I could do was control the bike and my lane, stay vigilant, and everything else would be beyond my control. I wasn't getting sleep; I had too many concerns. When I rechecked the time, it was 4 a.m., and vehicles were already starting to show up at the site to work, sitting in their trucks with their diesel engines idling.

Really? Are you coming to work at an LPG facility at 4 a.m.? What is this? Turn off your noisy trucks. I've got to get out of here.

So much waiting, worrying, and checking the time repeatedly. It was 4:48 a.m., and I developed a surge of rising energy. I reached outside of the tent, grabbed Starbucks in a can, and then guzzled a leftover can of warm iced tea. I expeditiously packed wet gear in total darkness, my favorite activity. More cars arrived but they didn't pull around back and didn't see me. I had infections on several body locations from random cuts and scrapes, so I applied triple antibiotic ointment to my legs and rolled out of the propane yard in total darkness. It wasn't raining but the road seemed paved with puddles. My shoes filled with cold water, making funny suction noises as I pedaled, and I laughed aloud.

I ventured out on Highway 167 east, then onto the back roads. Something unusual developed in my riding condition after Iowa. Sure, I couldn't feel my feet at all but now, a new phenomenon impacted my hips and legs. When I got back to riding after a break, after about 20 seconds, my leg muscles decided to stop working involuntarily. My legs were sapped of all strength for five to ten seconds, as if they were going into paralysis. After 30 seconds, all was fine. Every time I rested or stopped riding for any reason, the same recurring experience alarmed me. Why weren't the legs doing what my brain commanded them to do? I had to consciously and even verbally command my legs to pedal.

"Crank that crank! Turn the wheels! Hit the road and get SeaBos moving," I yelled at my thighs out of concern.

I wondered if I was beginning to have a stroke or some mental breakdown. I pulled into Toulon and encountered a delightful and attractive millennial. She told me about the Rock Island Trail State Park Bike Trail from Toulon that headed east along Route 17. I rolled out of Toulon only to find the bike trail unpaved, with no surface gravel. The rainstorm from the previous day resulted in soft, muddy conditions, sinking my tires a couple of inches and coating everything in gooey mud, including the chain. I rode nearly a quarter of a mile and returned to Route 17 to Wyoming, Illinois. Like Iowa, this section of the road had no breakdown lane, but there was little traffic. In a town named Wyoming, I couldn't resist sending pictures and texts to spoof my kids about how I became lost and an incorrect GPS setting put me in a big circle back to the West.

I pedaled south of Wyoming towards Speer. On the corner of Routes 17 and 40 in Speer, I stopped at Tanner Orchard, a large produce market. The place looked interesting, so I parked the bike and investigated amongst the bustling crowd. Somehow I was singled out by the owner's daughter, who wanted to get pictures of SeaBos and me in front of their sign for their Facebook page. They gave me free coffee and donuts, and the owner's daughter even offered me a place to stay at her house. Too bad I didn't know this the night before.

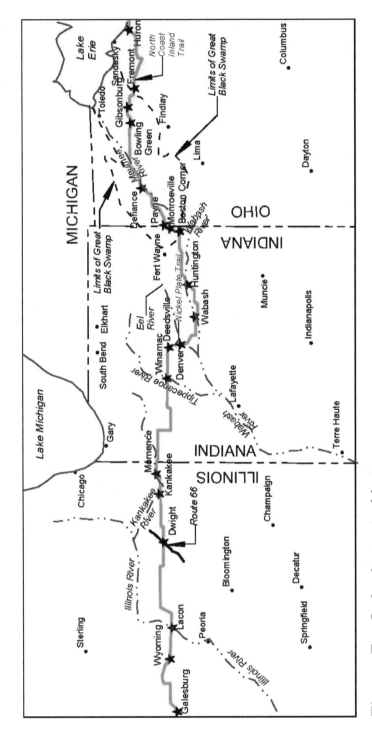

Figure 7 - Galesburg to Huron

I sprinted for about 11 miles from Tanners Orchard due east on Route 17 to Sparland, a small town along the Illinois River's west side. Around a big road bend, I spied the green truss bridge over the Illinois River to Lacon. Bridges are exciting but for me, simultaneously induce anxiety. Crossing the Illinois River to Lacon over a 1000-foot green truss bridge was the most dangerous bridge crossing yet on the entire tour. There was no lane to ride, and the top of the guard rail was about two feet above the road. This bridge was very narrow and tight for a single vehicle, never mind two and a bike.

Be bold and take the road lane across the bridge at 15 miles an hour, stay in the center of the lane, and the guy behind me can wait.

My nerves trembled but there were few cars when I got out onto the bridge and I hastily pedaled across into Lacon. I was wary of traffic on Route 17, so I dropped one mile south and found a pleasant alternative sub-parallel ride on County Road 6 North. I sped along through the corn at 16 miles per hour with a tailwind and minimal effort. Soon, I was cruising at 18 to 20 miles per hour on pavement as smooth as silk. Superior riding. For the first time in six days, I was thoroughly enjoying the bike experience again. The horrendous storm system that blew through Illinois the day before with tornado warnings slowed me considerably. But today, clearing winds from the west-southwest were my best friend.

I spent the afternoon touring delightful back roads, mesmerized by seemingly endless cornfields—what a joy to ride in Illinois. Every back road seemed like a bike trail, nicely paved, or had a well-compacted gravel surface. My goal was Kankakee, keeping south of Chicago traffic. Large, charming houses surrounded by large, graceful trees and perfectly manicured lawns dotted the landscape between alternating corn and soybean fields. Impeccably mowed grass alongside the cornfields added a neat touch. Old red barns appeared from time to time, amongst grain bins and grain elevators.

I rode towards Dwight because I needed a shower and dry out the wet gear. I stopped to look over an old jet airplane when I realized that my bike rack had broken in two places, which accounted for the noise I heard for hundreds of miles. I didn't have anything to repair the frame, so I stopped for supplies at a convenience store. I attached large paper clips to the broken bracket for rigidity and then wrapped metal tape around the clips, bike frame, and rack. It seemed sturdy but I still had many miles to pedal. At a Super 8 Motel, I showered and called my son Drew. As I talked to him, a guy down the hall complained loudly to the Super 8 front desk clerk that he didn't have any washcloths.

"How am I going to wash my butthole without a washcloth?" he repeatedly yelled in only a towel. I ducked out on foot to the Subway for dinner, and then returned to the room to write in my journal and clean my clothes in a washing machine for the first time, not in a river or with my feet in the shower. I laid out wet clothes and camping gear all about the room to dry. I rode 109 miles for the day and laid down my weary body.

August 20th - Dwight, Illinois to Wheatfield, Indiana

Around 6 a.m. I arose from a comfy bed after a great rest. I finished the laundry and took two showers just because I could. I had a marginal breakfast in the lobby and drank an entire pot of coffee, which seemed to have little to no caffeine. After breakfast, I had to reinforce the rack again with more duct tape and paper clips as it was still loose, and sewed up more tears in the panniers. Before heading out, I stopped by the post office to mail home more items acquired on the way.

I toured the side streets of Dwight before leaving town. Dwight is on Historic Route 66, a highway constructed in 1926 to connect Chicago to Southern California. The route, and its aura, was officially removed from the Federal Highway System in 1985, replaced by interstate highways. The Mother Road was well-traveled during the Dust Bowl days of the 1930s and inspired songs and a TV show that I vaguely remembered watching in my youth. I rode past a woman working by the street and stopped to chat. She offered me a brick from a pile stacked in her front yard, allegedly removed from the original Route 66. But really, a brick? I looked at the sewn-up panniers and thanked her. I pedaled down to the historic Texaco Station, a popular attraction on old Route 66. The Route 66 Texaco Station decor was more like a museum of early Americana memorabilia. I signed in the guest book and took pictures. It felt fun to goof around like a real tourist.

The storm brought cool, clear air for August and it felt like one of the first days of fall; warm sunshine with cool breezes that feel good on the skin. The 17 to 25 mile per hour gusts from the west pushed me along effortlessly up to almost 30 miles per hour.

Wow! I couldn't even imagine if I had to pedal into this wind. It's strong enough to blow over a bike. This kind of tailwind is every biker's dream; this never happens!

I pedaled east out of Dwight on Route 17 but the road was too narrow in the breakdown lane, so I dropped south onto the back roads through infinite cornfields. No matter where I looked, I saw beautiful homes surrounded by perfectly manicured grass. But the weirdest curiosity was that I never saw anyone mowing the lawns or margins of the fields.

When does all this lawn mowing get done? Who cuts all of these ginormous lawns and endless miles of grass strip along the cornfields?

I moved fast between cornrows, propelled by the strong wind at my back. It felt much like moving with the fluidity of a Class II river. Where the wind met a fixed resistance, such as dense stands of trees, near homes, or along cornfields, it would concentrate behind me and push me faster. To test the theory, I traveled on the left and then the right side of the road. When the wind forced me to move to the left side of the road, I would pick up about one and a half miles per hour without expending any additional pedaling energy. Some type of sail configuration would have been a real benefit. The roads were empty and it felt like I had entered the Twilight Zone.

Where did everybody go?

Most of the homes appeared unoccupied but well-kept. The vast emptiness and the unending flatness of the cornfields made for a pleasant and efficient ride. Roads were straight east-west, disappearing to the vanishing point in both directions, intersecting every mile with a north-south route also stretching to the horizons. The streets on a map look like a mega-chessboard and I was the rook. I stopped in the exact middle of an intersection and took pictures in all directions. Every way looked precisely the same, and there were no street signs for many miles. Suppose you got lost out here in bad weather without navigation. In that case, you might never know your exact location or which way to go because every route is identical. There was nobody out there; you could cruise in a vehicle at high speeds without fear of hitting anything but corn.

I couldn't believe the favorable tailwind combined with the smooth and easy biking terrain, flat as a pancake. Despite the monotony of the endless cornfields, I found the scenery to be beautiful and peaceful. At one point, I hopped off SeaBos to inspect the corn by pulling off an ear and shucking the husk. I was surprised at its horrendous condition. No one could eat this corn; it was way over-ripened. This type of corn is called "field corn," not the corn I was hoping for. How naive I was to think they grew this corn for human consumption on a cob. Here I was, out in the middle of the US corn belt, and suddenly realizing how little I knew about corn. Only one percent of corn produced each year is sweet corn, the kind we like to eat.

The ride should have been about 30 miles from Dwight to Kankakee but I added another seven miles by taking extra one-mile detours to the south or north on the giant chessboard to stay riding on the pavement. Just to the west of Kankakee, I swung by a pig farm. I stopped in to observe the pigs in a very neatly kept pen.

About seven miles out of Momence, I crossed into Indiana without any notice or state line signage. Only a small, square Indiana highway marker sign alerted me. I turned around and went back to a sports bar with a classic, aging Budweiser sign above the entrance. I locked the bike and went inside to get a Mountain Dew on ice. Roz, the bartender, told me she was concerned about me riding Route 10 because there were many trucks and the lane is narrow. After three sodas, I thanked and bid Roz farewell, then dropped a few miles south of Route 10 and headed east into Indiana for about 15 miles.

I came across a thick oak forest with a concealed dirt road that led back into darkening trees. The campsite was somewhat obscure and I was unsure of my exact location. For some reason, a random wooden ladder leaned against a large oak tree. I checked navigation and determined that I was about five miles southeast of Wheatfield. I was completely unfamiliar with the road coordinate system and my unfamiliarity posed an entirely new set of navigational challenges. It was a beautiful, warm, quiet night with a first-quarter moon peeking through drifting gray clouds framed by swaying oaks. Gone were the all-night sounds of traffic and railroads from the first half of the tour. I put in a casual 84 miles today, most of which was easy pedaling.

August 21st - Wheatfield, Illinois to Wabash, Indiana

I awoke early in the morning at 4:45, ready to roll, but laid in the bag, waiting for the slightest hint of light. The campsite in the woods was pleasing and quiet and I fell into the usual morning cold coffee routine, which did the trick. Caffeine was essential on the trip, along with nuts, squeeze-cheese in a can, Triscuits, a mix of granola, assorted M&Ms, and raisins. I sprayed the cheese on the Triscuits, then dipped it in the nut-granola-raisin-M&M mixture, and voila, a satisfying non-refrigerated snack with enough cholesterol, fat, pure sugar, and protein to jump-start a bonked zombie. Ten of these scrumptious gut bombs followed by four ounces of beef jerky, two liters of Gatorade, and topped off with Zip Fizz. Now that's a memory.

I packed up, checked the iPhone Google Maps App, picked a direction, and rolled out of the oaks onto Indiana Route 41. I took a right and headed south, then left to the east onto 900 North. Interestingly, I was now thinking differently; at this point, every day became a new miracle. I began to think of myself, my mind, my physical being, and the world of humanity differently as if they existed in another dimension from my reality. I knew I shared the same consciousness but I felt somehow unshackled and liberated in a way that lifted my spirit. Only by the grace of God had I made it to Indiana. For the entire ride, I had been navigating by Google Maps day to day, determining the azimuth, magnitude, and direction of my progress and plan a route for the next day. I had no plan except to be energized, vigilant, ride hard, and enjoy a new unique experience every day.

The maps I picked up at Adventure Cycling in Missoula would become useful today as I planned to connect with the Northern Tier Trail to the Buffalo, New York area. I was still a bit too far north, but I had successfully navigated a route from Seattle on my own by the seat of my pants. I had butterflies in my stomach. I headed east on County Road, which occasionally turned into gravel for stretches but was good riding for the most part. Sometimes I had to contend with thick, three-quarter-inch crushed limestone rock. I hadn't fallen for some time and felt confident at how well I could finally control the bike in those conditions compared with loose gravel back in Washington. I crossed the Tippecanoe River (Indian name for buffalo fish) and rode through the town of Winamac (Indian name for catfish.) The Tippecanoe River is over 180 miles long, flows southeast to the more massive Wabash River, and has the most considerable population of exotic and endangered fish. A fish advisory warned of the consumption of bottom fish impacted by PCB and mercury.

I pedaled hard from Winamac on Route 14 and worked my way east, then south on Route 17 to join up with the Northern Route near

Fletcher. Indiana was pretty but somewhat unremarkable to this point—the terrain showed slightly more relief than Illinois and the houses lacked the opulence of the homes back in that state's cornfields. The trees were mostly oak but the forests were changing with an increase in the frequency of pine trees.

After fighting a south wind, I arrived in Fletcher, a community with a small lake and a campground. I stopped at a soda machine, where the campground host said that many cross-country bicyclists pass through Fletcher and camp on the lake. It didn't look all that appealing, so I decided to keep riding. I pulled out the Northern Tier Bike Map and followed the directions to 1000 North to Deedsville. The route was a crappy, thick gravel road, which made me wonder why this was part of a bike trail. Ahead was a fast-approaching passenger car in the middle of the road, kicking up a dust cloud and accelerating straight at me. I made a quick, reactive move to the right and tried to move over quickly, and spun out sideways, hitting the gravel hard and instantly feeling a stinging pain in my hip. My legs were cut and bleeding.

Son of a bitch, what the hell was that guy thinking? I had the lights on, and I know he saw me. Hogging up the entire road, what a jackass.

I sat on the road, a little dazed, and then picked up the bike. The car's brake lights came on, he momentarily slowed, then kept going. Thanks, Northern Tier Map, for my first-mile inauguration. In Deedsville, I turned onto the Nickel Plate Trail. This fun paved trail led further south into Denver, Indiana, where I picked up Gatorade at a small store. Strangely, my bank card didn't work, so I went to the bottom of the pack for any spare change. I headed across the street and into the Denver Bar. The place was packed for dinner, and the bar was lively and thick with cigarette smoke. I sat at the bar, asked to have my water bottles filled, and told the bartender that I was riding to Boston. He filled up my bottles, gave me two free beers in cans, and then the owner came out and gave me $20. I refused, politely, but she wouldn't hear of it. I graciously accepted the cash, grabbed the beer and ice water, and pedaled out of town. I stopped to call my parents on the Eel River Bridge to let them know of my progress and that I was okay.

I passed the remnants of an old farm and ducked off the road into the deep grass and ingrown trees near the home foundation. It was a great spot, nestled between lilacs and thick vines growing to the top of a nearby windmill. This site must have been one of the original farms of the area, now fallen into ruin. As darkness set in, fireflies floated through the still air all about the campsite. I rode 96 miles for the day and scored the perfect camp spot in a beautiful secluded area. Sweet day.

August 22nd - Wabash, Indiana to Tappan, Ohio

Between 1 and 2 a.m., I heard bizarre, chilling, unexplainable noises in the distance. I wasn't quite sure what it was. At 6:15 a.m. I got up and I was startled by several giant hairy spiders hanging from the lilacs. I packed quickly, then savored my morning coffee. I stopped, paused, prayed for God's grace and safety on the road, and set out into a beautiful Indiana morning, pedaling on 200 North to Lagro. The strong headwind was a pain but the temperature was pleasant. I passed by Lagro, which I later regretted because I was running low on food and didn't stop for breakfast.

South of Lagro, I turned left into the Salamonie River State Forest. Salamonie is a translation of an Indian word meaning "*yellow paint*" for the dye extracted from the roots of the bloodroot plant, which grows abundantly along the river. This trail was a beautiful side trip into lush forests on nicely paved roads. I popped out of the woods and onto a large dam built by the CCC in the 1930s. The reservoir showed remnants of previous flooding that overfilled the lake, leaving a giant mud ring and killing off the trees all around the lake. I met two bike riders on the dam who told me that all three reservoirs in the area were utterly full two months earlier. The Army Corps of Engineers was nervous about potential dam failures from the 2015 runoff conditions.

Despite the map, I became utterly lost and ended up in Huntington, vice-president Dan Quayle's hometown. There I crossed the Wabash River's headwaters, one of the largest tributaries to the Ohio River. The Wabash is over 500 miles in length and drains almost all of Indiana, essentially flowing free to the Ohio River for over 400 miles below the Huntington dam. I pedaled along Riverside Road in Huntington, a delightful ride that ended up cutting off some miles. I headed up to Zanesville, picked up Gatorade, candy, and snacks, and discovered my bank card was no longer working. I was not sure why. The last time I saw a Wells Fargo bank was in South Dakota.

Fortunately, I had the $20 given to me from the Denver Bar owner. I left the store and pedaled east to Poe and Hoagland, grunting into a robust wind the entire way. I headed east on Hoagland Road, passing many farms with small ponds at each residence, pushing maybe eight miles an hour up to 14 or 15, depending upon the protection or the deflection from the wind hitting the trees.

The Flatlands, Indiana

At some point, I noted an unusual cemetery out in the middle of a soybean field. It was a family plot and the worn engraving dated back to the late 1800s. Each headstone leaned in a different direction, a metaphor in death as in life. About a dozen rocks were also equally spaced, probably indicating interred children. Each stone was meticulously edged and neatly surrounded by a freshly mowed lawn. Monroeville was my goal for the day, known as a crossroads for long-distance riders along the Northern Tier route, and I became genuinely stoked as I passed through Boston Corner. In two miles, I turned left and north up Route 101 with the wind now at my back, finally pushing me in the direction of Monroeville. I stopped to get pictures of SeaBos and me alongside a jet airplane on display outside of town at a park. I stopped at a gas station in Monroeville and the attendant told me to get information on camping at the local bar. I chugged a quart of Gatorade and headed to Toads Tavern, a local waterhole. They told me that I could meet someone with access to a shower and possibly get a place to crash for the night. I sat at the end of the bar and met a couple about my age named Ron and Patty. Each had several empty beer bottles and shot glasses in front of them. Ron was funny, talkative, and somewhat disconnected, but completely good-hearted. Patty was blonde, fit, energetic, with a rowdy personality.

They invited me to stay overnight at their house, which was about 13 miles away over the border in Payne, Ohio. I gladly accepted their offer because they seemed like a normal-enough couple. However, I noted how they bickered and snapped at each other, then immediately embraced warmly and kissed, which seemed odd. Patty and Ron decided it was time to go (after several pitchers of beer). I ran across the street to the liquor store to buy beer and tequila mini bottles to take to their home. I was supercharged after downing four Mountain Dews in the bar as I headed north out of Monroeville on Ohio Street, towards the Ohio border just 3.5 miles away.

Ron and Patty caught up to me on a Harley-Davidson Sportster and signaled me to pull over. We stopped at an enormous tree stump surrounded by an endless sea of corn. I sat on Ron's Harley, lay back on the motorcycle seat then turned around to see him rolling a large joint. Numerous cars passed by us and honked.

"Is that a smart thing to do out here on the open road?" I asked.

"Don't be so paranoid, man. There are no police on this last stretch before the border," he said as he fired it up.

But I was paranoid because this was completely illegal. He said no one cares. Breaking my own rules, I decided to chug a tequila mini even though it was still another eight miles to their house. The sun grew larger and blood-red in color as the day approached two fingers above the western horizon. The tequila shot hit me immediately as I gazed off to the west, knowing that I came from somewhere out there, now a seemingly unfathomable distance. Ron and Patty joined me in a toast with tequila shots. I was a little more than concerned about them on the motorcycle, especially after an extended stay at the bar. We hit the road, riding bar to bar, side by side, while I took a few selfies. They said that their friend had colon cancer, and Ron would deliver the remainder of his weed for his friend's nausea and pain. They roared off ahead and stopped at their friend's house about a half-mile from the Ohio state line. I passed by them, waved, and pedaled for Payne, Ohio.

When I got to the border, I rode along north-south Stateline Road with Ohio to the right and Indiana on the left. From behind, I heard the roar of an approaching Harley, and Ron and Patty pulled up to my left. Ron had a beer clutched in his hand. A few cars pulled around us and honked. The sun was down as I rolled into Payne and as I arrived in their driveway, a deluge ensued, seemingly out of nowhere. Made it just in time.

I smelled bad. I was filthy dirty from the gravel and dusty roads, and I hadn't had a shower in two states. Ron and Patty were welcoming, and I much appreciated their hospitality, but all I could think about was a shower. Ron said he was going out to buy more beer. I couldn't understand why we needed more beer. There were already plenty of beers in the refrigerator.

As soon as Ron went out the back door, Patty grabbed me by the hand and led me around the house for a tour, showing me every room. At that point, things became uncomfortable. In the bedroom, she removed my riding gloves. Then she met my eyes and took off my bandana, then little by little, she slowly started to unbutton my shirt. I became uncomfortably tense because this was not what I was expecting.

"Ron and I met way too soon after the death of my husband. I don't want to be serious with him anymore because we fight all the time. Every morning, we wake up in the recliners opposite of each other in the living room, and we are completely hungover," she said.

I was startled and reeled back. I realized Patty was hinting about romance.

"Hey, I'm flattered, but this isn't going to happen. I'm married."

I held up my left hand to show my gold ring. I took her hands off of my shoulders and gently put them down to her side. She gave me a funny look, then grinned. "I am going to make you a good home-cooked meal! You'll need it for your strength tomorrow!" she said.

That was an awkward moment, to be sure, and I raced to the shower, having just dodged a bullet. I thought maybe I shouldn't even be here. But the shower felt wonderful; hot and steamy. I washed my clothes with my feet and shampoo. About five minutes into the shower, I heard the creaking door open and slam shut as Ron came back to the house with beer. Then I heard them quarreling. Next, I heard Patty say something, followed by Ron yelling loudly.

"Why don't you just go screw him in the shower!" he screamed. *Now that, I heard. Damn. This is not good!* I went into survival mode, thinking of that Lynyrd Skynyrd song, *"Gimme Three Steps."* My mind raced. I'm a stranger on a bicycle, in an unfamiliar town, in a foreign state. It's dark and raining outside. How would I make a clean getaway without getting into a major confrontation? I finished my shower, dried off quickly, and then put on my riding clothes. It was time to go. I walked into the kitchen.

"Listen, I am going to leave, I shouldn't even be here, and I don't want to cause any trouble between you guys," I said. They jumped up quickly, waving their hands. "No, no, no, no, don't leave, we're just about to have dinner, so sit down and have a beer!" said Ron. I felt uncomfortable with the whole situation. Maybe it was only one of the two who wanted to have me stay over. Patty cooked fried chicken with home fried potatoes and peas. I wouldn't say I like canned peas, but for some reason, they tasted incredibly delicious. I quickly snarfed down everything on the plate, finishing the best home-cooked meal I'd had in a month. It was Ron's 58th birthday, and we opened more beers to celebrate. Ron left, came back into the room with two guitars, and we sat down and jammed for about an hour. I play lefty guitar, but I could still manage to remember some of the chords backward from my younger days when I just played righty guitars, up-side-down. For some reason, Ron couldn't stop talking. I wondered whether he was doing cocaine or some stimulant because neither of them ate dinner. It was quite strange. Ron, a trucker, kept talking about his fines and getting caught for being overloaded at the Point of Entry. After a while, his voice faded into Patty's story. Patty described her late husband, a decorated marine who served his mission in a dangerous Afghanistan region, which saw heavy fighting.

"About six years ago, my husband and I were at my parents' house, and my husband was pouring gasoline on a charcoal grill while smoking a cigarette. While he was pouring the fuel, the grill back-flashed to the fuel can. It exploded in his hand, setting him on fire, inflicting major burns over most of his body. He lay on the ground and told me he was going to die. I watched him suffer in the hospital over the next 48 hours," she said.

I was traumatized. Patty still grieved his death. She said she met Ron soon afterward, which would explain why she told me they got together too soon after her husband's death. The story affected me, much in the same way that Amber J's story affected me in Iowa. I fought back tears as she continued her story. Then Ron piped in again about his trucking problems and his overweight ticket story and cut off Patty. Ron was simply annoying at that point. I went upstairs to a kid's bedroom and crashed on a twin bed with Bart Simpson sheets. I put in 82 miles and I was dog tired. As I drifted off, I could hear them bickering downstairs. I didn't have any idea of what lay ahead in Ohio, but with the flatlands behind me, I contemplated the increase in towns and traffic meant that riding would become increasingly challenging. And I had to get out of this house.

SeaBos – Lake Erie and Cleveland, Ohio

CHAPTER 9 - THE DREADFUL and THE BEAUTIFUL MIDWEST

August 23rd - Payne, Ohio to Gibsonburg, Ohio

I woke up in a strange bed with a dry mouth and foggy head. It was one of those moments where you sit up in a peculiar place and look around and don't know where you are, then in a couple of seconds, it all regrettably comes back. Even the pictures on my phone were blurry. I got up and wobbled downstairs to the living room to find both Patty and Ron sleeping. They ended up in separate La-Z-Boy recliner chairs positioned diagonally across from each other. They were up squabbling late into the night, then passed out. I packed up rapidly and drank coffee in the kitchen as they slowly shuffled their way past me up the stairs, not acknowledging my ghostly presence.

I finished a Power Bar for breakfast, crept upstairs into their bedroom, jumped into bed between them and laughed to annoy them, as I promised the night before. Patty took off her silver necklace, placed it around my neck, and told me to wear it to Boston. It belonged to her deceased brother. Ron was asleep. We said our goodbyes and I was out of there. Note to self: No more mingling with couples in bars.

I rode around Payne first looking for food, then ended up circling the entire town back to where I started. I was a wee bit hungover and couldn't even navigate out of town. I rode Route 500 northeast to Paulding, following a creek on my right and pastures of horses and cows and farms on the left. All I could think about was food. About eight miles down the road, I took a right onto Highway 111, rolled for about seven miles to Junction, Ohio, and intersected the west bank of the Auglaize River. The scenery was delightful, and the river sported a particular shade of green I hadn't seen before.

For the last 30 miles or so, I pedaled through an area known as the Great Black Swamp, stretching from Fort Wayne, Indiana, to Lake Erie. This approximately 1,500-square-mile area once was a lowland formed by the retreat of the last of the glaciers. The glaciers left moraine behind, blocking the drainage of the Black Swamp to the north. Before its draining, the swamp had a forest of such incredible density, the sun couldn't reach the ground even during the summer months. Settlers experienced bouts of malaria and after they drained it in the late 1800s, the Great Black Swamp yielded some of America's most fertile, and muddiest, lands.

I followed the river north for about eight miles into Defiance, where the Auglaize River confluences with the Maumee River. General "Mad" Anthony Wayne constructed Fort Defiance and its namesake town in August 1794 to fight the Northwest Indian War, another war that pitted the U.S. Government against indigenous people to gain control of the Ohio Territory. I crossed the Maumee River and took a right on East River Drive, stopping at a delightful park by the riverside. The river water was a slimy fluorescent green stemming from an algal bloom laced with excessive nutrients (nitrates and phosphates) in the river water. I talked to a couple of kayakers who were pulling off the river and they said that the slime coating the bottoms of their kayaks was some pollutant, but they were not sure what it was.

"You just don't fall in, and it's okay for paddling," they said. "There are warnings not to swim in the river, though."

It's okay? Are you kidding me? How is this in any way acceptable in America? These rivers are appallingly impaired. When I was a kid, we called it "polluted." Mercury and PCBs are the main toxins in the rivers, with bacteria, phosphorus, and DDT posing additional environmental risks. I noted multiple warnings along the river that raw sewage could be present from time to time during rainstorm events. Raw sewage! The problem with some upper Midwestern towns is that some un-sewered communities cause river pollution. Though it is technically against the law to discharge raw sewage into a state water body, it happens anyway in areas with limited resources. Whether discharge is to a river, lake, or pond, the result is as you would imagine: smelly, nasty, toxic, cancer-causing water. The fish advisory on signs by the river stated that people should limit their fish consumption to one per month. It is a sickening state of affairs.

Riding along its streets, Fort Defiance had the feel of a classic Midwestern town. Ohio seemed like Iowa's estranged hillbilly cousin. Not necessarily friendly, based on my limited exposure to the natives at this point. I noted recurring wardrobe themes, tattoos, and multi-colored hair as I followed Highway 424 along the Maumee River for about nine miles into Florida, Ohio, another town with a confusing name. This route follows the Miami and Erie Canal, which once connected the Great Lakes to the Ohio River. The canal was built between 1825 and 1845 to improve commerce in Ohio, a difficult concept to imagine today with our complex interstate highway system. More or less, this canal concept was the primordial railroad and interstate highway system. Barges carried goods and merchandise to westward-expanding communities on these river channels, while locks facilitated changes in elevation across the Appalachian Mountains. The railroads, however, ended the use of the canals.

When I got to Florida, my solar panel quit working. It worked like a champ since Washington, so I pulled over and stopped on a residential lawn to make a phone call to REI. During the call, a young man came out of the house and yelled at me. "Hey, what are you doing on my lawn? Get the hell out of here! If you don't leave, I'll shoot you," he said.

Not taking him seriously, I held up my index finger up to motion to him that I was talking on the phone. "Just one minute, and I'll be with you," I said, not looking at him directly. He disappeared back into his house and came out with a handgun at his waist. "Get off my property or I am going to shoot you," he repeated in a more threatening tone.

"Holy shit!" I said, backing away, holding the phone and hands in the air, staring at his pistol. *What the hell is the matter with him. Do I look that menacing or threatening?* I ended the call, or at least I thought I did, but I accidentally speed-dialed my mother.

"Hello?" she said over the speakerphone. I realized my mistake. "I've got to go, Mom. There is a guy here who's going to shoot me. I'll call you back in a few minutes," I said frantically while continuing to fumble the phone. I left the property immediately and rode into town while he ran back into his house. *Why would anyone feel threatened by a guy on a bicycle talking on a phone? The last challenge I needed was to deal with a moron with a gun in hand.* Five minutes later, a red Ford F-150 pickup followed me through town. It was the same guy, stalking me. He pulled up to me in his truck and rolled down his window. I didn't know whether to get off the bike and run, but he only followed me to apologize for his behavior. "Hey buddy, I'm sorry I threatened you, but you scared me when I saw you on my property."

"Whatever, man, please leave me alone. I have done nothing wrong to you." As he drove away, I exhaled a sigh of relief. I don't know if I was more upset about the gun or the fact the solar panel was no longer functional. Essential, nonfunctional gear left me sore and frustrated. Four of my REI purchases failed after three weeks, including the sleeping pad, one of the taillights, the pump, and now the solar panel. I called my parents and explained the incident. They wanted to call the police but didn't know my location. It wasn't worth the added stress so I let it go and kept riding.

I followed the Maumee River to Napoleon past a sizeable courthouse building and the most impressive structures since the Des Moines capitol. I crossed the river and turned left onto Route 110, heading east for 13 miles along the river to Grand Rapids. I was making good time but not enjoying the Ohio experience, despite easy pedaling and the occasional accommodating breakdown lanes. Not all roads were bike-friendly, despite the fact I was following the mapped Northern Tier Route. At times it seemed I was doing better on my own before I started following their map.

I dropped south to Poe Road, which made for pleasant cruising through more corn and soybean fields. Even so, the traffic steadily grew more extreme at West Poe Road, where it became downright dangerous. This narrow road had no riding lane and I was heading straight into Bowling Green, which had just finished up the 2015 Annual National Tractor Pulling Championship. Traffic in town was at a standstill.

"No problem, I'll jump onto the sidewalk through town and pass everybody," I said unsolicited to a guy with his window down and a blank stare into traffic.

I typically never ride on sidewalks because it's dangerous, and cars don't tend to see a bike on the sidewalk. It's also illegal in many places. I passed several weird-looking, highly-modified "tractors" towed by large trucks. Some had giant back tires and in most cases, they didn't resemble tractors at all. Some looked more like drag cars. It's all about torque and horsepower.

I followed a canal along Poe Road out of town, then turned northeast on Scotch Ridge Road for about seven miles to Pemberville. My body was starving for food and it was getting late, so I took a break for dinner at Pisanello's Pizza Sandwich Shop in Pemberville. At the table next to me sat a lovely group of elderly folks who invited me to join them, where we laughed over an excellent dinner. When we finished eating, we went outside and took a selfie, and then they told me about a park that had camping outside Gibsonburg, still quite a distance away.

The skies became dark and threatening, accentuated by oncoming nightfall. I pedaled south for a couple of miles and turned east on Gibsonville Road towards Gibsonburg. Just about a mile south of Gibsonburg was the White Star Park Campground, a former limestone quarry. A simultaneous flash of lightning and crack of thunder followed by a rush of cold air descended upon me as I rode into the park. Then the heavens opened up like a fire hose, drenching everything while I was eaten alive by mosquitoes.

Perfect, just perfect, What's next, malaria? The romance of bike touring was fading and fading fast.

Through the torrent of drenching rain, I heard a "ding" on the phone. My daughter's text stated that our house back in Salt Lake City had experienced a fire in the utility room. The light in the laundry room had fallen into a pile of unwashed clothes and set them on fire. Most of the clothes burned up, along with damage to the furnace, washer, dryer, plumbing, and electrical wiring. I was beyond upset. The next text came from my wife:

"House uninhabitable. No electricity, staying in a hotel, all my clothes burned up."

My wife called the fire department and my family temporarily moved out of the house into a couple of downtown hotel rooms. I was at the breaking point. I immediately dialed up Shannon and she assured me the incident was under control. My wife and son Andrew put out the fire with extinguishers, which we kept at various home locations. I knew at this point that things were starting to unravel. In the soaking rain, I climbed into the wettest sleeping bag of my life. I rode 94 miles for the day and dozed off in a foul and soggy mood.

August 24th - Gibsonburg, Ohio to Westlake, Ohio

Sometime during the early morning hours, the sounds of pouring rain faded to chirping crickets and water dripped on my head inside the tent. It was still pitch black but it was about 6:20 a.m. My first thought was that of my wife's 48th birthday and that I wasn't there to receive her wrath—the house fire put me in the metaphorical doghouse- the final nail in my coffin. I sent a birthday card to her with money for the month to cover the mortgage and home expenses, but not enough to cover the current situation. And I was out of checks and out of money.

I rose from the tent and packed soaking wet gear while walking barefoot around camp in thick mud. The Great Black Swamp squished up between my toes. Everything I loaded into the panniers was a muddy mess. I added at least eight pounds of weight just from the overnight rain and mud. I didn't bother paying the $15 camping fee, which included no electricity, no water, no toilet paper, and an 8x5-foot mud pit to pitch a tent. Improved campsites were a complete joke, mainly where I listened to generators running all night and loud liquor parties. My idea of a good place to camp on a bike trip? Right behind a *No Trespassing* sign. Those are usually the best sites and who would look there for intruders?

I headed east on Township Roads 59 and 51 into Fremont on the Sandusky River. Fremont is a lovely town, rich in history, dating back to 1750 when it was a French trading post. Fremont is the birthplace of President Rutherford B. Hayes and home to his museum and library. Constructed in 1916, it was the first of the presidential libraries. President Hayes also died in Fremont. It is obvious why he liked this elegant town with large estates and brick-laid connecting streets and the most magnificent homes I'd seen in years. I tried to engage a few locals but they didn't seem interested in talking to a stranger.

I picked up the North Coast Inland Trail in Fremont, which paralleled the railroad southeast to Clyde. I passed many bikers on the trail but nearly all of them went by me without motioning even the slightest nod. This lack of acknowledgment bugged me because even back in the Wasatch Mountains, the ever-so-slightest nod was usually the norm between riders. After a couple of miles on the trail, I stopped for a break. A white Ford Explorer approached rather hastily, driven by a heavily armed Sandusky County Ranger. He hopped out of his vehicle and walked directly towards me suspiciously.

"What are you doing here?" he asked. To me, it seemed fairly obvious. I was on a bicycle tour and taking a break. I was tired and drinking water. What the hell did he think I was doing?

"What are you doing here, driving on the trail in a 4x4 instead of riding on a bike?" I replied. At that moment, two colossal black horseflies buzz-bombed his vehicle. I ducked as they zipped by my head. These were the most massive flies I had ever seen, the size of a small hummingbird. "What the hell are those!" I yelled, hands covering my head

"Those are horseflies. Haven't you ever seen a horsefly? Let me show you a trick you can do with these," said the officer. He scooped one of the horseflies into his hand after it landed and held it in a covered fist. Then he bent over, grabbed a blade of grass, removed the stem, and jammed it into the fly's rectum. Then he tossed the horse fly upwards. The fly ascended about ten feet with the dangling grass, then plummeted swiftly to the ground.

"It gives them a heart attack. What do you think about that!" he chuckled.

"I think you have too much time on your hands."

What could I say? That was frankly one of the weirdest things I'd seen in a while. I grabbed the camera and took selfies with the officer to commemorate my strangest encounter with the law so far. He was arrogant and suspicious initially, but he just turned out to be bored with his job and looking to entertain a stranger.

I left the North Coast Inland Trail in Clyde, where I met a worker on his smoke break at an impressively large Whirlpool Washer manufacturing plant entrance. He told me that the plant produces all types of washers, all shipped out by rail. I rode northeast on Route 175 and picked up Route 15 (Strecker Road) near a large limestone quarry. The confusing road names and township numbers changed at every county line. Some of the roads had little or no lane to ride, then the streets changed to 20-foot-wide riding lanes for no apparent reason. I stopped a couple of times to ask for directions and headed east on Strecker until I got to Avery, where I stopped for a Subway sandwich. From Avery, I rode on Route 123, the Huron-Avery Highway, which wasn't a highway but a beautiful cruise through agricultural and residential neighborhoods.

After six miles, I arrived in Huron and saw Lake Erie for the first time. The town had a beach community feeling. There was a large marina with dozens of sailboats and even a massive freighter ship at dock. Seeing Lake Erie for the first time was a mind-blowing experience, probably more so on a bicycle. Riding alongside water changed the feel of the ride altogether. Lake Erie was not the gross-looking water I envisioned, but a beautiful ocean of deep blue water extending to the horizon. It made me feel surprisingly small. The bike route followed Route 6 on the Lake Erie shoreline, past beautiful lakefront homes and closed businesses. At one time, this place must have been more popular than the present, as some of the man-made structures along the route appeared run-down. I pedaled past one beach after another, and at one location past multiple rows of greenhouses where the forest had grown through the glass. Only the fronts of the greenhouses were still visible. Some sections of Route 6 had a bike lane but much of it did not. I had a strong cross tailwind, which helped to push me along and everything was great until I hit a rock and got a pinch flat. The back tire was shot, my second back tire failure for the trip. The front tire didn't look good either. I had a spare but I was not ready to use it just yet.

Since Monroeville, most people I met seemed indifferent to talking to me. Most of the folks I met didn't look up from their phones or magazines to make eye contact. Many probably didn't realize the distance from Seattle but whenever I mentioned I was going to Boston, it always produced the same reaction:

"Boston?!! Are you kidding me?? That's really far away! How are you going to make it from here?" Yeah, and it was a long way to here from Seattle too.

The Northern Tier led me through Vermilion on the Lake, Lorain, and Avon Lake on Route 6, towards Westlake. The ride was delightful and exhilarating, and I felt strong as I stood up riding for much of the time. This section of the ride was a new chapter; I no longer felt landlocked. The ride now included a commanding ocean view of ever-present cornflower blue.

It was late in the day, the bike needed repairs, and I needed a shower. After a quick stop at the 7-Eleven for beer, coffee, and food supplies, I headed south on Columbia Avenue in Westlake by Highway 2 to a Super 8 Motel. In my cozy room, I turned up the heat, pulled out all of my sopping wet gear, and draped everything across the beds. I felt drained, but I stepped out of the hotel room to watch the first quarter moon rise. Just as I stepped away from the front door, a car rocketed around the corner of the building past me, missing me by inches and blowing me back towards my hotel room.

"Oh my hell, you son of a bitch!" I yelled at the car. A surge of adrenaline overtook me, sending me almost into shock. After all the dangerous road conditions since Seattle, I almost got run over within feet from my hotel door. I went back inside, brushed my teeth, and laid down. I rode about 90 miles and felt depleted.

August 25th - Westlake, Ohio to Painesville, Ohio

At 6:15 a.m., I curled my feet to see if there was any feeling. Still nothing, but it didn't matter because it didn't seem to affect my riding ability, so I brushed it off. Maybe just a casualty of the trip. I turned up the heat to ensure my gear was dry and sewed up more tears in my panniers, which were falling apart in the wet weather conditions. The back tire was bald as well, resulting in an increased frequency of flats. With no money and a bank card that didn't work, I needed a plan. I located Century Cycle in Westlake and cruised down after breakfast. I still had the American Express, but it was my business card, not for monkey business, and my accountants must have worked for the IRS because they were very picky about my expenses. I could get away with a hotel charge, but anything else might bring suspicion. Century didn't take AMEX anyway. However, I can't say enough about their kindness and integrity. The bike mechanic put SeaBos up on a work stand and checked the brakes, gears, spokes, and the entire drivetrain. They trued the back wheel and put on a "loaner" Gatorskin tire. I promised to repay them as soon as I got back to Salt Lake City. They didn't charge me for their services.

The debit card, which hadn't worked since Indiana, was distressing. I called Wells Fargo multiple times, but honestly, they didn't care. I was desperately low on money, scraping dollars in change from the bottom of my Camelbak. As I pedaled out of Westlake, dark cumulonimbus anvils formed over the lake but with a fresh new back tire and a positive attitude, I ignored the impending weather. I reached the town of Lakewood, passing beautiful homes and mansions. Where I could, I followed Lake Drive, a more scenic route with less traffic. To the east was Cleveland, topped by massive gloomy clouds and framed by trees and water. It was a stunning presentation that looked like the Emerald City in *The Wizard of Oz*.

Cleveland grew as a hub city after the completion of the Ohio-Erie Canal. The canal connected Cleveland to the Gulf of Mexico via the Ohio River and the Mississippi. I followed much of the canal route since Defiance and rode into Cleveland on an exceptional bike path alongside beautiful parks. The lake was white-capped from a strong northwest wind that induced four-foot waves. I walked the bike to the end of a long pier where two fishermen were trying their luck. They spoke a foreign language, but I thought they asked me if I was hungry.

"No thanks, I've already eaten," I responded. One man opened the cooler and offered me one of his fish, the smallest fish I had ever seen anyone keep, around three inches. I thanked him but told him I was okay.

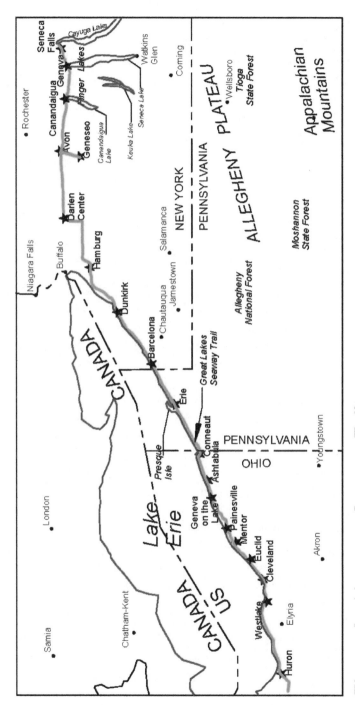

Figure 8 - Huron to Seneca Falls

I rode past sandy beaches packed with teenagers before the bike trail entered a tiled tunnel into Cleveland, and stopped by a painted mural of bike riders for pictures. I took some wrong turns and was lost as I approached inner-city Cleveland, ending up in a run-down part of town before reorienting myself back to the Northern Tier Route. The jumble of bridges near the water was visually fascinating. Drawbridges, steel truss arch bridges, cantilever truss bridges over bridges, bridges everywhere, one framed against another with the city as a backdrop. How difficult it must have been getting across here when the country was expanding westward. The only way to cross these big rivers was on a boat or barge. I avoided the Detroit Bridge, which spanned high above me, and instead rode underneath it carefully across a smaller grated metal bridge that was a challenge on thin tires.

I rode around the new Cleveland Browns football stadium and ended up at the Rock and Roll Hall of Fame Museum, a place that I always wanted to visit because of my love of music. The building is a pyramid glass and tower structure with seven floors and multiple exhibits and theatres. With less than ten dollars in change, this was the prime location for panhandling—tourists exiting busses, anxious to part with their cash in the gift shop. I greeted them all with a big smile, holding out my helmet, displaying a quickly drawn message of "Need Money" on a small cardboard scrap. *If they're going to throw away money, they may as well throw it at me.* I felt a little guilty, but not much, and I would never have in my wildest dreams thought I would ever be begging for money when I left Salt Lake. I ended up making about 26 bucks, which wasn't a lot, but I thought that I better quit after the first bus before I got busted. In front of the museum, workers were replacing a large pane of glass and I couldn't stand out there hassling people for long. I locked up the bike and walked through the window opening between the workers rather than through the front door. Inside, I was treated to Janis Joplin's Porsche, guitars from Jerry Garcia, Robbie Robertson, Eddie Van Halen, and many dated photographs of famous rock musicians. I didn't spend a lot of time but did stroll through the gift shop for a look. I walked back out through the missing pane, got on the bike, and left town a little wealthier.

I pedaled out of Cleveland towards Bratenahl on hectic city roads, then rode along the Cleveland Lakefront Bikeway, which I found to be a lovely bike path paralleling outstandingly beautiful mansions on the lakeshore. These stately homes contrasted sharply against trailer parks across the street. I stopped and called my bank again to check whether the debit card had expired or if the account was empty. They wouldn't say. They gave me locations where I could get a replacement card at the closest branch in Columbus, Ohio, hundreds of miles out of the way. *Seriously? Didn't I tell her I was on a bicycle?* She said she was sorry, but there was not much she could do for me. Screw it, I thought, one more problem to solve.

Pedaling out of Bratenahl towards Euclid felt like I was riding back into poverty. Here was a stark contrast between a neighborhood of predominantly poor African Americans in beat-up cars residing adjacent to areas with mansions and multi-million dollar properties. The disparity was incredible. I have never seen such financial discrepancy within such proximity. I rode past an abandoned McDonald's with shrubs and weeds growing through the parking lot and an apparent former amusement park that was closed and converted to high-rise public housing. Many of the cars on the street and in parking lots had severe damage, and some of the vehicles had bungee cords holding the doors shut. I noticed car windows made of plastic sheeting and fenders held on with duct tape. Was I in Somalia? I had not seen the like anywhere in the country. I had never been to and inside a grocery store where jersey barriers were placed right outside the doors to prevent shopping cart theft.

It began to sprinkle and the sky looked even more threatening. I pedaled to Eastlake along Lakeshore Boulevard, hugging the shoreline. Fog and mist whipped in from the lake. I rode through the town of Mentor on the Lake and got lost. The bike map showing the Northern Tier Route didn't follow the lake in all places so I worked my way around the town of Grand River in drenching rain. I put on the Gore-Tex coat and after a few minutes of riding, the waist cord on the jacket tore through the fabric and went up under my legs, hobbling me. I became desperately cold and miserable. My phone battery was running low so I stopped at a McDonald's, where they had removed the outlets from the lobby and refused to charge my phone. Well, screw McDonald's, I gave them two years of minimum wage service in college. Outside was a downpour of epic proportions as the rain continued to drive in from Lake Erie in squalls. It was survival time, so I just sucked it up and went out into the rain and the darkness of night. It was August and I was freezing. I called my parents and assured them that I was okay, which I wasn't, then blew out of town on a puddle-laden road and illegally crashed in a swampy conservation area outside of Painesville. It was still pouring rain but I managed to set up quickly and comfortably. Somehow, the mosquitoes still managed to find exposed skin.

August 26th - Painesville, Ohio to Erie, Pennsylvania

Rain, rain, rain. It was blowing fog. I poached the sparsely-treed campsite in the dark without realizing I was camped in the Grand River Conservation Area, a 16-acre floodplain on the Grand River flowing into Erie. The area was once the site of an apartment complex that flooded out in 2006. They removed the buildings and the land was restored to green space. I miraculously set up the tent on the only high ground in the area in the dark and driving rain. This was the worst day of the trip. I was no longer "living the dream" on a bike. I was plain miserable. I hated packing up wet gear and longed for the dryness of the West. It was difficult to see in the dark as I pedaled an unlit road and my shoes became instantly saturated as cold water squished out, refilled, and emptied again with each pedal stroke. The sewing job on the Gore-Tex jacket paid off by keeping me dry on top despite being splashed by every passing car. Incredibly discourteous drivers traveling way too fast for the conditions blew past, pounding me with dirty spray from puddles. I stopped into a minimart for hot coffee and then sat out front with a couple of unemployed carpenters dressed in torn work clothing.

Back into the downpour, I zigzagged north, then east, then north and east again a dozen times before getting back close to Lake Erie. The routes routinely changed numbers between counties and sometimes the roads were marked, sometimes not. It was challenging navigating in the rain with passing cars, a paper map, and an iPhone. At one point, the route was interrupted by bridge demolition; I could see the construction workers only a few hundred feet away. Still, the river was too deep to cross, so I followed detour signs for almost four miles out of the way to gain that 200 feet across the river.

I rode through North Perry on Route 20, noting two large hyperboloid cooling towers for the Perry Nuclear Station, one of the country's largest power plants. I followed Route 20 to Geneva, then pedaled north on Route 534 to *Geneva-on-the-Lake* and stopped at a gas station for more coffee. Interesting that the Ohio towns added the suffix "*on the lake*" to the town names. The cashier told me he used to own one of the bars in town, but the 2008 recession killed off all of his business. He said things never recovered back to pre-2008 conditions for this area. He also said the town could get tremendous snowstorms and significant accumulations from the lake effect, so the summer season is pretty short by the time the snowpack melts. I did not doubt the amount of moisture the lake could generate.

I cruised the boulevard east on Lake Road, past dozens of bars, pizza parlors, and open-air arcades that lined the street for about half a mile. It was 9:30 a.m., but everything looked altogether shut down, and almost no one was on the road. I caught glimpses of the lake from time to time. I stopped to use a restroom in a park, but somehow I got turned around and rode back to the west a half a mile before I realized that the lake was on the wrong side. I felt a moment of panic and confusion before I realized the mistake.

Was that decaf coffee I had at the gas station?

I pedaled through Ashtabula past several ghostly coal-fired power plants, substations, and water towers that had fallen into decay and were in the process of being dismantled. This place was indeed a messy industrial area. The power industry, especially coal, took it hard with all of the national focus on global warming. I headed over to Bridge Street into downtown Ashtabula where the road narrowed considerably and had to move the bike into the main flow of traffic with several cars behind me. I had no choice; they would have to slow down and be patient with my speed. I was not going to hug parked cars and risk getting doored.

I cranked about 20 miles an hour through downtown when a semi-truck pulled right up on my behind. He down-shifted and revved up his engine, honking his horn to harass and intimidate me. I stood up pedaling, as he moved up close, right up to my back tire before the bridge. At the last split second, I cut to the right onto the pedestrian walkway and rode the pedestrian access across the bridge. I was incensed but kept my composure and kept riding.

What a jackass! No gestures, no middle fingers, control emotions, and stay calm and under control. If anything bad happens to me, I'll be in the doghouse when I get home.

I took Lake Road into Conneaut, Ohio, a town on the border of Pennsylvania, and pulled over to take a selfie with the Pennsylvania welcoming sign. However, when I came to a stop, I lost my balance and crashed and fell to my left side again. This fall was the fifth severe fall on the trip, and every fall was to the left. A passing vehicle stopped and a man jumped out and asked me if I was okay. It certainly wasn't the trucker from earlier in the day. I immediately liked Pennsylvanians.

Less than two miles into Pennsylvania, Route 5 splits off Route 20 to the northeast towards Lake Erie and the Great Lakes Seaway Trail. This was a great riding section with a beautiful bike lane. After nearly ten miles I arrived in Lake City and rechecked the navigation. Two lycra-clad bicyclists named Kaish and Hans approached. They were from the Netherlands and touring the U.S. for the second time. Hans wore a green ball cap with a sizeable yellow *U.S. Border Patrol* logo. Both were neatly adorned with matching blue and white racing outfits, shorts, and short sleeve shirts. I was riding in full Gore-Tex and wool. They started their tour in Seattle twelve days before me, and somehow, I had caught up to them. They couldn't believe I left Seattle on July 24th. Both Hans and Kaish were skinny as rails and could no doubt ride circles around me. We had a friendly chat about their touring experiences, both in the U.S. and in other countries, and I sensed a little swagger in their attitude. Kaish told me this bike tour experience would stick with me for a long time. It was genuinely good to hear this. I knew what I learned from my cycling experience would have to carry me through some challenging times ahead. We took off together and rode about four blocks, where they stopped at a fast-food restaurant for a sandwich, and I never saw them again. I hate long good-byes anyway.

Not long afterward, I met another bike tourer named Radley near the town of Avonia. Radley was riding west on an old bicycle to visit his nephew in Arkansas. Even though he came from Burlington, Vermont, he took a bus with his bike and gear to Erie, Pennsylvania to start his first bike tour. His journey was just getting started. He complained that his knee was giving him fits and his Brooks saddle was uncomfortable to ride and falling apart. He also mentioned he was carrying about 80 pounds in his panniers. I should be the last person to critique other bike riders but Radley didn't look like he was actually up to the task. His Huffy bike had large fenders holding four overloaded panniers and a solar panel tied on with string.

"That solar panel will surely fall off by the end of the day," I mentioned in passing.

"It's made it this far. I'm not worried," he said.

He's lucky it made it ten miles. I wished him luck; he looked like he would need it. I refocused on the road and appreciated that I was no longer riding the Midwest's flatlands. Route 5 was rural, delightful, and scenic, presenting an accommodating bike lane with many good pavement stretches. Vast grape vineyards replaced the cornfields of Ohio and the riding was pleasant. My legs were strong from a month of daily travel. Still, that recurring, peculiar paralysis onset after starting from a dead stop was now becoming more severe and increasing in frequency. It occurred nearly every time, not just on occasion. Out of an abundance of caution, I decided that my routine would include less frequent stops.

I reached West Erie, and Route 5 split into four lanes. With nowhere to bag a campsite, I checked into the Presque Isle Comfort Inn, went up to the room, and started perusing the city street layout on my phone. Erie is Pennsylvania's fourth-largest city and yet another town whose history included wars between Indians and white settlers during the Napoleonic Wars of 1812 to 1815. Erie's most prominent geographic feature is Presque Isle, a French term meaning "*almost an island.*" The peninsula is unique to the south side of Lake Erie. At just over six miles in length, the park consists of dunes and intervening ponds, a remnant of sandy sediment left behind by a retreating glacier from about 13,000 years ago.

After showering and changing into my only non-biking clothes, I rode over to the Ugly Tuna Bar. As usual, I brought the bike inside with me. A handful of attractive young servers were busy slinging drinks and attending to about 30 men, seated at tables behind me. There were no women patrons. I sat alone at the bar and glanced back to SeaBos by the oversized fireplace as a drop-dead gorgeous platinum blonde, who didn't look 25, took my order and poured a big tequila shot and a beer. Not a minute later, the door behind the bar swung open, spewing out an enormous bald, muscle-bound man who looked like Mr. Clean on steroids. He pointed at SeaBos, breathing heavily, seemingly disturbed by the presence of a bicycle in his establishment.

"Who owns that bike?" he yelled. I motioned with one finger that the bike was mine without lifting my head or looking at him. "Get that bike out of my bar and put it in the bike rack outside," he barked in anger.

The bar fell silent. All eyes were on Mr. Clean. I gazed over to *SeaBos,* about 30 feet away, resting up against the fireplace, and I saw something more than a bicycle covered in stickers and duct tape. That two-wheeled miracle machine was the physical manifestation of my freedom and my best friend. I was a little loosened-up after tequila and irritated by Mr. Clean's bravado and his ridiculously tight tee-shirt. Now the customers looked directly at me.

"I'm not going anywhere, and the bike's not going anywhere either. That's my date. I'm not moving it." He raised his voice even louder, pointing a finger to the door. "Get the bike out of the bar now," he shouted.

"I'll leave...when I finish my beer," I calmly said and gave him a passing smile and looked back at my beer. The girls behind the bar looked mortified. I heard crickets. He briskly walked into the back room and slammed the door. I thought I might be on borrowed time, so, time to drink up.

"Oh, well!" I said with a smile to the girls. The bar resumed back into motion as the bartender refilled my glass of tequila nearly to the top. Then she smiled at me and wrote up the bill for $5. I left her a $20 tip on my AMEX, angel that she was. The damn accountants will just have to figure out a new business category in Quickbooks. I downed the shot quickly and exited the establishment before Mr. Clean decided to return in an angrier mood.

After 87 miles of hills and three drinks on little food, I pushed the bike back to the hotel, too intoxicated to ride. However, after the exchange with Mr. Clean inside the bar, the adrenaline offset most of my impairment. I couldn't understand his obsession with one bike and I wasn't in the least bit intimidated by him despite his macho display. Something in me had changed.

Back in the room, I worked late into the night on the phone with my daughter trying to complete monthly reports and keep juggling clients while secretly on the road. It was hard to think about work when after 20 years, my once-successful company was faltering and my personal life was deteriorating. Two years earlier, I walked away from a lucrative client to save my marriage and spend more time at home. Shrinking income and enthusiasm left me without a forward business plan. It was now clear that these events precipitated an emotional climate that made riding the bike so cathartic.

CHAPTER 10 - THE EAST

August 27th - Erie, Pennsylvania to Hamburg, New York
The hotel bed was comfy and I slept four or five hours before the alarm went off. It felt like the East, waking to a day of cloudy, damp weather. I studied the map of the Northern Tier Route. The East has many cities, towns, traffic, congested areas, and a higher concentration of highways. Uh-oh. I went down to breakfast and consumed as many calories as my stomach would allow, including two bowls of Raisin Bran, three yogurts, two Danishes, three juices, four cups of coffee, and four pieces of toast.

Packed with fuel, I checked out of the hotel and rode around Erie, then out to Presque Isle to see the dunes. I liked Erie and found it easy to ride in traffic. I dropped off one more package at the post office to send home as the rain began to dissipate. The weather report called for clearing and looking back, I was fortunate to have had favorable weather for most of the ride, not to mention I rarely had to negotiate direct headwinds.

The scenery became incrementally more rural as I pedaled out of Erie on Route 5, revealing views of intensely blue Lake Erie as I climbed onto higher bluffs. With multiple shades of green and azure blue water to the horizon, the panorama resembled a placid ocean landscape that could have been anywhere in the world. I had a small tailwind, cool temperatures, and an easy lane for riding, ranging in width from a few feet up to nearly 20 feet. Pennsylvania seems to take pretty good care of the major roads. There were a few hills, but I rarely shifted to the small chainring.

After about 18 miles, I reached the New York border and my enthusiasm spiked.

New York, Gateway to the East

I rode another ten miles and stopped in at a Minimart gas station for supplies on Route 5 in Barcelona. I took a break on the bench outside to eat, rehydrate and put up my feet. I met a couple who were traveling from South Carolina and camping near the beach. They stayed in a new motor home and the man said he couldn't fathom riding more than a few miles on a bicycle and that he l-o-v-e-d his motor home. I get it.

Nice, good for you. But I think there is an underappreciated fulfillment that stems from traveling as a minimalist that he could never understand. Although, it's hard to argue the benefits of a comfortable bed and a shower. I packed up and jumped back onto Route 5, pedaling northeast along the lake for about 12 miles to Van Buren Point. It was another five miles to the harbor town of Dunkirk, the home of William Carpenter, the Army geologist with General

Custer's party, who discovered gold in the Black Hills. *I was just there a few weeks ago!* Small country.

I pedaled northeast on Lakeshore Drive for another 10 miles to Irving, making some great time. But soon I was bonking and stopped for a Subway 12-inch tuna sandwich, where I told my bike story to the two employees who came outside and sat with me. They were both interested in the places I had passed through in the West. When I said I was riding to Boston, they were dumbfounded. "Wow! That's so far away, do you think you can make it?" they asked.

It seemed odd that most people did not realize that I already pedaled more than 80 percent of the way. Seattle was much farther away than Boston. I left the Subway and passed through the Cattaraugus Indian Reservation, which would have been a great place to camp, but I kept going, following the old shoreline route past Point Breeze and Sturgeon Point. The sun was setting over Lake Erie and for a few fleeting minutes, it broke through a hole in the clouds, spreading sunbeams across a shining saffron yellow surface. I was far above the water now as the road closely followed along the edge of the cliff. I was treated to spectacular lake views; another shoreline and the silhouette of the Buffalo skyline.

I passed Graycliff on the Lake Estate, a house designed in 1931 by Frank Lloyd Wright, then turned off Lake Shore Drive in Pinehurst, bidding farewell to Lake Erie. I picked up Pleasant Avenue east under the New York Thruway and cycled towards the town of Hamburg. Night came quickly and I needed to find a place to crash. Posted "No Trespassing" signs were ubiquitous as the suburban population grew increasingly dense with every passing mile. In diminishing light, I spotted a noxious weed patch at the edge of a neighborhood behind a thick stand of bushes with a small opening. I was grateful to have found anything. I started to feel better about the tour, having left the rain and Ohio behind. I pedaled 92 respectable miles for the day, and it felt like it.

August 28th - Hamburg, New York to Avon, New York

On a couple of occasions during the night, someone pointed a flashlight beam on my tent fly. I was pushing my luck and grateful the neighbors or the police didn't confront me. This was the first camp where I felt like I might be in someone's backyard. I heard the neighbor up early, rolling out the trash can before dawn, and someone had parked a car next to me on the other side of the bushes while I lay quietly on a deflated pad. I chugged cold coffee and completed my usual routine—pack gear, pump tires, pray for safety, and then time to grind. I no longer needed light for these tasks; it was automatic. I even impressed myself. I rolled SeaBos out through the bushes and brushed past a man on the street, getting into his car.

"Good morning!" I said with a smile as I rolled past him. He was startled by my sudden appearance. I turned on the lights and pedaled into town. My legs went into quasi-paralysis, then kicked in as I pedaled towards town beneath a ceiling of low-hanging clouds. One mile outside of Hamburg, the first seconds of brilliant sunlight illuminated treetops against brooding clouds. The ethereal display of light ignited a renewed enthusiasm for riding which I had not felt in days. In Hamburg, I stopped and looked over a collection of coal-driven steam locomotives and train cars, then stopped at three different stores looking for a map without success. I was off the Northern Tier Route and entered some of the country's most confusing road systems. The clerk at the 7-Eleven told me to take either Route 20 or Route 20A eastbound, noting that Route 20A had many more hills. I don't know what I was thinking at the time, but Route 20A sounded like a fun challenge.

I pedaled out of town on Newton Street to Chestnut Ridge Road. About three miles outside of Hamburg, I started to climb at grades exceeding six percent and wondered if this was the right choice. I pedaled into Orchard Park and checked the navigation. I thought, *How hard could this be? I rode over the Cascades and the Rockies and across America!* Over the next 20 miles, however, I found out the answer. I climbed in elevation from about 900 feet to over 1,500 feet, pedaling at a pathetic three miles per hour, grinding hills in severe strain, and coping with strange leg issues. Memories of those horrible Iowa hills flooded my head while sweat poured from my body. New York was a different ride altogether. After a 600-plus foot climb and vanquishing four summits, I was done with Route 20A and anxiously looked for a different route. I checked navigation and saw that Route 77 connected to the north to Route 20. I struggled up to the top of the last hill, covered with wind turbine generators, where I came upon a large, full-scale white elephant monument on the roadside next to a farmhouse.

What the hell is this doing here? So incongruous with the rural

countryside, so oddly out of place. I cycled Route 77 through
Bennington to Darien on a rollercoaster route. After just 1.5 miles, I
approached a giant hill that tilted up at grades exceeding ten percent.
This monster may have been one of the most challenging climbs since
the Rockies, as I was genuinely suffering at the hillcrest. The Midwest
made me soft and weak, I got too used to the flatlands, and now I had
no residual Western acclimatization.

The Relentless New York Hills

But I made it and coasting down a long descent on the other

side, I stopped at a car pulled off the road. I wasn't sure what was happening but it was on the brink of rolling over. The driver's door opened up, a man stepped out, and the car lurched. I pulled up behind the car, dropped my bike, and rushed to stabilize the vehicle."We pulled over to let the kids out to pee, and I didn't see this ditch in the weeds." He was clearly confused by the situation. The enormous ditch swallowing their car was completely obscured. The back tire lifted off the ground with every movement inside the vehicle.

"You've got to get them out of the car!" I yelled. I counterweighted the car with my body's full weight as the two boys in the back seat climbed up to the driver's side and jumped out, followed by a woman. A nearby farmer working the adjacent field rolled in on a tractor to offer assistance. I picked up my bike and left quickly, as this scenario ended as well as it could have. There was little doubt that one tug on that car with the tractor would end in disaster.

I rolled downhill to Darien Center, where I turned right onto Route 20 towards Albany. Only 33 miles left to Avon, where I planned to spend the night. I had a good tailwind, cruising with enough momentum to get up the next hill. It was an exhilarating ride, I felt good, and the road conditions were superb. Near Alexander, I saw five bike riders ahead and stood up on my pedals to pass them. They were all millennials in their twenties and thirties and it felt good to whiz by. I pulled into a gas station and grabbed junk food and Gatorade, and they pulled in behind me just a minute later. All five riders were from Buffalo, New York. The oldest of the group was pulling a trailer. He worked for a non-profit co-op bike shop in Buffalo, which rescued old bikes and rebuilt them. They also taught biking and bike safety skills to elementary school kids. After our snack break, they departed to the south while I continued east on Route 20.

Two miles outside of Avon, I heard a loud pop. My rear derailleur stopped working, and I assumed the shifter cable broke off somewhere in the grips. I could still pedal in 9th and 18th gear, but what a grunt. I pushed the bike for a relatively long distance to the top of a hill, then coasted downhill to Avon, switching off Route 20 onto Route 5, and stopped in at a gas station to inquire about a bike shop.

"There is a bike shop, but it's in Geneseo. That's about nine miles south on Route 39. They probably close soon, so I'd check with them."

I bolted expeditiously to the south on Route 39, grunting it the entire way on a gentle 200-foot climb. Despite the arduous ride in high gear, it was a beautiful road through farm country to Geneseo, a small college town. When I reached the bike shop, the owner was just about to close but he threw SeaBos up onto the bike vice to check my cable. I can't give enough praise to a bike shop that understands the urgency to help a long-distance biker with mechanical problems. He struggled with vice grips and needle nose pliers, as the cable had unraveled and made a real mess, breaking up deep inside the shifting lever. He said he could fix it, but it would take about a half-hour.

I needed money, so I went to a couple of banks in town and try to get cash out on my American Express Card with no luck. They all shook their heads at the first bank, and I could tell the teller was sorry that she couldn't help me. I went to a second bank with the same result. They ran the card, then called the manager. Out she came, they both squinted at the computer screen and began shaking their heads, and said they couldn't help me. They only provided lame excuses for why none of the cards could be used to give me cash. A table behind me was loaded with snacks, candy bars, cookies, and juices. The teller motioned me to help myself, at which point I did not hesitate. I loaded up my Camelbak until the backpack compartment was full. Then, I lifted my shirt and filled it with as many juice boxes as I could carry, folding it like a pouch. I ran from the lobby like I stole something. In a Walter Mitty fantasy, I imagined robbing the bank, riding away out of town on the bike, and getting away with the loot. In reality, I turned to see her give me a thumbs up and a smile. I jogged back across the street to the bike shop, and Big Mike had just finished repairing the rear shifter cable, only charging me $20.

"Wow, thanks, buddy!" I said as I handed him $23 in cash, leaving me with less than $15.

I packed up and reversed course to the north on Route 39. For some reason, the road seemed uphill in both directions. In Avon, I picked up groceries and a beer with cash and stopped at the Hilltop Motel, a dated small hotel on town's outskirts. I figured that I could use my AMEX just a few more times for a hotel room only, since these were noticeably not work-related expenses. I was greeted by the owner and her large Labrador Retriever. I went to my room to unpack wet gear and turned on the television. I watched breaking news in complete horror about a young bicyclist killed by a car in a nearby town. A sick feeling overcame me when I realized it might have been one of the boys I met earlier that afternoon at the convenience store. I reached deep into my pack and pulled out a mini bottle of tequila stashed from a few days before, mixed up a drink, filled the sink with ice, and iced down a beer. I laid back in the bed, completely distraught. I rode 98 miles for the day and was dog tired from the colossal New York hills. This leg of the trip was genuinely challenging. But the load was now a bit lighter because I carried less water and clothing.

August 29th - Avon, New York to Jamesville, New York

I was up at 5:15, thinking that I could get used to a motel room for the rest of the trip. At the same time, a nub of sadness began to slowly develop in my gut. This was the melancholy feeling that always seems to accompany the last few days of a great vacation. With most of the miles behind me and far fewer ahead, I faced the reality that my adventure was winding down. Ironically, I longed to reach Boston and now that it was within my grasp, I didn't want the experience to come to an end. When it did, I knew that this life as a vagabond would end as well; as sudden as death, it would be over. I would be, and feel, just like anyone else, back to living in a house, working a daily job, following the rules, sucked back into the day-to-day banality of society. Not the passionate guy on a bike, living in the moment, escaping everyday reality on plan-free adventuring. Simultaneously, I felt the magnetic pull of the proverbial horse back to the barn.

I contemplated the news of the fatal bike accident on the previous day and lingered for a few extra prayers for the deceased biker and his friends. Afterward, I felt sporty and cranked hard out of Avon on Route 5. I wanted to get some real mileage. But right outside of Avon, I encountered enormous climbs.

"Kill those son-of-a-bitch hills, let's get this done!" I screamed at SeaBos, staring at the road ahead, standing and pedaling on deadened feet, which at times made riding feel a little weird below the knees. I rode over horrible hills in Iowa, so what could be worse than Iowa? The answer to that question became apparent in New York. About 24 miles before Canandaigua, I struggled over several hills, with elevations ranging from 650 to about 1100 feet. Canandaigua is on the north end of Canandaigua Lake, the fourth largest Finger Lake[i]. The Finger Lakes are eleven deeply-carved glacial lakes that were formed by advancing glaciers about 18,000 years ago. These glaciers originated from massive ice sheets on the north slope of the

Allegheny Plateau[ii] that gouged, deep north-south aligned gashes into the bedrock. The Finger Lakes are among the deepest bodies of water in the country, with a few bottoming out below sea level.

I felt strong and to my amazement, I was pulling smaller hills in 10th gear. *Not bad.* I stopped at McDonald's for breakfast, water, and ice for the Camelbak. I was getting pretty sick of fast food and gas station goodies. It was astounding to me how much junk I had consumed and still lost more than 25 pounds at the same time. Nutrition wasn't a key focus of my trip. Many of you may criticize my choices; I saw it as cheap gas.

I cruised out of town, feeling strong, thinking that I had this ride licked and that it would be an easy pedal to Albany. Four miles out of town, I reached a hillcrest, then sped mostly downhill for 13 miles, dropping 500 feet into the city of Geneva. I pulled off of Route 5 onto the sidewalks and cruised through a lovely park by Seneca Lake. The bike pathway, paved with brick, was a pleasing touch. The day's weather couldn't have been more delightful, with a comfortable on-shore breeze from the south. The lake is 38 miles long, the largest of the Finger Lakes, and the deepest at over 600 feet. I took SeaBos out to the end of the pier to take pictures.

I cycled east on Route 5 through relatively flat suburban terrain, passed through Waterloo's town center seven miles later, then continued for another four miles to Seneca Falls. The big fat riding lane disappeared in each city, where it was replaced by nine-inch granite curbs, which made riding more confining in traffic. Granite curbs were a distinct change in conditions from what I experienced across the country. I had to trust the drivers passing me and make sure the tire never accidentally touched the curb. I didn't find New York drivers to be bike-courteous; in fact, some of them were real dicks. I was boxed between cars on several occasions in the town sections. Several vehicles cruised by slowly on the open road, then throttle their engine next to me and pass, leaving me in a black cloud of diesel smoke. One truck did this, then turned right immediately in front of me without a turn signal.

"Just keep pretending you are invisible," I thought, a concept embraced from many years of motorcycle riding. Not all cars notice a biker, and pretending you are unseen makes you extra cautious with your position on the road. I pedaled east on Route 20 from Seneca Falls, then to the north around Lake Cayuga, the second-largest Finger

Lake where I finally entered familiar terrain. Cornell University is located at the south end of Cayuga Lake, where my three brothers, Matt, Peter, and Tim, all attended college.

About one mile west of Auburn, Route 5 and 20 transformed to a congested freeway with heavy merging traffic. Suddenly, I was riding in the middle lane of high-speed traffic. In a panic, I got off at the first exit and rode the back streets heading towards Genesee Street, the main route through the center of town. I pedaled through sub-neighborhood roads and back alleys, noting that some parts of Auburn looked pretty run down. Looks of desperation and unhappy faces fronted dilapidated porches and homes in disrepair. I stopped in front of a prominent gray stone facade of St. Mary's Catholic Church and gave a prayer of thanks, and asked for my continued safety on the road.

The Mohawk-Hudson Bikeway

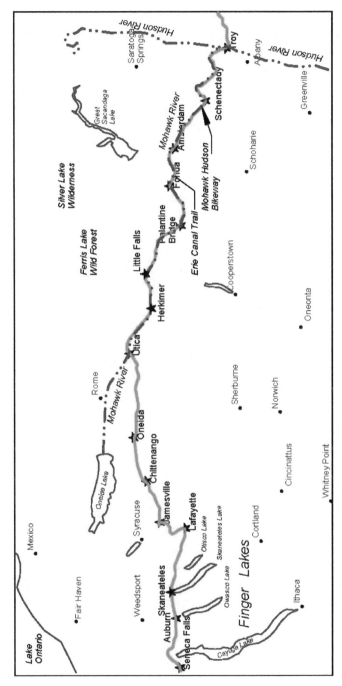

Figure 9 - Seneca Falls to Troy

I pedaled east on Route 5 and 20 for about seven miles, climbing over 300 feet to Lake Skaneateles. About five miles east of Skaneateles, I coasted down into a valley, then climbed another 500 feet up unpleasantly steep grades. I approached the mother of all hills just past Cardiff, rising over 700 feet in just more than a mile. I groaned, standing up, pushing in first gear at the perilous point of losing my center of gravity. My muscles cramped up for the first time since the West. I got off the bike and pushed the last 200 vertical feet up 13 percent grades, wondering what the highway engineers could have been thinking.

Exhausted from an unbearable climb and embarrassed for walking the hill, I pedaled into a gas station near Lafayette. I needed a new course because there was no way I could continue this route. I asked for directions from a young man named John, who was filling up his truck. I suspected that he was a local, judging by the muddy pickup truck and enduro motorcycles in the truck bed. "I saw you were pushing your bike up that last hill," he chuckled. "I once worked at the farm on the last hill and rode those hills on a bike once, and it just about killed me. I never tried it again."

"I'm looking for a better route to bike east across New York to the Hudson River," I said.

"Your best option with the least number of hills is to head north to the Mohawk River Valley by Syracuse and follow the Mohawk River to Albany. Otherwise, you are headed for the misery of relentless hills on Route 20."

He gave me directions to Jamesville, paralleling Interstate 81. I pedaled up Route 11 to Kennedy Road and while poorly executing a quick right-hand turn uphill onto Sentinel Heights Road, I lost my balance. I instantly fell to the left again, landing directly on my arm and elbow. I was geared too high heading uphill. Dreadful pain ran from my fingers to my shoulder and through my body, and I cursed aloud. I tried to shake it off. Blood ran down my arm and gushed from my left knee and down into my sock. I thought I had undoubtedly broken my arm.

"Dammit, is this the end?" I wondered, palpating my elbow and tearing up. With SeaBos undamaged, I shook it off and rode Graham Road to Lafayette Road to Route 173. I took a right and headed for Jamesville, where I spotted a perfect place to crash in the woods directly across the road from the Clark Conservation Area. The campsite, located in dense trees, was well-hidden from the road and nearby homes. I set up camp, then walked across the street to the state park, looking for a men's room or anywhere to plug in the phone. The bathroom was a bonus, complete with a clean toilet and running water, but there were no power outlets. I crossed the road back into the dark wooded burr-laden camp and crashed in the tent for the night, exhausted, while my arm throbbed from the crash. I laid on the mattress as it slowly deflated. Ridiculous that no one has designed a better light-weight sleeping pad when cars are now driving themselves.

August 30th - Jamesville, New York to Palatine Bridge, New York

I awoke to the sound of light sprinkles of rain striking the fly at 5:10 a.m. Throughout the night, the distant lights of Syracuse to the north illuminated the tent. I debated whether to get up or whether to keep sleeping when I heard the rain. I sat up, downed cold coffee, and packed up as light slowly filtered through the clouds. Burrs stuck to my clothes and socks, and my phone was completely dead. I rode into Jamesville and searched for a power outlet. After hunting around churches and several buildings, I located an outlet in front of the homeless food pantry. I plugged in my lights and phone, sat down on the pavement, reclined against the building, and waited. I looked at my reflection in the dark glass window and saw someone in need of severe personal grooming.

A man with two dogs approached. He introduced himself as Kurt, a local lawyer. I questioned him about living in Jamesville." Jamesville is a lower-income town. Few folks here have any disposable income. The local cement factory made a colossal mess and went out of business and closed down in the early 1980s. Everybody moves out of town, except those working the prison."

The economy in upstate New York was indeed in dire condition. Home sales in the area went cheap as people moved out of the city looking for better opportunities. Decay, desolate streets, litter, overgrown vines, and ivy evoked ghosts of the past. Hypodermic needles and liquor bottles occasionally littered the roads. According to Kurt, upstate New York taxes on properties were paying for New York City. People generally looked beaten down by the pressures of unemployment and had little hope or no opportunity. It struck me deeply to the core. I pedaled from town on the bike on Route 173, crossing the river and climbing steeply up 300 feet out of the river valley in less than a mile. I got off the bike and pushed some of the hill climbs, again much to my embarrassment. New York hills are killers. I got back on the bike on a semi-flat section and finished the last climb, passing the prison on the right and the abandoned cement factory on the left.

Not far past the prison, a white speeding half-ton pickup truck approached on a side dirt road, and it was apparent we were on a collision course. Even though we made full eye contact, he didn't even slow as he blew past the stop sign. I braked hard and turned sharply to the right, almost skidding underneath the back tire. I went to the ground onto my face in dirt and gravel as the truck sped away, leaving me in a cloud of dust. Adrenaline pumped through my body, while anger poured into my head and shook my body. I wanted to get up and scream. But I didn't for fear that this guy was purposely trying to injure me.

I rolled into the town of Manlius and ate breakfast at a fast-food venue, desperate for calories, then pedaled northeast up Route 173, climbing about 600 feet for about three miles, and descended nearly 700 feet to Chittenango, the birthplace town of L. Frank Baum, author of the Wizard of Oz. I picked up Route 5 for another six miles to Canistota. Route 5 was a marked bike route, with an excellent riding lane in most places. Six miles later, I passed through Oneida, close to Oneida Lake, the largest lake within New York and a remnant of glacial Lake Iroquois, predecessor to Lake Ontario. Passing Oneida, I climbed for about 11 miles, then dropped down into Kirkland and on to Utica, finally entering the relatively flatter and more bike-friendly Mohawk River Valley.

The Mohawk River is about 150 miles long and the largest tributary to the Hudson River. The valley was formed about 13,000 years ago during the rapid draining of glacial Lake Iroquois, a Pleistocene age proto-Lake Ontario. The Mohawk confluence with the Hudson River is just north of Albany. The cities of Rome, Utica, Little Falls, Canajoharie, Amsterdam, and Schenectady all sprang up because of their proximity to the river and the Erie Canal system. The Erie Canal connected the east coast to the Great Lakes near Buffalo. The Mohawk River Valley was an essential early passageway through the Appalachians. I was so relieved to ride a river valley's gentle grade versus the massive, unrelenting central New York hills.

Somewhere just to the west and outside of Utica, New York, Route 5 became a nightmare, morphing into a full-blown New York freeway with traffic signs posted "No pedestrians, No scooters, No bicycles." Oops. I panicked as I rode down the middle of the highway with two lanes to the left and two merging lanes on my right. I pedaled for about five miles in the breakdown lane, but merging onramps forced me into traffic lanes. I wondered how long until a cop came along and arrested me. I finally exited the freeway in Utica and followed Genesee Street to the northeast through town, over Interstate 90, and back on to Route 5 East. The route follows just to the north of the historic Erie Canal. Utica was once a thriving textile town that was settled after the American Revolution but fell prey to political corruption and organized crime in the nineteenth century and was dubbed "Sin City." Arthur Savage, a town resident, developed the hammerless lever-action Savage "Model 99" rifle, first manufactured here in 1899. My Dad owned a half dozen of these sleek lever-action rifles. By the mid-twentieth century, Sin City was weakened by globalization.

Route 5 parallels Interstate 90 between Utica and Herkimer. These towns became more depressing as I progressed to the east. After 15 miles, I passed through Herkimer, famous for the Herkimer diamonds that weather out of a 500 million-year-old dolomitic limestone[iii]. These gems are not diamonds but crystal clear double-terminated quartz crystals found in voids in the rock that closely resembles their harder namesake. This quartz crystal habit[iv] is only known to exist in a few places on earth. Before Little Falls, I came upon a trailer-less 17-foot fiberglass speedboat that was pushed in the woods. I laughed at the boat's name, *"Who Knew,"* which I assumed was the owner's reaction when he arrived home. I stopped, took pictures with the bike, climbed inside the boat, and had a good laugh.

In Little Falls, I was greeted by a massive brick factory, a shuttered paper mill named Burline Specialty Tissue Papers. Little Falls was named in the early 1700s for a small waterfall on the Mohawk River, which had to be portaged. The town was an integral part of the old Erie Canal in the early 1700s and, more recently, Bill Warner's birthplace. He set the world speed record on a motorcycle at over 300 miles per hour. Riding through town, I noted a few syringes in the street gutters, liquor bottles, and bar cups along the main street.

I headed southeast along the north side of the Mohawk River, passing through St. Johnsville.

After another 9 miles, I rode into Palatine Bridge. Occasional cautionary road signs with "horse and buggy" images were posted, something I had not seen. I passed a historic church comprised of gray stone built in 1770. I was deep in Amish country, a sect of people who live a modest, simple life and shun modern technology's conveniences. They still travel using horse and buggy carriages on the roads. I checked into a cheesy motel room in Palatine Bridge. I pedaled 91 miles for the day, and I was drained. The young man at the front desk sent me over to the grocery store about a quarter-mile away. I walked on numb feet in flip flops, picked up cold beer, some supplies for dinner, and headed back to the motel. The room checked all the boxes for the definition of a dump. The carpet was chewed up, exposing foam padding, there were a few paper towels to use for a bath mat, the cold water was on the hot water side, and there was no soap. I turned on the TV, and there were four channels and static. I reclined in a comfortable bed, the only good aspect of the room, and jotted down thoughts in my journal, eventually drifting off to sleep with the TV on.

August 31st - Palatine Bridge, New York to Grafton, New York

I woke up at 4:20 a.m. to a static TV screen, looking around and not recognizing my whereabouts. The bed was comfy, but I got up and showered again just because I could. The paper bath mat stuck to my feet, and I couldn't get it off as I stomped around the room in a daze. I ate Pop-Tarts and flipped the TV channels. When daylight arrived, the fog was so heavy that I couldn't see more than 20 feet into the parking lot. I packed up and patiently waited, thinking the fog might lift. Time passed, with nothing but wet, heavy, dense fog creeping about. I was not feeling strong. My leg muscles were weak, more so than I had sensed for the entire trip. For the first time on the journey, I thought my body was cannibalizing itself. With excess body fat nearly gone, I didn't have much reserve in the tank. I packed up and left the motel heading east on Route 5 and pedaling through the low visibility fog blanketing the Mohawk River. Occasionally the road pavement was cracking off and sloughing away towards the river because Route 5 was built on soft riverbank mud sediment in some locations. Sometimes the breakdown lane was missing altogether because it had merely slid away with the guard rail. After 12 miles of smooth pedaling, I cycled through the town of Fonda. My fatigue faded as the dense fog disseminated, revealing a cloudless blue sky. I pedaled into Amsterdam, exploring the neighborhood side-roads through town, avoiding the increasingly narrowing roads and increasing traffic with every mile.

At the east end of town, I stopped for some badly-needed coffee at a convenience store. A tanker truck driver delivering fuel came over to talk to me after noticing SeaBos and gave me a $20 bill to buy lunch. I didn't want to accept the money from him, but he insisted that I take the cash. "Take it, man, I won this playing fantasy football. Good karma," he said.

The downtown sections along the Mohawk River offered little room to ride because of the granite curbs and densely packed cars. Riding through the centers of these towns unnerved me the most. The possibility of someone dooring me could end it all. Occasionally, I jumped onto the sidewalk to avoid these situations, but sidewalk riding is a dangerous thing to do, too, because cars traveling in both directions don't see you. I was mindful not to jump out onto the street with oncoming cars due to the limited space.

I continued down Route 5 for almost nine miles to Rotterdam, then crossed the Mohawk River at Bridge Street, joining Route 5S. Here I discovered a great road with little traffic and a generous riding lane that followed the Mohawk River's south side with a munificent tailwind. I felt healthy again, exuberant.

I left Route 5S and picked up the Mohawk Hudson Bike Trail, which appeared to be part of the Erie Canal Trail. Along this section, I enjoyed the most delightful ride, winding my way along the edge of the Mohawk River. It was a picturesque trail ride through thick woods following the old railroad grade but each time I stopped, I was attacked by an onslaught of mosquitoes. The forests were so dense I hardly noticed the busy interstate highway just to the south of the trail, which meandered to Schenectady Community College. North of town, I picked up the course once again by the Mohawk River. Occasionally, the old Erie Canal and the historic canal locks could be seen in the woods by the trail, overgrown with weeds, thick ivy vines, and consumed by the forest. I followed the path to its end in Cohoes at Alexander Street, abruptly pedaling into a residential neighborhood, then steeply descending to the Hudson River. I cycled along the Hudson River into a run-down neighborhood in the town of Green

Island. This particular area is known for leading New York State in crime. I observed some nefarious activity, including a few apparent drug deals going down in plain sight. I was careful not to meet anyone's glance on the way through town.

I followed the bike path signs under a large bridge and met up with a crossing at the Green Island Bridge, which looked doable. I was incredibly excited. Pedaling into Troy, the route took me up steep Federal Street and right onto 8th Street. I took a left onto College Street, which was over 20 percent grade, so I got off and pushed the bike up the hill. I decided to meander my way up through Rensselaer Polytechnic Institute's campus, searching for more accessible paths to gain elevation, and stopped in at a student lounge to get coffee. I asked some of the students for directions to Route 2 towards Massachusetts. Still, none of the students were familiar with off-campus road directions.

I pedaled to Orchard Street and intersected Route 2, after climbing 300 feet in less than one-half mile. My leg muscles strained to the point of cramping. Route 2 is serpentine, steeply graded with no breakdown lane, no room for bikes, and blind corners. The ride was loud and intimidating, with a constant stream of fast-moving vehicles. The road finally widened near Eagle Mills into a full-sized two-lane road, and I reached Grafton after a 1,400-foot climb in less than 15 miles. I stopped and charged the phone out in front of the town firehouse station, then called my parents to let them know I was spent, but okay.

My legs were cramping and my body was cannibalizing the remainder of my fat reserves. About a mile past Grafton, I saw a thick hardwood forest across from an elementary school. I carried SeaBos over the stone wall and pushed SeaBos deep into the woods. I camped in a place where a barn may have once stood in colonial times but had long-since collapsed and been reabsorbed back into the forest. The sun went down as a fiery red ball, filtering through the tall trees and dispersing contrasting shadows on a crimson forest carpet. For the first time, I felt truly alone. I peered through the fly tent netting, entranced in the richness of colors penetrating my wooded surroundings. The hardwoods' enveloping density, crisscrossing stone walls, meadows, and swamps stirred deep memories of childhood daydreams that set this adventure in motion. I remembered that just outside my driveway in South Natick, a cycle path connected Massachusetts to the Pacific through an intricate network of roads. Now that realization wasn't as far-fetched as it once seemed to a young boy. Nostalgia overwhelmed me. Massachusetts was only a few miles away. Darkness fell and I drifted off to sleep with thoughts of childhood adventures somehow more clearly remembered than ever before.

[i] Finger Lake - Long, narrow rock basins occupied by a lake.

[ii] Allegheny Plateau - An uplift area caused near the end of the Paleozoic Era and into the early Mesozoic Era.

[iii] Dolomitic Limestone - Dolomitic Limestone - Limestone that contains higher percentages of magnesium, a calcium-magnesium carbonate.

[iv] Crystal Habit - The characteristic shape determined by crystal faces, relative shapes, and proportions to an axis

CHAPTER 11 - MASSACHUSETTS

September 1st - Grafton, New York to Millers Falls, Massachusetts

I awoke just before 6 a.m. to the sound of vehicles whizzing by along Route 2. I was overcome with doubts about who I was and what I was doing on this adventure. I lay on a flat mattress and stared through tent netting as my thoughts rambled.

What am I doing out here on the road anyway? Am I completely nuts? Who am I? Is this recklessness I will regret, or did I need this? I just rode 3,300 miles on a bicycle. So what, who even cares?

"Man, pull it together and stay focused. You're pedaling into Massachusetts on a bike from Seattle. Own it, and let's see some focus here," I whispered to myself.

I shook off my uncertainties, packed quickly without coffee, and recited my prayers. Being enveloped by cool, fall-like foggy air was something that I had not experienced in years. Even worse, the caffeine withdrawal left me in a bewildered state of mind with sub-performing body coordination. I felt like I was functioning at 11,000 feet in the mountains. I donned two coats and pulled SeaBos from the woods across the ancient stone wall. My legs were now experiencing the 20-second paralysis at pedal start-up every time.

It was a long chilly downhill run on Route 2, with about 800 vertical feet of drop in less than five miles. I arrived in Petersburg at the bottom of the valley, cold and desperately in need of hot coffee. My mind was hazy as I stopped to ask a man getting into his car for directions to a cafe. He responded in an undecipherable burned-out mumble, which I couldn't understand. I crossed the Little Hoosick River, reduced to a trickle of orange-brown liquid, and climbed steeply up narrow Route 2, a.k.a. the Taconic Trail. The road ascends about 1,450 feet in 5.5 miles at grades ranging between 4 to 13 percent with no traffic. The road's edge was either sloughing away, broken up, or covered with gravel, which made the riding dangerous. After four long, sweeping switchbacks through hardwoods, the grade flattened at the summit. The view from Petersburg Pass was magnificent as the early morning sun pierced yellowish-gray clouds. I was less than a mile from the New York-Massachusetts state line and just a few miles south of the Vermont border. I pedaled into the dirt parking lot, which was the former Petersburg Pass Ski Area entrance. This historic ski area went bust in the 1980s, and the ski slopes were now well on the way to being reclaimed by the forest. I signed the trail register, which marked the Taconic Crest Trail.

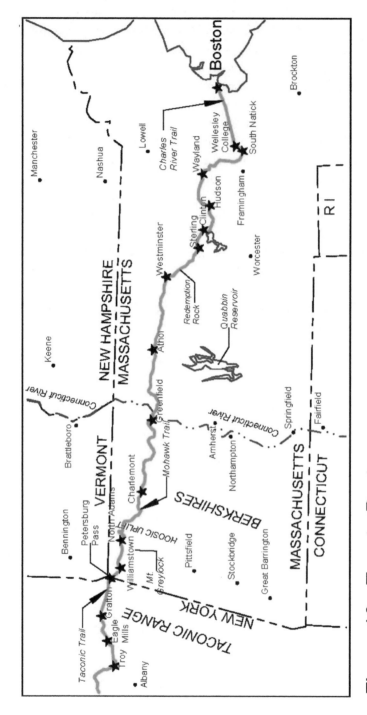

Figure 10 - Troy to Boston

I was euphoric with one more major pass and mountain range behind. Only the Berkshire Mountains remained between Boston and me. I guzzled Gatorade and gazed east into Massachusetts. These ancient, eroded hills were as tall as the Rockies at one time. The Berkshires are older than the Taconic Range, formed over 500 million years ago, exposing some of the East's oldest rocks. The Berkshires themselves are the most eroded hills in the Appalachian Mountains chain, worn down to their crystalline roots. Despite all this erosion, I found the mountains just as challenging as riding in the West. I walked to the register and left a note inside, marking the journey.

I picked up speed off the pass, crossed the Massachusetts line, and stopped for pictures. A great wave of emotion swept over me. What a tremendous relief finishing New York, the second most challenging state to ride behind Iowa. Tears flowed as I coasted at 40 to 45 mph, dropping 1,250 feet in about four miles through a dense maple forest, intersecting Route 7 in Williamstown. This particular stretch was one of the most exhilarating downhill bike rides of my life, second only to the downhill drop to Vantage on the Columbia River in Washington. Williamstown has an elegant presentation of historic buildings and is home to Williams College. I took time cruising the main street to check out the town, then stopped at a coffee shop. I plugged in all my devices while listening to a pretentious Williams professor bully his colleagues with academic challenges. With the lights and phone charged, I was geared up to ride to the Berkshires.

I stopped to pick up food supplies and more caffeine, then cycled through North Adams, enjoying great views of Mount Greylock, the highest peak in Massachusetts. It was about 85 muggy degrees, which felt much warmer than an equivalent temperature in the West. I cranked out of North Adams up Route 2, climbing 1,300 feet in about four miles to the top of the Hoosick Uplift, a high ridge that defines the Berkshires' western edge. The route is steep, ranging from about 4 to 10 percent grade, with no riding lane and blind corners. My strategy was to maximize my visibility and ride closer to the center around bends in the road, so I didn't surprise vehicles when they came upon me from behind. Despite the steep climb, I felt energetic and remarkably healthy, emboldened with a new well of energy, and feeling sporty. I passed a State Trooper controlling traffic by a road construction crew.

"Hello, ladies!" I yelled at them while standing up on the

pedals, cranking at 25 mph.

The cop turned and looked displeased. After the 3.5-mile mark on the Mohawk Trail, I reached a significant switchback, which was the same location where I stopped many times before in my college days on my motorcycle. Today, the sky was a brilliant blue with just a few clouds. A rolling emerald green panorama spread out before me, just as beautiful and impressive as I remembered from my youth. Mount Greylock loomed imposingly in the foreground. I pondered the compressed passage of time between those college days and laughed at the thought of meeting a younger me at this same spot on that old Honda.

I hopped on the bike, experienced the 20-second paralysis, and screamed at my legs to get going. Grunting the last mile up the hill to the border of Florida, Massachusetts, I reached the top of the Hoosick Ridge. The maple trees provided much-needed shade in the sweltering heat and humidity. After a few miles, Route 2 included a more bike-friendly riding lane. I rolled downhill for about 14 miles to Charlemont, dropping about 1,400 feet in elevation alongside the Deerfield River. It was exhilarating, but the long hills cut both ways, and these are serious hills. After another seven miles of riding, I crossed the Deerfield River and arrived in Shelburne Falls. I stopped by the rusty reddish-brown river to look at the mostly dry waterfall. I climbed for another 5.5 miles past Shelburne, then stopped to rest by a church before descending more than 600 feet into the Connecticut River Valley to the town of Greenfield.

The Connecticut River is wide in places, over 400 miles in length, flowing from near the Canadian border to Long Island Sound. This part of the Connecticut Valley was the glacial Lake Hitchcock site, which filled the valley approximately 15,600 years ago. The valley was settled by several native tribes. I had no idea how to cycle across Massachusetts from Greenfield. I searched the internet and located a bike shop across town east towards Route 2. I called the shop for riding directions, and the manager was quite abrupt.

"There is no easy way to ride across Massachusetts. It's challenging from the standpoint of traffic, drivers are terrible, and there are many roads where bikes are excluded. Besides that, the hills in Massachusetts will wear you out."

"You're kidding me, right? I just rode through New York." He did offer some good advice about following Route 2, so I headed east out of Greenfield on busy streets and turned towards Turners Falls. The Connecticut River was the last major river crossing before Boston. The bridge was too narrow and there was no riding lane. The guard rail was low, and it was a long way down to a dry river bed, so I took the centerline across the bridge, holding up traffic.

Cycling farther down Route 2, I found a secret place to crash in the white pines close to the Millers River. The camp was replete with a thick bed of long pine needles overlying soft sandy ground. Night came on with dense fog, and I drifted off to sleep. But my shallow rest was continuously interrupted by a deflating mattress and a harrowing 2 a.m. text message from my wife.

"I can't find Andrew. He was supposed to go to lacrosse and never showed up. Now he's not responding to my texts or attempts to reach him."

"Call the police!" I texted back. Then my phone died.

September 2nd - Millers Falls, Massachusetts to Stowe, Massachusetts

The sleeping pad was a nightmare. I refilled it three times during the night. I looked out of the tent into a world of fog. Completely out of sorts about Andrew with no communication and void of caffeine, I packed up quickly at first light. Pushing my way out through the dense fog and deep sand, I realized I could hardly stand my body odor. Everything smelled terrible, including inside the tent. I knew I looked like hell too. People would keep their distance from me today. My feet were completely numb, so I was consciously watching where I stepped—the same routine. Get on the bike, pedal, an onset of temporary leg paralysis, then up to speed and cranking.

A plastic manufacturing facility appeared through the fog about a mile down the road. I stopped and went into the office to ask permission to use their power outlet. The secretary was sweet and brought me coffee and a state map, then made copies of the Massachusetts and Boston metro maps for me. When the battery power came back, I called my wife for the first time.

"I found Andrew. He was asleep in his bed all along. I guess I didn't look very closely. I want you to know that I am very proud of you," she said.

Her voice had a detached, chilly tone, something I had never heard. It sounded almost alien. It was creepy. I told her I had to go and ended the call. It left me emotionally drained and made my body feel tired and weak. I had to reach deeper down to find whatever untapped reserves were left in me. After fully charging my gear, I headed east on Route 2A as the fog gave way to heat. So far, the hills were merely annoying as I tried to carry speed down one hill and over the next. I became notably weaker. The legs struggled with start-up paralysis and my hands were cramping and sore. I stopped in Athol at a Dunkin Donuts and wolfed down two giant donuts with a large coffee. I had been pretty careful not to eat much sugar on the trip, so this gut bomb gave me an instant sugar rush. While relishing the Dunkin experience, I chatted with a Korean War veteran at the next table about politics. His heavy Boston accent was distinctive, and my heart knew I was close to the finish.

I took off out of Athol following Route 2A, then out onto Route 2. A 500-foot climb in about 3.5 miles took me out of Athol toward Orange, which got my heart pumping. Route 2 turned into a divided turnpike after another mile or so, and the dreaded No Bicycles yellow sign appeared. I pulled off onto Patriots Road to Route 2A, riding through Templeton, Gardner, and Westminster's towns. From Westminster, I dropped south onto Route 140. This area of Massachusetts is full of low amplitude hills, hardwoods, and numerous lakes and ponds. It was a delightful afternoon ride through thick hardwoods on a narrow road. It was hot and muggy, and my legs were tapped. The endless hills numbering about four to the mile wore me down. The angry bike shop owner's words about riding in Massachusetts wasn't off the mark. However, it mattered little now. I was on a magnificent ride through picturesque forests with glimpses to the west of Mount Wachusett Ski Area. At one point, the entire mountain came into view near Wachusett Lake.

About three miles south of Mt. Wachusett on Route 140, I stopped at a sign marking Redemption Rock. This ledge was the site of Mary White Rowlandson's release in 1676, who was captured by the Narragansett Indians during the King Philip War. The sense of history was palpable. The rock, the surrounding woods, the sky probably looked just like this in 1676. I dropped my head and said a prayer for my redemption. The sacrifice, stress, physical exertion, and constant concentration after 35 days of riding were now shaping my perspective on life. I refocused my efforts and pushed the bike back to the road.

From Redemption Rock south on Route 140, I dropped about 400 feet in elevation for another five miles to Beaman Road. Out of the woods, I crossed under I-90 while my thoughts wandered back to summiting Snoqualmie Pass back in Washington. Beaman Road and Route 62 took me to Sterling as the road narrowed with continuous blind corners. I followed Route 62 east from Sterling to Clinton and Berlin, all picturesque beautiful Massachusetts towns and all with narrow downtown streets requiring me to ride in traffic. I thought it rather odd that I had spent the first 20 years of my life in Massachusetts and had never traveled to or even heard of these towns.

Somewhere Outside Athol, Massachusetts

I stopped at a Subway in Hudson to charge my phone. The Subway girls were friendly teenagers, chatting with the customers and whirling about behind the counter. They were amusing because they didn't even know the name of the next town heading east. There was no direct route east because the Assabet River National Wildlife Refuge was a geographic obstacle. I could go north or south towards Wayland. It was nearly 5 p.m. by the time the phone was charged. I headed out of air-conditioned comfort into late afternoon high heat and humidity onto Hudson's narrow streets to find the Assabet River Rail Trail. Still, there was no river, and the trail was just over a half mile in length. Stopping in the parking lot on the east end, I looked back in disbelief and thought, "What a joke of a trail that was!" Then I abruptly fell to my left without unclipping from the pedals, resulting in a bloody leg. I cut my left hand and blood seeped out of my glove. I applied some pressure, quickly got up, and looked around to see if anyone had noticed. I didn't know how many more of these falls I could endure.

I cycled towards Stowe on Route 62. At Gleason, I pulled over into thick woods across a bridge and downriver from a large industrial factory complex on the Assabet River. The river was black, stagnant, and covered with floating leaves. The spot looked like the best option for the night. A thick layer of crunchy light brown oak leaves covered the ground, and thick waves of mosquitoes filled the air. A well-built stonewall surrounded the campsite. Large stone gate posts adorned the openings, all of which were cloaked in the darkness of thick stands of oak. I knew these stone walls well, crossing them repeatedly in my youth in Massachusetts. There may be as many miles of stone walls in New England as miles to the moon. New England settlers built stone walls between 1775 and 1825, as roughly 70 percent of the New England landscape was deforested and cleared of large rocks for farming. These glacially deposited rocks were tilled up, moved, stacked, and lined up for miles, requiring millions of manhours of labor. By the late 1800s, the industrial revolution attracted the younger generations to abandon New England family farms for other more lucrative opportunities than farming marginal New England soils. Abandoned farmlands were reforested with white pines, which became New England's most essential and valuable timber commodity. Around the early 1900s, the old field white pines were heavily harvested via clear-cutting methods and succeeded by hardwoods. Today, only the stone walls remain; a testament to the early New England pioneers' work.

I set up camp while two guys in their late twenties arrived in a beat-up pickup. A 14-foot aluminum rowboat hung out of the back of the truck bed. With little care, they yanked the boat from the back, crashing it to the ground, then dragged the boat over a stone wall with loud scraping sounds accompanied by laughter. I walked over and asked them if it was okay to camp there, and they shrugged and smiled. These guys seemed like they hadn't a care in the world. They were heading out to go night fishing. One of them handed me a cold beer. I opened it, and we toasted to the life of vagabonds and fishermen. I wondered whether there were any fish in this shallow river. Even if there were, would it be safe to eat them?

It was too hot and too humid to lay in the sleeping bag and I was pumped with adrenaline and restless as the mattress deflated. In the middle of the night, the two young fishermen dragged their boat through the camp again, scraping it back over the stone wall. I checked the phone and it was about 3 a.m. I hardly slept.

September 3rd - Stowe, Massachusetts to Wellesley College

I was up early, well before sunrise, after a terrible night's sleep. Everything smelled bad, including me, and I had to get out of the tent for fresh air. The bridge crossing was noisy early as people dashed off to work. Not me. I took my time packing up, said prayers and started the day, passing the Assabet River Wildlife Refuge along stretches of straight road through swamps and overgrown cattail ponds. I stopped at a lake covered with lily pads, watched two large swans floating gracefully, and reflected on the tranquility of the moment. I pedaled through Sudbury and stopped at an intersection, waiting with traffic as parents in crosswalks escorted kids to their first day of school.

I followed Route 27 from Sudbury to Maynard on narrow roads and sidewalks around blind corners, stopping at a Starbucks in Maynard to charge up my phone. I finished up my coffee and headed south on Route 27 through Cochituate, then on to Natick. An avalanche of childhood memories overtook the moment. Many of the landmarks had changed or closed, including the Natick Mills, where my mom previously bought fabric, now an apartment building. The Harwood & Sons Baseball Factory that once manufactured all of the major league baseballs closed in 1988. I passed Saint Paul's Episcopal Church, where I was confirmed at 12, and the Friendly Ice Cream restaurant where I landed my first job at 15, now a Dunkin Donuts shop. I cycled by the Leonard Morse hospital, where I received my first stitches. I pedaled past the home of my childhood sweetheart, who sat behind me and vomited on my back in third grade—all good memories.

I took back roads off Union Street to my nephews' house in South Natick, where both Alex and Teddy greeted me with various questions about my trip. I needed a shower and to do laundry. Everything I had was filthy, but neither of them knew how to use the washing machine. I walked into the bathroom, closely followed by the twins. "Guys, I need to take a shower now." They nodded in agreement but didn't move. "I'm going to take it by myself, so I could use a little privacy."

They laughed, looked at each other, and retreated from the bathroom. I finished a long, well-appreciated shower, watching a stream of dirt flow to the drain. I didn't feel normal; I was dizzy, possibly from lack of sleep and 39 consecutive days of riding. I packed up and headed to South Natick center, stopping first at the Charles River's falls. The falls were my old fishing hole where I caught my first fish. I crossed the bridge and rode to my childhood home, a modest white cape-style clapboard house with green shutters and two dormers. Cedar shingles placed on one side of the house by my father and me in my youth had faded to gray. No one was home.

It was a bittersweet moment. Dozens of deep memories came rushing back, including my first thoughts about riding a bicycle across the country. The passage of time and long-ago memories assailed my emotions as a lump formed in my throat. The pines that once lined the backyard were all gone, but the sycamore near the driveway remained. They replaced the post and rail fence with a tasteful white picket fence placed between perfect granite posts. My bedroom was extended with a deck. The house never looked better. I took a few pictures and deep breaths and pedaled away, down Dover Road to Grove Street and to the Wellesley College campus to meet up with my daughter Shannon.

Wellesley College is my Mother's alma mater, and Shannon was following in her footsteps. I checked into the Wellesley College Club, removed all of the gear and packs, then pedaled to Wellesley Hills to get some beer to celebrate. When I came out of the store, my front tire was flat. The tire was completely worn out as well. Of course, I left the tube repair kit in the room, so I walked the bike two miles back to campus with warm beer. At 4:30, Shannon sent me a text that she was on her way, and I ran outside to greet her. Our eyes locked, and we ran into each other's arms in tears. It was her words at the beginning of the ride which inspired me and kept me going.

"Dad, I knew you could do this!" she said, so positively that all doubt was gone and I felt completely validated.

"I know you did, and tomorrow I will be in Boston!" I beamed.

How she knew that I could do it was beyond me. I went to Shannon's dormitory for dinner. Afterward, Shannon and her roommate left for evening activities. At the same time, I walked around Lake Waban and called my friend T Bone. I went back to the room, changed the flat, and put on a new tire. I was ready for my unheralded grand finale in Boston. I was too excited to sleep, but as I sunk into the comfortable bed, my thoughts drifted back to my youth. It was a slacker day. I pedaled only 19 miles, but it was a day of overflowing reminiscence and reflection, which was emotionally fulfilling.

SeaBos – Wellesley College

CHAPTER 12 – BOSTON

September 4th - Wellesley, Massachusetts to Boston, Massachusetts

I woke up at 6 a.m., literally shaking with excitement to ride into Boston. I donned my Transamerica biking shirt that I carried from Missoula. It was my first real bicycle shirt, and now that I was across America, I wanted to celebrate the accomplishment in style. The shirt fit perfectly. At 8:30, Shannon knocked at the door, and we headed down to the breakfast room where we were alone, allowing us to discuss school and home issues. I thanked her for helping me keep my business alive while I was on my extended walkabout. We went back to the hotel room to look at my pictures. SeaBos was packed up and ready to ride to Boston. Around 10 a.m., it was time to go and finish the ride. Shannon walked me out. As I watched her walk away, I sensed an extreme wave of sadness and heartbreak. My family was growing up, I had passed the point of no return, and my life ahead would never be the same as before.

Now get your act together and get your mind together. You are 15 miles from Boston and it is time to finish this. You worked for this. This ride is something you have earned.

My excitement erupted like a volcano and I felt like I had just won the lottery. A strong yet peaceful feeling supplemented with sheer adrenaline overtook me. This ride was my epic journey, one incredible experience, with memories that no one could ever take away. As Kaisch, the cross country biker, told me back in Pennsylvania, "*This journey will stick with you for a long time."*

I crossed the Wellesley campus one last time when a guy in a golf cart pulled me over. Word of my bike trip had made its way around campus. His name was John Brown, and he also grew up in Natick. I called bullshit on him because I had never met a John Brown before, never mind one from Natick, until he showed me his ID badge. Off I pedaled onto Route 16, crossing the tracks to Wellesley Hills, where I traversed back onto Route 16, Washington Street, and headed over Route 128 to Newton. I knew this route well from my childhood and didn't need a map. I traveled with gusto at 25 to 30 miles an hour, beating traffic into Boston. I felt no fatigue whatsoever, running on pure adrenaline. I had more energy than my first mile in Seattle. Cars gave me plenty of space and I was riding on pins and needles. I flashed exaggerated hand signals at cars in intersections. I was too close to the goal post now for an accident.

Don't think about it, just pedal hard and pay attention to the traffic, you idiot. My emotions ranged between crying and laughing, hyperventilating, and feeling crazy, like Christmas morning on steroids. *Slow down your mind and get a grip. Be mature. You have worked hard for this. Complete this ride.* The traffic became more onerous as I progressed further down Washington Street, and then I picked up back streets to Galen Street and onto the bike path adjacent to the Charles River's south side.

Could it be this easy now to make it into Boston? I pedaled into Brighton and arrived at the Community Rowing Boathouse, a unique building with wood clapboarding that appeared like ripples on water. I locked the bike to a boat trailer and went inside looking for my nephew, Tristan. He was in the back room with his dog and Dave Snowden, who rode his bike from Boston to the west coast. Big smiles and high-fives went all around.

My phone rang. It was Sarah Roberts calling from the Boston Globe to see whether my story was worthy of printing. My emotions played while I relayed some of the more poignant details of my trip. I choked up several times, realizing how grateful I was for the opportunity to fulfill a most exceptional adventure of a lifetime. I told her that it was my childhood dream. The interview lasted about 30 minutes. In the meantime, Tristan cooked up cheeseburgers for the crew. I was beyond stoked. I bid farewell to the boathouse crew and pedaled onto the trail, greeted by the smell of saltwater. The Atlantic

Ocean's breeze created a headwind, just one last deterrent that didn't bother me in the least. I was off-the-wall delirious with excitement, and nothing could come between me and the end zone. Sailboats and sculls darted across the Charles River. I pedaled through parks and between dozens of unyielding Canada geese.

Harvard University, where my dad attended, appeared on the north side of the Charles. I decided to pedal over the bridge and onto campus, working my way through Cambridge's one-way streets into Harvard Yard. In front of the John Harvard statue, a crowd was taking pictures as I rolled in with SeaBos.

"Hey, I just rode from Seattle to Boston and I need someone to take my photo!" A cheer came from the crowd. Right away, a young student took the camera and started snapping pictures. Subsequently, several others took photos of me with the bike. A couple of girls surrounded me and took selfies. After five minutes of jocular selfie indulgences, I had to go. I rolled out of Cambridge, picked up the trail, and cycled further into Boston. I passed the Boston Museum of Science and kept traveling east until the Bunker Hill Monument stood straight ahead. I was within the tidal zone on the Charles River near Boston Harbor. No need to touch the ocean. This endpoint was far enough. I made it. I arrived at the Boston State Highway Patrol headquarters and stopped to take the end of the journey pictures with a young Bostonian.

So this is how it ends? I looked around and time moved in confusingly slow motion. I couldn't get my mind around this instant in time; it was the one-minute of self-congratulations I had been striving, grinding, bonking, falling, going broke, and suffering for, many miles across America. There was no trophy here, no celebration, no crowds, no fame, no physical rewards, no partner, just strangers surrounding me. It was over. That one-second in time represented one of the most remarkable accomplishments of my life and there was no one there to share it. It was not the moment that I expected. Crowds of people walked by me on the sidewalk without even a glance. I felt invisible. Then I laughed. Something inside me changed forever. I turned SeaBos around and we headed back to the boathouse, stopping for a few more Boston pictures near Copley Square and the iconic

Prudential Center.

Journey Complete and Happy Parents – Boston MA

What now? A big letdown? How will I handle this? I pondered my future and slowly worked my way back to the boathouse in Brighton. I pedaled around the end of the building and found Tristan, who ran inside to get my parents. In the meantime, I talked with Dave Snowdon about his cross-country bike experience and asked him what might happen to me next.

"What happens now?" I asked.

"There will be a few weeks of excitement, and then as your monumental adventure fades from memory, you will return to the boredom of everyday life. You will slowly get absorbed back into the system," he said.

"How will I deal with the transition period back to everyday life?"

"Who knows?" Dave said, "There will be an emotional letdown. You will talk about it too much, then as time goes by, you might mention it less, then not at all. But the experience will stay with you for a long time. Then maybe a year or two down the road, people will hear about your ride, and they will want to share your journal and experiences, they will want to contact you and possibly to do something along the same routes."

My parents were all smiles. We took a few group pictures and Dad kept commenting on the incredible distance traveled on the mighty SeaBos. "My God, John, I can't believe you rode all of those miles. That's just fantastic and hard to imagine." I broke down the bike and my dad brought the car. We loaded up the bike and panniers, hopped in the car, and took off from Boston towards New Hampshire. Dad took a few wrong turns and we became lost on familiar roads around Newton. I smiled and thought about all my wrong turns made along the ride. They didn't ask me much more about the trip. We were off to New Hampshire, and I experienced an overwhelming feeling of relief. My journey was complete.

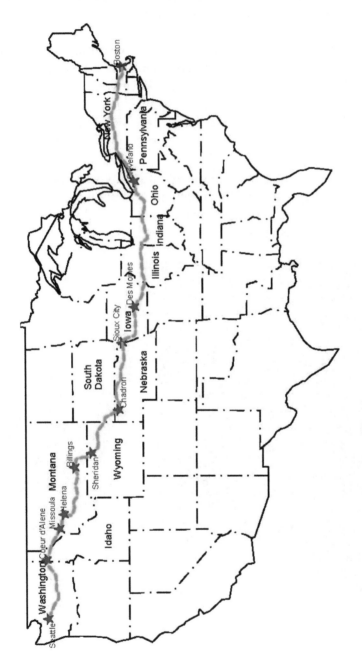

Figure 11 - The Cycle Path

CHAPTER 13 - BITTERSWEET REFLECTIONS

Members of my New England family came to visit over the next several days. We spent the weekend relaxing, cutting the grass, and replacing a 30-foot wooden flagpole in the front yard. On the following day, after everyone left, I felt restless. It was hard to stop cold turkey after 43 consecutive riding days, so I took a tour around Lake Sunapee. New Hampshire has beautiful countryside, with low but steep rolling hills and mountains. The trees were changing to fall colors. The next day I took SeaBos on a big lap down to Route 11 past Mount Kearsarge and down around Pleasant Lake. I climbed up the long hill on North Pleasant Street past Pleasant Lake to the center of town then around Colby Sawyer College in high spirits. My parents couldn't understand why I continued to ride.

On the following day, my dad and I picked up a box to ship the bike back to Salt Lake City. I cherished this brief time with my parents because I didn't get to see them much after moving to the West. I cleaned gear and packed up everything for the flight back home. The local New Hampshire newspaper called and asked me questions about my trip. The Boston Globe article was published and it was exciting to see a few of my pictures in the Boston paper. The interview for the New Hampshire paper lasted about 15 minutes. The next day, my parents drove me to Manchester, where I boarded a plane home.

When I got off the plane in Salt Lake, Channel 13 News was there to greet and interview me before I picked up my bags. It was a brief interview and a bit weird. My longtime friend Charlie picked me up at the airport and drove me home. It was a subdued and somber ride. The caustic stench from the house fire overwhelmed me as I walked in the front door. Everything, including the new furniture, looked unfamiliar.

EPILOGUE

The ride didn't change my life. It changed me. My experience taught me that bike touring is one of the most rewarding challenges life has to offer. All you need is some strength, a lot of determination, and just a wee bit of insanity to pull it off. Safety is not guaranteed on a bike in America; it is up to you. You have to be ready for anything. It could be a nervous stranger with a loaded gun, menacing dogs, arrogant semi-truck drivers, narrow bridges, rattlesnakes, strafing crop dusters, angry bar owners, bull shitters, or drivers intending you harm. But the love, kindness and generosity of individuals that I encountered more than made up for the bad stuff. I began the journey with doubt and uncertainty of my abilities and my life in personal and professional disorder. I left with no plan or route. While it is advised to reasonably plan and coordinate a solo tour well in advance, I rolled the dice, which added to the excitement daily. I learned from the experience that following my gut instinct worked better than a determination by the most sophisticated algorithm. I discovered another reality that I never knew existed—life at the speed of a bike. My marriage? I think you can guess how that turned out. But, I did, finally, get feeling back in my feet.

There was an immense satisfaction and indescribable enlightenment that I still recall, but cannot now feel in the same context. If I had to do it all over again, I would. I cherished the vagabond lifestyle, living in the present with a sense of unparalleled joy. There were incidents along the way which can't be translated into words. I always felt that God rode with me, giving me a sense at times of safety, strength, and fearlessness, sparing my life, and someone to talk to. This heightened sense did not derive from apparitions or hallucinations. This awareness was hidden in signs, written in numbers, perhaps found through coincidental manifestations of everyday matters or items entirely out of the ordinary. It came through the people I met. I felt a connection to the long-distance touring riders who understood this lust for pedaling. It was a genuine spiritual experience. It was as if the blinds of another life had been lifted away, allowing me to feel and see the world differently. Perhaps my understanding of this took some solitude and a bit of physical suffering.

The visions in my adolescence were right on. All of those towns and cities across the country connect in a dot-to-dot pattern, no matter how you decide to ride it. If you once daydreamed like me to seek adventure and happiness, go experience your walkabout. I almost waited too long, and life is too short. Don't lose sight of what is essential to your happiness. We can do more with less. And it's later than you think.

Until the day I die, I will always remember how it felt, cranking away with the biggest smile on two wheels. I lived only in the moment through the most beautiful country imaginable. Just me and SeaBos under an open sky, pedaling past faraway mountains, lakes, and rivers, through thick forests, towards unknown horizons once dreamed of as a child.

ABOUT THE AUTHOR

An avid outdoorsman and adventurer, John Strater Brown grew up in New England and moved West after attending the University of Massachusetts, receiving a B.S. Degree in Geology. John is a hydrogeologist and spent his career mapping and drilling all types of water wells and remediating Superfund and Hazardous Waste Sites in the West. He loves backcountry skiing, camping, hiking, river running, bicycles, riding his motorcycles, and virtually anything that takes him out of doors.

John resides in Salt Lake City, Utah with his beautiful companion Jolene, who also shares his passion for the outdoors and music. When they are not out on the trails or slopes, they hold neighborhood jams with musician friends and enjoy some of John's homemade specialty beers.

Made in the USA
Columbia, SC
20 November 2021

49400008R10135